B77-BH

Books in the macabre field by Basil Copper

Non-fiction
The Vampire: In Legend, Fact and Art
The Werewolf: In Legend, Fact and Art

Short Stories
Not After Nightfall
Here Be Daemons
And Afterward, the Dark
From Evil's Pillow
Voices of Doom
When Footsteps Echo
Whispers in the Night

Fantasy Novels
The Great White Space
Into the Silence
The Horror on Planet X

Gothic Novels
The Curse of the Fleers
Necropolis
The House of the Wolf
The Black Death

The Solar Pons Series
The Dossier of Solar Pons
The Further Adventures of Solar Pons
The Secret Files of Solar Pons
Some Uncollected Cases of Solar Pons
The Exploits of Solar Pons
The Recollections of Solar Pons

The Black Death

Basil Copper

Illustrations by
Stefanie Kate Hawks

Minneapolis, Minnesota
1991

THE BLACK DEATH

Copyright © 1991, by Basil Copper

Illustrations: Copyright © 1991, by Stefanie K. Hawks

First Edition

All rights reserved. No part of this book may be reproduced in any form or by any means without written permission of the author, except for brief quotations in critical articles or reviews. Address all queries to: FEDOGAN & BREMER, 700 Washington Ave., S. E., Suite 50, Minneapolis, MN 55414

ISBN: 1-878252-04-6 (Trade Edition)
ISBN: 1-878252-05-4 (Limited Edition)
Library of Congress Number: 91-075396

Book design by Felix Bremer

CONTENTS

Part One: Indian Summer

Prologue: Arrival 5
1. Thornton Bassett 12
2. An Unexpected Toast 18
3. First Warning 24
4. Death in Sunlight 29
5. Twisted Souls 35
6. Evening at the Inn 43
7. Pollard, Bassett 48
8. The Man on the Mound 53
9. Pollard Speaks 58
10. Night Visitor 64
11. A Message From Jeremy 68
12. The Rector is Reticent 74
13. An Unexpected Meeting 80
14. Fiona 87
15. Simon Hemmings 92
16. The Commission 99
17. The Collection 105
18. Baron von Kempelen 110
19. Hands is Fearful 118
20. The Black Death 123
21. Carter is Troubled 130
22. An Invitation 135
23. The Dragoons Arrive 140
24. Signs of Winter 145

Part Two: Autumn

25. Hemmings is Enthusiastic 153
26. The Moor-Riders 160
27. Rats' Castle 167

28	The Captain is Put Out	175
29	The Catacombs	181
30	The Metal Man	186
31	Lights on the Moor	193
32	The Hounds Gather	200
33	At the Rectory	206
34	On the Tower	213
35	Fiona Again	224
36	Questions from Pollard	233
37	The Thing in the Stream	238
38	The Broken Lock	247

Part Three: Winter

39	Work in Progress	257
40	Accident or Design?	264
41	Golden Dreams	271
42	A Deadly Gift	275
43	Friendly Stranger	281
44	Anti-Christ	287
45	The Feast of Asses	292
46	Good News	297
47	Flame in the Darkness	302
48	The Goat, the Skull, and the Ass	310
49	Satan's Hounds	316
50	Hunted	322
51	Plans	328
52	The Stone is Lifted	337
53	The Tunnel	344
54	The Guardians	351
55	Silver Sabres	356
56	The Goat-Priest Speaks	360

Epilogue: Pillars of Fire 370

I am grateful to my old friend Patrick Moules for his expert advice concerning Victorian railway companies operating on and around Dartmoor at the time of this story.

Basil Copper.
Semur-en-Auxois, Cote d'Or

The Black Death

Part One

Indian Summer

Prologue
Arrival

1

JOHN CARTER ARRIVED at his destination in the golden haze of a perfect October day. It had been a long and time-consuming journey which had begun at Paddington in the morning when he had travelled by the Great Western Railway to Plymouth. There he had changed trains, still on GWR lines, to the Launceston branch and had again transferred, this time on to the single-track Princetown railway at Yelverton.

By then the character of the country had altered drastically, the strange and sometimes fantastic outlines of Dartmoor beginning to climb up the horizon. The rugged terrain was all splashed with purple and gold, which the young architect supposed to be the autumn colours of the gorse, while the jagged outlines of the prehistoric rocks known as tors jutted up into this bizarre landscape like weird Gothic cathedral spires, limned sharply against the black and blue distances which led to the fastnesses of the moor.

This wilderness seemed absolutely deserted except for the occasional flight of a bird but Carter knew it must contain human habitations, farms and communities, even large villages and towns hidden among the mysterious hummocks and, despite his tiredness, he had gazed with great interest as the small tank engine drawing its half-dozen or so non-corridor carriages had carried him along the last ten miles to Princetown itself.

Here there was evidence of some softening hand of civilisation at work upon the moor—a metalled road, three men toiling alongside the line, a solitary pedestrian plodding forward, his shadow thrown upon the ground by the hazy sun, and once, a pony and trap driven at a spanking pace in the direction of Princetown.

The railway swept around in great curves so that Carter, his face close against the open window, heedless of the soot and sparks which danced in their wake, was able to see across the wide blue spaces of the rolling moorland which swept up from the village.

He felt exhilarated by the wildness of the scene and when a half-dozen of the small, stocky Dartmoor ponies, their tangled manes and tails flying in the wind of their passage, galloped alongside the train for a while, sure-footed on the jumbled rocks, he felt the last links that held him to the grimy bondage of London fall away from him.

This euphoric mood did not last, for the bleak convict prison of Princetown slid past a few moments later and the young man's eyes glanced soberly over the dun-coloured granite walls which the gold of the sun could do nothing to soften, and was lost in the blackness of the sloping slate roofs which must conceal the suffering of so many men.

Most of them, he knew, probably deserved such a fate, but it was a melancholy beginning to his new life and as he gathered his small heap of belongings together on the platform preparatory to commencing the final stage of his journey, it was re-emphasized by the dull grit of boots upon the roadway and there came a file of convicts; listless, bowed figures, marching back to their grim lodging; flanked on either side by mounted warders who rode easily, loaded rifles at their saddles.

They had no doubt toiled all day at some roadworks upon the moor and, hard as their lot must be in this warm October weather, it did not require much imagination to realise how much more gruelling it would be in the depths of winter. The shuffling line of figures in their coarse clothing had soon disappeared down the single village street and Carter's thoughts were lifted on to a more pleasant plane by the stationmaster, a tall, bearded man with a white face who hastened from his office with a message for the solitary passenger.

His conveyance had been delayed but would arrive within a quarter of an hour; in the meantime he was welcome to wait in the stationmaster's own office. Carter smilingly declined the kind offer and said he would rather remain in the sunshine. He amused himself for a while watching the fussy operations of the tank locomotive which was prepared for its return journey down the same strip of line over which it had just travelled.

Carter had paused in front of the station waiting-room and the sun, low now, but still hot, flung back his reflection in the dark surface of the glass as though in a mirror. He studied his own image critically; he saw a strongly-made man of thirty-three, with pleasant, open features and dark, wavy hair. He was wryly aware that his smart city suit made him stand out in these rustic surroundings; he should have invested in some country tweeds and thick brogues.

He would remedy that in due course. He supposed there would be tailors' establishments and similar amenities in the neighbouring towns. It was something he would have taken care of except that his new appointment had come about in such a sudden manner, all within three weeks, and he had really little time for such things. For some while Carter had laboured in the lower ranks of a great City firm in which he had little scope for advancement. He had, in fact, seen the announcement for a partnership in a recent issue of *The Builder*, and, as the interviews had been conducted in London, had hastened to secure an appointment.

It was the action of a bored, frustrated man, he realised, and his friends in the profession had told him he was mad to accept the readily proffered position without at least travelling to see his new offices and the place in which he would live.

But Carter was a good judge of character and he had warmed immediately to his new principal who had conducted the London interview. He was a kindly, efficient man, good-humoured and forward-looking; a man in late middle age who had built up a large and scattered practice which spanned the length and breadth of Devon and Cornwall.

Carter's surprise at the firm's establishment in such a relatively small and remote town as Thornton Bassett was re-echoed by the principal himself, who told Carter that the founder of the firm was his father-in-law; he had taken over when the latter retired, and as his wife did not wish to leave her native surroundings, he had acquiesced in her wishes.

He had chuckled at Carter's expression and had remarked that the firm was a unique one; the Head Office was in a small town and the branch offices in Plymouth and Exeter. Carter had immediately closed with the offer, and did not think he would have any reason to regret it.

He turned away from the window, his reverie interrupted by the sharp impact of hooves on the tarmac surface of the station forecourt. He picked up his baggage and moved across the platform, just in time to see the smart-looking pony and trap the train had earlier passed upon the roadway draw to a stand at the station entrance.

2

A tall, bearded man with a hard hat drawn down across his iron brow jumped down quickly and saluted the young architect by putting the forefinger of his right hand to the brim of his headgear.

"Mr. Carter, sir? I'm sorry to be late on your first day. I hope you have not been inconvenienced."

Carter smilingly shook his head.

"Not at all. A beautiful day, is it not?"

The tall man lifted Carter's heavy valise and two other pieces of baggage as if they were featherweights and stowed them in the luggage compartment at the rear of the trap before helping his passenger up to sit beside him. He slammed the rear door of the vehicle and cracked his whip smartly, the little brown pony stepping out eagerly along the moorland road.

"It is that, sir. My name is Slade. I work for your firm and carry a deal of confidential documents for the principal. We shall be seeing much of one another and I trust that you will find your appointment a congenial one."

Carter muttered an assent, secretly much amused at the attitude of his new companion. He was obviously a man of superior intellect for his somewhat lowly position, but Carter was pleased at the obvious warmth of his welcome and once again felt he had made the right choice as the beat of the little pony's hooves carried them farther and farther into the fastness of the moor.

There was a shrill whistle as they breasted a rise and, looking back over his shoulder, Carter could see a thin plume of blackish smoke as the tank loco started back on its ten-mile journey.

"Is it far to Thornton Bassett?" he asked his companion, who had jammed his hat down farther over his ears and was handling the reins with the smooth confidence of the veteran.

"A little over five miles," Slade replied. "Nice enough on a day like this but not so much fun in winter."

He glanced at Carter critically.

"You'll need stout shoes and some more practical clothing before then, sir. Particularly in the waterproof line."

Carter smiled.

"I'll see about it. Mr. Pollard said he would arrange lodgings for me."

Slade nodded.

"That's all in hand, sir. You'll find Mrs. Tregorran an excellent woman. The house is only two minutes from the office."

Carter nodded. His new employer was a man of marked contrast to some of those in the City of London with whom he had been involved in past years. Though it was obvious that Pollard would have difficulty in finding someone of the right calibre for a practice in such a remote corner of England, it had been reflected in the generous terms of the partnership arrangements. Carter had been left an unexpected legacy by an aunt who had died in Australia. With this sudden windfall he had sought to secure a more soundly based future and he thought he had found it here.

It was not many men who could count on a full partnership at the early age of thirty-three and he felt he had made a sound investment. There were only three principals beside himself and he understood there was a large staff in the drawing office. Pollard had provided extensive documentation and Carter's own solicitor had carried out exhaustive searches in the matter which had merely reinforced the young architect's belief in the soundness of his choice.

Slade had reined the pony in to a walk now. They were going down into a valley and presently they crossed a foaming river by an ancient stone bridge which was all crusted with lichen and moss. It was a dark, gloomy place and Slade gave his passenger a wry smile from beneath his hard hat.

"There's more darkness than sunshine on the moor, Mr. Carter, for most of the year, and that's a fact."

He read the unspoken question in the young man's eyes as the pony clattered across the bridge.

"The River Dart, sir. It gets very swollen here during the winter rains. But Thornton Bassett is high up and in a very healthy position."

He smiled again, revealing strong yellow teeth.

"Fog, rain, and wind, sir. You'll be well weather-beaten by this time next year!"

Carter joined in the other's laugh and, at the latter's suggestion, they got down from the trap as the road went steeply up the opposite shoulder of hill in the north easterly direction.

As they breasted the rise and regained their vehicle, Carter saw with a thrill that they were in a strange and remote countryside, the hills all scarred and channelled as though with courses made by the winter rains, granite boulders littered across the inhospitable landscape, while here and there the earth heaved up as though at some gigantic volcanic eruption, the crests of hillsides crowned with the jagged heights of the tors.

Water gleamed silver in the low light as it went its crooked course down the valley and on the hillside the green, gold and mauve of the gorse caught the last of the sun. Once the road passed close to great groups of tumbled stones and Carter gazed with interest, realising he was looking at the ancient dwellings of prehistoric man.

Far to the east, at the foaming crest of a stretch of green moorland stood the jagged silhouette of what looked like a ruined castle, black against the sky beyond. Due east from them, the hillsides fell away and then black belts of trees began, extensive and spreading wide, so far as Carter could see.

"Dartmoor Forest," Slade said in satisfied, proprietorial tones.

"I see I shall have much to occupy me on my spare-time walks," Carter observed.

The driver shook his head slowly.

"I should be very careful, particularly in the winter-time, sir. There is a deal of danger on the moor for the inexperienced."

Carter caught the nuances of the man's tones with quickening interest.

"Danger? What sort of danger?"

Slade shook his head again, a worried expression in his eyes.

"From the weather, from the roughness of the terrain. One could wander for miles and die of starvation. Mr. Pollard will tell you all about it. But there are congenial companions in the office who know the moor well and would accompany you."

"I see," said Carter slowly.

He had been so absorbed by the novelty of his surroundings that he did not at first notice that they had come to their destination. Now Slade slowed the pony to a walking pace and the passenger saw that they were on a sort of high plateau. Behind them the ground tumbled and again far to the west and the east.

But directly ahead the narrow lane, bounded by a dry stone wall, wound its way down into what looked like a largish town; comfortable, solidly-built granite houses lined three or four substantial streets; a stream ran foaming in front of them, crossed by a large stone bridge. A church tower peeped from the shelter of some ancient trees, the first Carter had seen in many a mile across the moors; and smoke ascended like the scribblings on a child's slate from half a hundred chimneys into the golden autumn air.

There was pride and quiet satisfaction in Slade's tones as he pointed with his whip.

"Thornton Bassett, sir."

ONE
Thornton Bassett

1

AN ATMOSPHERE OF great peace descended on Carter as the trap clattered into the town, the mellow stone of the houses catching the golden evening light, the chimney-smoke fragrant in his nostrils, the faint murmur of human activity rising above the sharp clopping of the little pony's hooves.

But there were few people about and Carter then became aware of a faint, sweet chanting which arose from somewhere beyond the belt of trees. He looked quickly at his companion but a curious change had come over his driver's face. He looked almost furtive and then did a strange thing, reining in the pony abruptly and taking off his hard hat, to reveal close-cropped black hair beginning to be fringed with grey.

Carter was already bare-headed, but he noticed that two old men standing near them on the pavement at the beginning of Thornton Bassett's principal street had also removed their headgear. The trap had already crossed the bridge into the town but on turning in his seat Carter could see the parapets were thick with people who had appeared, silently and mysteriously, as though by some subtle natural process.

He was about to make some commonplace remark to his companion, who sat with eyes cast down, but the explanation of this behaviour occurred to him almost immediately as he saw that they were nearly opposite the entrance of the church, whose tower emerged from the sheltering trees. A funeral procession was debouching from the lane, led by a man in a white surplice whom Carter judged to be the Rector or the minister of the parish.

The coffin followed behind on a farm-cart and then a long file of mourners, walking with heads bowed. The procession passed on over the bridge, the people lining the parapets moving to let it through, and then bringing up the rear of the procession. Carter guessed that the cemetery lay somewhere up the hill, off the road down which they had just come.

"I am sorry you had to see that, sir," said Slade, urging the pony on again. "It makes a melancholy greeting for your arrival."

Carter thought it a curious conceit but kept the notion to himself; after all, the funeral arrangements in a place like Thornton Bassett could not be organised to take into account the arrival of a new junior partner in a firm of local architects.

But he muttered some polite disclaimer and looked about him with deepening interest as the trap traversed the streets, Slade greeting various people on the pavements as they passed. It was obvious that he was well-known in the place and such knowledge might be invaluable to a newcomer like Carter.

They soon came to a large paved square, which was evidently the town centre; the buildings were widely spaced and handsome here and the young man made out a prosperous-looking inn, a few public buildings, shops and other places of business, and several more streets diverging from the main thoroughfare.

There was another handsome stone bridge here, which spanned the swiftly running stream of clear, cold water; evidently the same river looping round from the bridge at the town entrance, crossing the line of the buildings twice.

Before the bridge which the pony took at a fast trot, as though glad to be home, Slade pointed with his whip at a large granite building of three storeys which stood to the right of the square. It had an imposing entrance porch with a palladian-style portico and gold-leaf lettering on the doors and windows glinted in the sun.

"Those are our offices, sir," the driver said with quiet pride.

Carter was impressed and he felt the conviction grow within him that he had done the right thing. Mr. Pollard's business was obviously prosperous and prestigious, and he would have a far more interesting and lucrative future than if he had stayed in London. The trap had crossed the bridge and was traversing a small section of side-streets, gay with baskets and stone urns full of brightly coloured flowers, as these thoughts passed through his head.

There were tiny gardens here, sprinkled with butterflies and carefully tended plots; sweet-scented plants perfuming the air and clustering round porches; while newly-cut grass lay in drying swathes on lawns and banks which surrounded the houses and cottages. Slade drew the trap up in front of a fretted iron gateway giving on a crazy-paving path down which a woman in a long gown was hurrying. Carter glimpsed a quiet, ordered life, refreshing after the harsh bustle of London.

Slade was already down, quieting the pony, handling the baggage with practised efficiency. He opened the gate courteously for his passenger, ushering the young architect through into the green tranquillity of the walled garden.

"Here is Mrs. Tregorran, sir. And I've no doubt she will have a substantial supper ready."

2

Mrs. Tregorran turned out to be a smooth-faced, elegant-looking woman with sad eyes and a kindly manner. Carter took to her at once and as Slade carried his baggage into the hall, she handed the architect a large metal door-key and assured him of the freedom of the house. The young man guessed that she relied on summer visitors to the area and that in the winter lean times might ensue; therefore, any long-term visitors such as himself would be more than welcome.

The sun had declined behind the hills now and a warm, limpid dusk glowed in the air as she led him indoors, through a clean, bright hallway in which vivid flowers blazed in copper pots and pans. The furniture was sparse but good and Mr. Pollard had no doubt chosen the landlady for his new junior partner with some care.

"If there is anything you need, Mr. Carter, you have only to ask," she said expansively, leading the way up a broad, carpeted staircase to the upper floors.

"I have given you a large room in front, where you will have a good view of the town and the moors. Dinner is at seven and you will no doubt wish to wash after your journey. You will find everything prepared."

Carter mumbled his thanks, conscious that he was fortunate indeed to find such salubrious quarters. He was an orphan, with few living relatives, and his lodgings in London had often been cramped and far from satisfactory.

They were on the upper floor now and Mrs. Tregorran led him forward toward the doorway of the first room on the left, which opened to reveal the burly form of Slade. He smiled briefly, his eyes thoughtful above the beard.

"I hope everything will be satisfactory, Mr. Carter. If there is anything further you require during the week-end, Mrs. Tregorran has my address. Just send me a message and I will come round at once."

"I am greatly obliged," said Carter.

He had his hand in his pocket but the big man smilingly shook his head and went off down the corridor. Mrs. Tregorran waited silently in the doorway as he appraised the room. It was indeed satisfactory in every respect, the bed looking large and comfortable, the furniture plain but serviceable, the floor warmly carpeted. Slade had piled his luggage neatly on a beechwood rack at the end of his bed.

There were two large windows, with a broad writing desk set between them; that would indeed be useful in case Carter needed to do any drawing out of office hours. He wandered over and looked down; the landlady had not exaggerated. The view was quite sensational. He could see a great deal of Thornton Bassett from here and beyond the village, the moorland rose steeply and spectacularly.

The sun had almost gone now and a thin mist was rising from somewhere, probably emanating from the stream which bisected the little town in two places, as he had already noted. He turned to thank his landlady but she had quietly quit the room. He crossed to the door and looked along the corridor, but she had disappeared. He closed the door, locking it with the key he found inside. He glanced at his watch, noting that it had turned six o'clock.

There might just be time for a turn about the streets before dark if he hurried. He made a quick toilet, finding hot water ready prepared in the jug on the wash-hand stand. Ten minutes later he was about to descend the staircase to the ground floor, when a door on the opposite side of the corridor suddenly opened and the figure emerging almost cannoned into him.

It was another young man, obviously a lodger like himself. He was tall and well-made, with thick, sandy hair and a wide, humorous face. He was about twenty-six, Carter would have said, and was dressed in a smart suit of subdued country tweeds, and wore a sedate gold stickpin in his cravat. The two apologised simultaneously, the other holding out his hand impulsively.

"You must be Mr. Carter. You were expected, I know. My name is Jeremy Hands. We are colleagues, as I work in your new office."

He paused diffidently.

"Forgive me, Mr. Carter. I appreciate you are the new junior partner. I am an articled pupil, working directly for Mr. Pollard. I hope to qualify as an architect myself next year, when I have taken my final examinations."

There was something so frank and pleasant about the newcomer's manner that Carter returned his hand-clasp vigorously. He had not yet spoken, and so far young Hands had given him scant opportunity.

"Are you taking a turn before dinner? I'd be glad to show you around. I am just going down to the square to get my evening newspaper."

He laughed infectiously.

"It is really a morning paper, but by the time it comes up by the late train it passes for evening."

He led the way down the stairway with a heavy clatter, Carter following on a little less boisterously. As they passed through the hallway, Hands called through the half-open door of a side room.

"We will be back before seven, Mrs. Tregorran."

He opened the front door and ushered his companion through. The two young men passed across the walled garden and out the iron gate, latching it behind them. The air was somewhat chilly now and, the sun being shaded by the great rounded humps of moorland that hemmed the town in, Thornton Bassett lay in semi-darkness.

It was such a contrast to the scene which had greeted Carter but a scant half-hour before that he felt quite startled. Hands had noticed his expression as they strolled together down the side-street.

"Odd, is it not? Darkness comes early here, especially in winter, despite the fact that the place is on a sort of plateau."

The two men walked in silence down past the houses with their brightly-flowered gardens, toward the bridge which spanned the quickly flowing stream. Carter realised that he had not spoken a full sentence to his new-found colleague once since their meeting and he hastened to make amends.

"It seems a pleasant spot, nevertheless. And how is the office?"

Hands smiled.

"Oh, well enough," he said carelessly. "And the people there are capital for the most part."

A shadow seemed to pass across his face as he glanced sideways at the junior partner as the two men paused on the stone bridge midway across the stream. Carter gazed blankly at the swiftly racing water which glinted now black, now silver, as the liquid mass foamed and swirled against the stones and boulders which littered the stream bed.

A murmuring noise interrupted their brief discourse and Carter glanced up, conscious of large numbers of people who were now drifting up the street. There was a melancholy on Hands' face which had not been there before. Carter realised that the people he had seen emerging from the churchyard earlier were now coming back from the burial service on the hill above the village. He had momentarily forgotten the incident when Slade had driven him across the first bridge at the entrance to Thornton Bassett.

"Another funeral," said Jeremy Hands softly.

"Another?" Carter queried. "I do not understand."

Hands expression lightened.

"Nothing, Mr. Carter. In any event, it is not a matter for your first evening in Thornton Bassett. Allow me to conduct you on a brief tour of the town."

And he hurried his companion across the bridge, the two men walking with averted faces through the mass of mourners who had now spread out to disperse to their individual homes.

Carter was left with an indelible impression of hopelessness and sorrow which he had never noticed on such sombre occasions in the past.

Two
An Unexpected Toast

1

CARTER SUDDENLY REMEMBERED that it was Saturday night. Though some shops were still open here, he could not imagine a greater contrast with the life which he had been used to lead in London; he remembered the rain gleaming on the thousands of roofs; the glitter of the great hotels; the sparkle of cutlery in the elegant restaurants; the patience of the long rows of horses harnessed to the hansom cabs, waiting for custom; of the raucous din of the musical hall, and the refined crescendo of the opera-house; and the lonely, impoverished faces of the human derelicts who thronged the inhospitable streets at all hours.

Nevertheless, he was young and ambitious and he looked about him with a keen eye as his new companion guided him through the streets of this miniature metropolis. What he saw pleased him—not to say astonished. For here was no rustic, sleepy centre but a small, bustling town which was elegantly laid out, business-like, and obviously thriving and prosperous. He made some cautious observations on these lines to Hands, the latter nodding assent, rubbing his fingers together in a gesture the young architect was beginning to find characteristic.

"Oh, yes, Pollard is no fool. He knew what he was doing when he set up here. You have a partnership for life if you are so disposed, Mr. Carter. And the range of work is interesting in itself. Churches, warehouses, businesses, farms, docks, the list is endless. It would be no exaggeration to say a hundred miles from east to west, and from coast to coast north and south is our beat. I'm certain you'll find it absorbing."

"I'm sure I shall," Carter observed drily, his eyes fixed on his companion's face as they came off the bridge.

"And do you find it interesting?"

It was a shrewd question and for a moment he fancied that Jeremy Hands' face coloured as they passed beneath the flaring gas-jet of a street lamp set on the cobbled approach to the bridge.

"A difficult question, Mr. Carter," Hands replied quietly. "There is a contrast, you see, between the sort of assignments likely to come the way of a qualified architect and junior partner and that of an apprenticed junior who is mostly doing surveying work."

He gave another of his ready laughs, startling a group of oldish women in black, who were just passing in the opposite direction.

"Pig pens, labourers' cottages and cow-barns are more likely to be my lot at the moment, Mr. Carter. You will find things a deal more elegant and lively in your department."

Carter smiled in his turn. He was beginning to like his companion more with every minute that passed.

"Come," he said deprecatingly. "I'm sure you exaggerate a little. And besides, I expect to do my fair share of the less interesting commissions."

Hands put his forefinger alongside his nose and gave his new acquaintance a knowing wink as he led the way briskly forward to the block of offices in the main square which Carter had earlier noticed.

"This is our billet, Mr. Carter. Mr. Pollard trusts me with the keys. Would you like me to show you round?"

He paused beneath the vast stone palladian porch but Carter arrested his movement with a quick gesture of his hand.

"It is kind of you, Mr. Hands, but I think not tonight. I would rather come to the business fresh on Monday morning. And perhaps Mr. Pollard would prefer to do the honours himself."

There was disappointment on Hands' face, immediately erased by his ready smile.

"You are no doubt right, Mr. Carter. As you wish. But I'm sure you'd agree that even from the outside we have a smart-looking business here."

The architect had already come to the same conclusion but now he contented himself with following Hands along the spacious façade, noting the gleaming windows, the freshness of the paint, and the gilded lettering on doors and casements, to which his own name might one day be added.

They turned now across the main square which led to the bridge and Carter was surprised at the size of the town; he had no time for more than a perfunctory glance, for their timepieces told the two young men it would soon be necessary for them to retrace their steps in the direction of their landlady's approaching meal.

There were a number of side-streets as yet unexplored as well as the remainder of the town which Carter had approached on his drive in, but that could wait until the following day. For the moment he was content to dawdle with his agreeable companion while they glanced in shop windows, Hands occasionally saluting an acquaintance or perhaps a client of the firm. He did not offer to introduce Carter to any of these people nor did the young architect desire it for the moment.

There would be time enough for such things on the Monday. He was content now, agreeably tired after his long journey, to drift along in limbo, wherever the steps of his companion directed him.

He noted with satisfaction the spaciousness and comfort of the great hostelry, The Bassett Arms, at the corner of the square with its welcoming lights; crowded bars and coffee rooms where, Hands informed him, some of the senior members of Pollard, Bassett made select little gatherings on certain evenings of the week, particularly during the winter months.

He was suddenly more tired than he had imagined as they began to retrace their footsteps, the sound of their progress echoing back from the cobbles on to the granite façades of the buildings of the little town; mingling with those of other passers-by so that for a moment one might have fancied an army on the march.

The simile was a curious one and Carter shrugged it off; they were back by the dark waters of the stream now and hurried across the bridge as a large wagon jolted over, taking up most of the space between the high stone parapets. The reverberation seemed to linger in Carter's head for a long time as the two young men regained the crazy paving path and went in to their supper.

2

They were alone for the meal, which they took in a large, high-beamed room in which a coal fire burned. Mrs. Tregorran ate her supper at a small side-table near the fire, from where she could direct the comfort of her guests. The young men were served by a tall, attractive girl with dark hair and dark eyes which darted impudently whenever either caught her glance, only to be lowered again when the landlady became aware of their scrutiny.

The meal was an excellent one; well-cooked and well served, with ample portions and Hands' conversation light and agreeable; Carter realised he had been fortunate indeed and he wondered whether his first good impression might not be later overlaid by some unseen drawbacks by way of compensation, if one could use such a term.

He hoped not. He had hardly dared admit it to himself but his expedition into Devonshire was by way of being a final gesture flung in the face of fortune. If he failed here all was lost, for his inheritance was now swallowed in the coffers of Pollard, Bassett and could not be recovered except through long and costly legal proceedings.

Time alone would tell whether he had been prudent in so disposing of his assets; but he was at least a partner, if a very junior one, and if he did not succeed here it would be his own fault. As he had earlier postulated such a chance did not often come a young professional man's way; if he did not prosper here he would not succeed elsewhere.

He had been brooding in this way for some minutes when he became aware of the awkward silence and realised his companion's eyes were fixed upon his face. He lowered his fork with a clatter to the plate, realising that both the landlady and the girl who had been serving them had now quit the room.

"I am sorry," he said by way of explanation. "I am tired after my journey and I must confess my thoughts were fixed upon Monday morning."

Hands gave another of his ready smiles; to Carter, who was a little more reserved, it seemed as though he had an inexhaustible supply.

"If that is all that is bothering you, Mr. Carter, think no more about it," the young apprentice assured him casually. "You will not find a more amiable crowd than those at Pollard, Bassett, from the directors down to the office-boy."

He paused and then leaned forward, lifting his glass of wine to his lips.

"That is, of course, providing one comes up to snuff professionally. We had a young chap two years ago who could not do the work. He lasted no more than three weeks. But I am sure you come with the highest recommendations."

"Have you been here long?" Carter said to change the subject.

Hands shrugged.

"Three years," he returned in his open way. "It seems a good deal longer. I was with Blakeney Gorstin in London before that. It was a good training ground, and by next year the five will be up, if you follow my meaning."

Carter nodded, reaching for the fresh glass of madeira his companion had just poured for him.

"And then you will be moving on, perhaps?"

Hands' eyes caught his, held them there in an awkward silence.

"Perhaps, Mr. Carter," he said simply. "But there is a young lady. Daughter of a local landowner."

He coughed as Mrs. Tregorran's shadow danced over the door-panel, her figure then materialising in the mellow lamplight.

"I am sure you understand," he said hastily, as though he had already said too much.

"Is everything to your liking, Mr. Carter?"

Mrs. Tregorran was standing by their table now, her white, rather beautiful hands folded across the front of her gown as she gazed at the young men.

"Really excellent, Mrs. Tregorran," said Carter.

"I am so glad."

She smiled briefly.

"We have managed to satisfy Mr. Hands these past years. And if we can do that I think we can cater for most people."

"Come, Mrs. Tregorran!" Hands protested, though he was laughing at the same time. "You must not exaggerate."

The landlady smiled amiably, her glance moving from the youngest of her guests to the latest. What she saw in the newcomer must have pleased her because she said softly:

"You must have some more of the apple-pie and cream, Mr. Carter. I'll send Pauline through in a moment. And perhaps you'd care to join me for coffee in my parlour afterwards."

"It will be a pleasure, Mrs. Tregorran."

The two men waited until the landlady had re-seated herself near the fire.

"A pleasant woman," Carter ventured in a low voice.

Hands nodded, his eyes more serious now beneath the thick thatch of sandy hair.

"Pleasant enough. I've known her now for a little over three years and you may rely upon her as you would your own mother."

It was a strange phrase to use, Carter thought, and he wondered what circumstances might arise in a quiet place like Thornton Bassett for a man to apply such terms to his own landlady. But he said nothing, gratefully applying himself to the extra portion of dessert the tall, vivacious girl brought through from the unseen kitchen beyond.

"Are there any other guests here?" he asked presently, as coffee was being poured.

"Precious few, even in summer," Hands replied casually. "Although we might take ten for a night or so in the holiday times. It's a big house, you see. But there are four permanent, now that you've arrived. Two clerks that work for the principal bank in the town. They're away on their annual holidays at the moment, on a walking tour together."

"So it will be quiet? Carter said.

Hands smiled.

"If you think this is quiet you should wait for the winter. Make the most of the gaiety while you may!"

Carter was aware that his hostess was waiting patiently in the doorway, and re-filling his coffee cup quickly from the earthenware pot on the table, he got up with a muffled apology to his companion and joined her in the hall.

She led the way across to a door just inside the entrance, opposite the dining room, and Carter saw that her parlour was comfortably furnished with good antique pieces, including a desk, a padded chair, some shelves containing leather-bound volumes of the classics, and a quantity of numbered ledgers in bound red morocco. He guessed that Mrs. Tregorran also used the room as her office. He sat down at the other end of the desk at her invitation and watched while she brought out two liqueur glasses and a bottle of cognac from a walnut corner cupboard.

Not for the first time in their brief acquaintance did the thought cross his mind that she was an unusual landlady. She poured a small measure into her coffee cup and a demi-portion into her own glass before filling his generously to the brim.

She lifted the small green goblet in salute.

"I drink to your arrival in Thornton Bassett, Mr. Carter. And give you a warning at the same time."

THREE
First Warning

1

"A WARNING, MRS. TREGORRAN?"

There was puzzlement in Carter's eyes as he lifted the glass to his lips. The cognac was excellent and he was conscious at once that his surprise had led him to allow a little too much of the fiery liquid to escape down his throat.

But there was no amusement in the landlady's eyes as she stared at him sombrely. She put one of her finely-made hands on his own as it rested on the end of the desk. It was a reassuring, friendly gesture, and he did not take offence at it.

"You must forgive a stranger's frankness, Mr. Carter," she said gently. "But you remind me of someone I once knew a long time ago, in happier circumstances. I meant no harm and mean no harm in what I am going to say."

"I am sure I take none, Mrs. Tregorran," Carter replied, though the puzzlement remained in his eyes. He picked up his coffee cup, sipping cautiously to soothe the passage of the badly judged draught.

"Dartmoor is a strange, wild place, especially for city people," Mrs. Tregorran went on, her eyes still fixed on his face. "This is your first visit?"

"That is correct."

The landlady nodded, a frown on her face. She got up abruptly and went over to the half-open door, closing it softly before returning to the desk.

"It is all gentle and smiling now, Mr. Carter, under these mild October skies. In winter there are fogs, moorland swamps, sudden floods, even landslides. Once off the road a man—or a woman—can be lost. A person could break a leg and lie there for years before he might be found."

Despite himself Carter felt a faint frisson of fear pass across the back of his neck. It was not the first time such cautions had been given during the initial brief hours he had spent on Dartmoor. It was hardly reassuring.

"I am not sure I quite understand, Mrs. Tregorran," he began cautiously. "I can assure you I have no intention of going out across the moors without guidance from an experienced companion."

Mrs. Tregorran smiled reassuringly.

"Excellent, Mr. Carter. This is all I wished to emphasise. I feel a responsibility for my guests, you see. And I have had some city people here from time to time who have done some exceedingly foolish things."

She leaned forward, the steam from the coffee passing through the light of the lamp making little freckled patterns on her face.

"The moor is a vast, empty, frightening place, Mr. Carter. Yet there are tangible things out there too, brooding, ancient things which must give a man pause in the present imperfect state of human knowledge."

Carter was startled at the woman's vehemence as well as her erudition but he tried not to let it show upon his face.

"You mean creatures, Mrs. Tregorran? Snakes, ponies, deer and other wild animals?"

Mrs. Tregorran nodded, her eyes a little wild and anxious, as though she had said too much.

"Those things as well, Mr. Carter."

She broke off, her head on one side and Carter thought he heard a creaking footfall in the hall outside.

"What I am trying to tell you, in a far from subtle way, is that Mr. Hands, though a most amiable gentleman, is inclined to be a little wild and foolish in his activities upon the moors. He means nothing by it but I am sure he has no idea of the dangers he runs."

She lowered her voice and bent forward across the desk.

"Last November, for example, he spent an entire night upon the moors in pouring rain. He fell into a moorland stream and was almost drowned. Fortunately, someone in Thornton Bassett knew roughly the path he had taken on his walk and a party of volunteers went out, led by the Rector. They found him and brought him in."

She looked at the young architect grimly.

"I should not like to think something similar might happen to you, Mr. Carter. So please keep to the roads. It is by far the safest procedure."

Carter smiled at her earnestness, though he was deeply conscious of her concern.

"I am indeed obliged to you, Mrs. Tregorran. I can assure you I will take good care."

He glanced toward the door.

"And I will regard our talk as confidential, of course. And do my best to curb Mr. Hands' impetousity."

Mrs. Tregorran let out her breath in a sigh of relief. She put her hand back over her guest's again.

"I am glad to hear you say so and I hope you did not take it amiss."

"Not at all," Carter said warmly.

He drew out his wallet, looking at his hostess significantly. "And now, I think we have a little business to transact."

2

Another quarter of an hour had passed before Carter quitted his landlady's parlour. As he had expected, he found the dining room empty. Hands had finished his supper and gone up to his room. Carter was still standing there, his empty cup in his hand when a shadow stirred in a corner and the tall girl Pauline stood there. "You'd like more coffee, sir? I have fresh here."

"Thank you, yes."

Carter sat down again, near the fire this time, while the girl leaned over him with the pot to fill his cup. He was disturbingly conscious of her proximity, of the animal warmth of her body, and of the faint perfume of her hair.

"If there is anything else you require, sir, you have only to ring."

Carter felt there might be a provocative double entendre in the innocent-seeming suggestion but he could detect no guile in the dark eyes or any pertness in her attitude toward him. He realised he was out of his depth where women were concerned; though he had had affairs, most of which had terminated badly in one way or another, he was really an innocent for his age.

He found it almost impossible to read the subtle signals that girls sent out to men, signals that for a man of his upbringing and temperament needed a receiving apparatus almost as delicate and receptive as the antennae of an insect. He felt a quick flush start to his cheek at the thoughts the girl's remark had engendered and he moved sharply, forcing her to stand upright as she looked down at him.

"I will remember that," he said gently.

The two remained staring at one another, their glances locked, for at least ten seconds; the moment was broken by a sudden clatter of footsteps in the hallway outside as Mrs. Tregorran quitted her office-parlour and the girl moved quickly away with a lithe, cat-like movement that reminded Carter of some beautiful animal he had once seen at the London Zoological Gardens.

He drank his coffee in hasty gulps and then left the empty dining room, walking with quick, nervous strides up the staircase in the direction of his room. Jeremy Hands was leaning against the wall in the passage outside his own room, looking down over the balusters to where the girl Pauline was disappearing in the direction of the kitchen quarters.

"A nice little girl," he said blandly.

"Indeed," Carter replied non-committally.

Hands was partly blocking the stairhead and made no move to withdraw. "Mrs. Tregorran gave you her standard lecture on the dangers of the moors, I suppose?"

Carter had to smile at the comic, semi-pompous manner his colleague had adopted.

"I think she meant well," he said quickly.

"Of course," Hands said.

It was impossible to read the expression in his eyes, the passage was so shadowy here.

"Well, you must be tired after your journey. I will probably see you at breakfast. And if you want a stroll out later perhaps we might go together."

"I will look forward to it," said Carter, without committing himself in advance.

"Goodnight, then."

"Goodnight."

Carter remained in the passage deep in thought a long time after Hands had gone in and closed his door. He was still there when the young apprentice opened it again. He did not seem at all surprised to find his colleague in the same position.

"I forgot to tell you. The bathroom is the last door on the right at the end of the corridor. A light burns there for the benefit of those staying in the house."

"Thank you," said Carter, inwardly amused at the mundane information.

Tiredness suddenly descended with all the weight of a heavy blanket, stifling his breathing, dragging his eyelids down. He got to his own room, scarcely conscious of how he came to be there, and locked the door behind him. Perhaps it was the wine he had drunk at dinner, coupled with the cognac Mrs. Tregorran had so kindly given him.

He had no need of his lamp. There was plenty of light coming into the room from the street lamps burning near the bridge spanning the stream farther down. He opened one of the big windows, that to the right of the desk, suddenly conscious of the coldness and dampness of the air. A thin mist was rising and a golden October moon rode high in the sky, outlining the bare curves of the steep moorland slopes that rose menacingly to westward.

The light made blurred, drowned images in the stream which looked as though it was dragging threads of tangled gold through the darkness and the plash and hurry of the water sounded chill and struck heavily on the young man's soul. There came the very faint music of an accordion—or was it a piano—from a distant tavern, perhaps from the big hotel in the square, and the occasional footfall of some homeward-bound person against the cobbles.

There was something else too; something which made Carter stay for a long time at the window, unconscious of the cold air and the dampness from the stream. At first he made it out to be the sounds of some night animal. A high, shrill keening noise that might emanate from a dog, a rat, or even a bird under the right circumstances—whatever they might be.

Carter was still standing there when it ended abruptly, with a sharp cracking noise. It was not until he had sought his bed that it came to him; and the sound had long ceased. It had been the high, bitter sobs of a woman racked by grief. His dreams were troubled when eventually he slept.

Four
Death in Sunlight

1

PERHAPS BECAUSE HIS sleep had been disturbed, Carter lay abed late the next morning; the sun was high when he awoke and the sound of church-bells flooded in. No-one came to his room and he then remembered it was Sunday. He did not know whether Mr. Pollard would wish him to be diligent at service or expect him among the congregation at some local church this morning so he made a hasty toilet and descended to the dining room.

It was already nine o'clock and there was no-one there but Mrs. Tregorran who sat in her usual place by the chimneypiece, reading the previous night's London newspaper as she toyed with her coffee cup. She greeted him amiably, and the young architect saw that the table was already laid.

He had just time to sit down before the girl Pauline came in to serve him with downcast eyes. Carter saw a subtle smile curving his hostess' lips as she raised her cup to her mouth. There was no doubt she was well aware of her employee's flirtatious nature and kept a close eye on her two young men in the house.

The landlady and the guest exchanged a few banalities from the separate tables when the girl had withdrawn and as Carter sipped his coffee and munched his hot buttered toast, he gathered that Hands had already breakfasted at eight o'clock and had gone out soon after on some business for the firm.

He had said nothing to Carter about the matter on the previous night but it was, in any event, no concern of his. It either bespoke great enthusiasm on the young man's part for his chosen profession, or a hard-driving hand on the reins for junior members of the staff at Pollard, Bassett.

Diffidently the guest broached the matter of Sunday worship. Mrs. Tregorran's eyes flickered and she evidently felt some inward amusement, though she answered Carter's question frankly enough.

"I do not think there would be any necessity, Mr. Carter. Mr. Pollard is too broad-minded for that. There is no coercion of the sort here in Thornton Bassett."

"It was just that I wished to do the right thing," Carter explained.

Mrs. Tregorran nodded, putting down her cup decisively.

"Of course, Mr. Carter. I quite understand. There are many Baptists hereabouts, of course. And the Church of England Minister, Mr. Sennen, could set you right about his services."

She smiled again.

"He sometimes comes here to enquire about the souls of my young men."

Her eyes caught Carter's and he realised they were a vivid blue at that moment.

"In the nicest and kindliest way, of course. He is certainly no bigot."

She drained her cup and rose.

"But you'll no doubt see the church at the end of the town, if you care to stroll down. You can't miss it."

Carter thanked her, and she went out presently, leaving him to finish breakfast in peace. Hands had still not returned so Carter went out in his turn without going back upstairs. He had not seen much of the girl Pauline this morning; he was somewhat relieved as her manner disturbed him. He could not have said why, but he felt awkward and uncomfortable in her presence.

He put it down to his lack of experience with women; being an orphan from an early age had meant he was not exposed to large, mixed families which so many other people enjoyed, and which had acclimatised them to the often seemingly arbitrary reactions of the opposite sex.

He turned down toward the bridge, realising fully for the first time the import of his colleague's remarks on Thornton Bassett in the winter-time. Though the sun was shining brilliantly, it caught only the high green slopes of moorland to the west which reared and towered over Thornton Bassett, their scattered flocks of sheep giving the impression of tears in a large sheet of green velvet.

But down in the valley below and on the small plateau which contained the little town there was dark shadow which enfolded the buildings and gave them a sombre aspect and Carter noticed that lamps had been lit in the interiors of some of the houses which were screened by their neighbours' roofs from even the high beams of sunlight which penetrated here and there.

Mist was still rising from the dark waters of the stream and Carter hurried over the bridge, realising that the air was dank and chill. There were few people about and he was glad to regain the square which, owing to its geographical situation, gained more of the sunshine. The shops were closed today, of course, but even so Carter was puzzled to see so many private houses and establishments shut tight with no sign of life.

He took his watch from his waistcoat, noting that it was now ten o'clock. He had stayed late at breakfast. He pressed on across the square, walking aimlessly, perhaps hoping to gain the downland which would again give him the splendid view of Thornton Bassett and the surrounding moorland that he had enjoyed on his drive with Slade the previous evening.

He had crossed the square without yet exploring the side streets and was back on the wide main thoroughfare again when he became aware of a faint, sweet chanting, as though a choir of children's voices were raised in some sad lament.

2

From here he could just see to the eastward, where the green hills were tipped with sunlight, the jagged silhouette of the ruined castle he had noted the previous night. From this position he could not make out the Dartmoor Forest of which his guide had spoken, but he knew it must fall away from the bluff on which the castle was set. It was hidden from him now by an intervening shoulder of hillside.

The morning was so quiet and still; the streets so empty; the only sound the faint, far-off clatter of distant footsteps sounding sharply over the fretting of water from the invisible stream which circled the little town; that Carter felt a great peace invade his soul. How long he stood there he did not know but he was roused again to consciousness of his surroundings by the echo of the children's voices once more.

Again he noted the tower of the old church piercing the belt of trees, on his left now, as he was walking back toward the town entrance, where the larger, more ornate stone bridge spanned the stream.

To his surprise, he saw that the square behind him and the parapets of the bridge ahead were becoming black with people; where they had come from or how they had appeared so silently he did not know. It was astonishing, almost as though they had appeared literally from the air. He presumed they had emerged from the houses and cottages round about, others from the side-streets and the margins of the stream, which were laid out with railings for riverside walks.

The people stood staring silently, completely ignoring Carter, heads bared, men, women and children erect and reverent, their eyes turned to the ground. Somewhat awkwardly, Carter adopted the same posture. He could hear the faint shuffling of feet now and the creaking of a heavy cart, the wheels rumbling over the rough surface of the unmade road to the church.

There was the children's choir all in white, a grey-haired sacristan walking in front with an ornamental cross held at the end of its long staff. The choir continued the same sweet low singing which seemed to Carter of an unbearable sadness. A coffin covered with flowers lay on the farm-cart and behind came the same clergyman the young architect had glimpsed the previous evening.

It was a strangely accurate repetition of last night's sombre ceremony made even more melancholy by the brightness of the day, the sweetness of the children's voices, and by the harsh ravages of grief on the faces of the mourners which the sunlight so pitilessly delineated.

Carter wondered for a moment whether there was some epidemic in the town—cholera, perhaps or some other dread pest—which was carrying people off in twos and threes. He hoped not; he was sure that Hands would have mentioned it. And Mr. Pollard would surely have warned his prospective junior partner of such a deadly danger.

Carter was being carried forward slowly now, as the mass of people in the square gathered behind the mourners; for the cart had turned out of the lane and was crossing toward the bridge which presumably gave on to the graveyard road atop the hill. All these people were quiet and stricken; they moved like automata; and their febrile breathing was muted, as though they feared to break some spell.

Alone among all these people, the Rector or minister seemed strong, unafraid and sure of himself; his firm voice, raised in prayer, echoed and re-echoed from the granite façades of the buildings round about. Carter managed to edge aside from the throng and temporarily isolate himself from their repressed grief as they gained the bridge. He wedged himself into the sheltering flank of a stone buttress and watched the drifting tide surge slowly past.

No-one took any notice of him; there was not one sign of recognition or interest in the faces of the people who passed, they were so immured in grief or anger; it was hard to tell which. Carter even felt a faint flicker of fear pass across him at some of the expressions he tried in vain to read. Grief or anger; it was certainly a strong emotion which animated the crowd, probably representing more than half the town.

Carter had turned now, and watched the cortege cross the bridge; he then noticed someone he knew. Mrs. Tregorran was standing a little in front of him, sideways on, at the edge of the parapet. She gave him a gesture of recognition and leaned toward him. By inclining his head he could just make out the low, muttered words.

"Please forgive me, Mr. Carter. I had forgotten the funeral when I recommended you this walk."

Carter warmed at the human contact and the tones in which his gracious landlady expressed herself. He made a deprecating movement, as though to indicate they would speak of the matter later, and watched the procession out of sight. The bridge was almost clear now and Carter was about to withdraw when he was arrested by the singular posture of a tall man who stood among the waterside sedges below the bridge parapet.

He was turned away from Carter who did not at first recognise him. He obviously could not have seen the procession from his present vantage point but it was in clear view of him as it began to mount the hill at the opposite side of the stream. The figure pressed its right hand on to the flexed knee of its right leg and said in low anguished tones that impressed themselves indelibly on the architect's mind: "Another, and another, and another! Where will it all end?"

He had no sooner taken in the import of this cryptic question when he realised with astonishment that the figure and voice were those of Jeremy Hands. He was about to make his presence known and question his colleague when the latter raised his face which was so strained and haggard that it thrust the intention from Carter's mind.

He hastily withdrew from the fringes of the crowd without revealing himself to his new friend and made his way back toward his lodgings.

FIVE
Twisted Souls

1

CARTER WAS UNPACKING the remainder of his belongings and setting out some of his surveying instruments on his desk after lunch when Mrs. Tregorran ascended to his room to announce a visitor. Carter's first thought was that his new employer had come to bid him welcome but Mrs. Tregorran smilingly disabused him of that. The Rector had arrived to pay his respects and to welcome him to the parish.

It was with mixed feelings that Carter descended the stair. He was glad he was alone this afternoon. Hands had not returned to the lunch-table and Carter had understood from his hostess that he was lunching with the family of the young lady of whom he had spoken to Carter earlier. Neither had he returned to his lodging after the strange incident on the bridge or Carter would have questioned him on the matter.

But here, he realised, as he followed Mrs. Tregorran to her parlour, was an excellent opportunity for innocuous-sounding questions to the Rector, who might well have the answer to some of the matters which were beginning to trouble him.

"You will wish to be alone, Mr. Carter. If you require anything, please ring."

The young man thanked his landlady who went back across the hallway to those regions the visitor had never yet seen. He opened the door to the little parlour to find a short, stocky man of about fifty or so, who rose from an easy chair with a quick, jerky movement to greet him.

"David Sennen, sir. Rector of this parish. I am delighted to meet you and welcome you to the district."

"That is very kind of you, Rector," Carter said, struck by the other's manner.

The two men shook hands warmly. The Rector gave the architect a shrewd look from humorous eyes which were almost lost in masses of wrinkles.

"You do not object to a pipe? One of my few weaknesses."

"Please go ahead, sir. It does not trouble me though I do not smoke myself."

Carter sat down again on the chair at the corner of the landlady's desk while the Rector resumed Mrs. Tregorran's chair. Carter was beginning to feel as though events were destined to repeat themselves, with subtle variations upon the originals. In less than a day he had seen two funeral processions, conducted by the self-same Rector who sat before him; and he had had two conversations at the desk whose smooth green leather surface stretched between them.

Like Slade, the man who had driven him from the station, Sennen had thick black hair which was already becoming sprinkled with grey. But there the resemblance ended. This man had some secret sorrow on his features which was burned and branded into them, as though with an iron. As Carter had already noted it was a humorous, characterful face, but something in the man's life had caused him untold suffering, he would have said.

The visitor finished lighting his stubby black pipe from the head of the sulphur match and puffed clouds of fragrant blue smoke into the scented afternoon air.

"I discerned some alarm on your face when you came in, Mr. Carter. Have no fear that I have come to convert you."

Carter joined in the other's smile.

"I am nominally Church of England, sir, but not a very diligent churchgoer of late years. Though, as a member of Mr. Pollard's firm, I am prepared to attend one service each Sunday if that were thought sufficient."

There was no doubt of the humour dancing in the Rev. Sennen's eyes now.

"Quite sufficient, Mr. Carter," he said blandly. "But is was not really on religious concerns that I came to consult you, though I always welcome new parishioners as a matter of course."

Carter sensed rather than saw a slight darkening of the atmosphere in the parlour, though the bright light of afternoon gilded the blinds and peaceful country sounds came from the street outside.

Perhaps he was thinking of the woman's dry, racking sobs he had heard last night. They had almost faded from his consciousness until now.

"To consult me, Mr. Sennen?"

The Rector raised his eyebrows at the surprise in his voice.

"You are an architect, are you not? Your principal is a great friend of mine, I fancy. And you are a specialist in church restoration, I understand?"

2

Carter felt confused and flattered at the same time.

"It is certainly true that I have taken some small part in the restoration of the fabric of a number of London churches, Rector. But I would not describe myself as a great expert or as a specialist of any sort."

Sennen smiled, flipping his match-stick into the grate where someone, probably Mrs. Tregorran's maid, had laid a fire of newspaper, sticks and coal against the evening chill.

"You are too modest, my boy. Mr. Pollard thinks highly of you. If you could take time to stroll down to the church I should be obliged. I could then show you the little problems I am anxious to deal with before the winter rains set in."

Carter was only too eager to prolong the conversation and he rose to the suggestion at once.

"Why not now? I have nothing pressing today; certainly nothing that could not be equally well done tomorrow."

The Rector got up with the brisk, bustling movement that was characteristic of him.

"Capital! Come along then. It is merely a few minutes' walk."

Pausing only to let Mrs. Tregorran know their destination the two men walked back down the street together, across the bridge and into the square. To Carter's mild surprise the Rector, who seemed to know everyone in the place, turned to the left and led the young architect through a series of cobbled alleys and side-streets.

"It is quicker this way," he explained. "Besides, you will need to find your bearings about Thornton Bassett if I know Mr. Pollard. He has one of the finest practices outside London if I'm any judge of such things."

"And are you, sir?" Carter ventured, stepping into the roadway, to avoid an old lady who was lifting a basket of hens up onto the pavement, preparatory to transferring them within her garden gate.

Sennen chuckled, giving Carter another sharp look.

"I once had a hankering for architecture at college," he said modestly. "But I hadn't the brain for it. So, as they always say, the fool of the family went into the church."

Carter smiled at the man's easy, good-natured banter, but he hastened to add, "I'm sure that's a libel on your character, sir."

"Well, well, I may have had my moments," the other retorted as they came round the corner of a small section of terraced cottages, where he opened a neat gate in the dry-stone wall.

"Here we are. The old churchyard was overfull and inclined to flooding in winter-time, so they shifted the dear departed half a mile farther up the hill."

Again, his good-natured features bore such an expression that no-one could take offence at the words and Carter realised there was a good deal more to the man than appeared on the surface.

The two men paused amid the worn, lichen-encrusted gravestones that leaned at crazy angles about them, Carter's eyes fixed on the soaring church tower that pierced the grove of trees ahead.

"That was what I wanted to ask you, Mr. Sennen. Is Thornton Bassett a very unhealthy place?"

A strange expression had passed fleetingly across the Rector's face, and he did his best to disguise it by briskly knocking the dottle from his pipe against an adjacent gravestone.

"Unhealthy, Mr. Carter? That is a rather strange term. What made you use it?"

Carter stood his ground.

"It is just that I saw you conducting a funeral here on my arrival last night. This morning, as I was coming to the church, I saw another one. I would appreciate a straightforward answer to my question. Is there some sort of epidemic in the parish?"

The Rector's face cleared, though it was still strained and marked with the stamp of sorrow Carter had noticed earlier. The dark-haired man put out his hand and clumsily patted the other's shoulder.

"No, Mr. Carter," he said soothingly. "It is nothing at all like that, I am glad to say."

His eyes were hooded now, his lips grim as he fixed his glance upon the ground.

"There have been some unfortunate accidents, that is all. I say that is all, but they are tragic enough, God knows. I have had my fill of epidemics in the slums of our great cities to last me a lifetime."

He smiled briefly.

"There is nothing for you to concern yourself with, Mr. Carter. Come along now and look at this roofing problem."

It appeared to Carter as though the Rector had quickly seized the opportunity to gloss the subject over but he did not return to it, merely followed the older man along the path between the tangled gravestones, keeping his mental reservations to himself.

The problems the Rector pointed out, both in and outside the church, absorbed him and Carter was glad to get to grips with something a little more tangible. He borrowed some sheets of an old sermon the Rector produced from somewhere within the massive stone pulpit and busied himself making technical notes upon the back of them, to the Rector's evident delight.

"We are not a rich parish, Mr. Carter," he said, as the two walked down the echoing nave, "But I've no doubt we shall be able to meet your price."

"Mr. Pollard's price," Carter smilingly corrected him.

The other's face lightened.

"My Rectory is just yonder through the trees. It is a little early perhaps, but I'd be honoured if you'd take a glass of sherry and a biscuit with me. I must not forget my manners. And I do not know what Mr. Pollard will say when he learns that I have been working you on Sundays."

Carter could not resist the rejoinder.

"But you work on Sundays too, sir."

The little cleric stared at him for a moment and then burst into laughter.

"Excellent, Mr. Carter. So I do! I see we shall get along famously. This way, sir, and let us discover what my housekeeper's cupboard will produce."

The two men walked easily along another path from a side door of the church, which led to a handsomely appointed house of some three storeys, just visible through the trees and over the top of the high hedge which separated the dwelling from the old graveyard. Carter guessed that there was a less sombre approach to the house via a drive running alongside the stream, and so it proved on his return from this entertaining expedition.

Sennen again paused as they reached the old timbered gate which opened on the driveway to his private garden.

"There was another small matter, Mr. Carter. Partly the reason for my visit this afternoon."

He glanced at an intricately chased silver watch he took from his waistcoat pocket.

"Let me see. I have just forty-five minutes before evensong. Time enough."

But he made no move to pass through the gate, his worried eyes still fixed upon the other.

"Your work will take you about the moors a great deal, Mr. Carter. I hope you will allow an older man to give you a little advice."

Carter inclined his head.

"Surely. But I think I know what it is. Mrs. Tregorran has already broached the subject upon my arrival last night."

The Rector relaxed his expression but his eyes were still sad.

"Ah, then it lightens my task, sir. Dartmoor is a dangerous and treacherous place for the unwary. I hope I make myself clear."

Carter nodded.

"Perfectly, sir. And I do appreciate all this advice which is being pressed upon me when I have not been in the town more than a few hours."

The Rector looked at the young man sharply but apparently read no offence in the words. He smiled thinly.

"It is a beautiful October afternoon, Mr. Carter. Sunny, smiling, the moors turning a delightful and innocent face to the visitor. That is all you see. But I have spent a good many years here. I know the people well. Most of them are good and kind, as willing to help a fellow-man as you and I."

He frowned ferociously at the ground.

"But there are others, Mr. Carter. Those with twisted souls and warped desires."

He put his hand out to the architect's arm again.

"Mrs. Tregorran will have told you about the dangers of the moor, Mr. Carter. Of floods, of treacherous bogs, of landslips and such. There are those and more. But I speak of other things. Of vengeance and murder. If you had seen the drowned bodies; of men drunk at cards who literally beat each other to death for the sake of a few shillings, of a wife strangled by a remote hill farmer for daring to look at another man—"

He broke off suddenly, aware of Carter's shocked disbelief at his outburst.

"You must forgive me," he said in quieter tones. "I have seen things that would turn the hair of a young man such as you grey overnight. I do not see the kindly, smiling face of the moor but other things, things that brood and fester beneath this charming rustic surface and erupt into violence and hatred. That is my Dartmoor, Mr. Carter, and I pray you do not live to see it as I have."

Despite Carter's astonishment at the Rector's soliloquy he was moved and shaken by the passion beneath it.

"Believe me, sir, I thank you for your concern," he said. "I know nothing of Dartmoor, as you say. But you can rest assured that I shall observe great care whenever I venture upon it, either by day or by night, just as my duties take me."

The Rector smiled grimly, taking out a silk handkerchief with which he dabbed his brow.

"Well said, Mr. Carter. Pay no heed. I spoke more warmly than I had intended. Perhaps I have been upon the moor too long."

He led the way rapidly across the driveway, oblivious of the babbling torrent that roared over the stones in front of them. He opened the garden gate for his visitor to precede him. Carter remembered then that the Rector's tirade had effectively prevented any more questions on his part about the two funerals he had witnessed on no less than two consecutive days.

The two men drank sherry and ate the dry, sweet biscuits brought by the Rector's housekeeper, in a shady arbour in the garden.

Carter dimly realised something of what Slade, Mrs. Tregorran, Jeremy Hands, and now this vastly experienced man had been trying to tell him. He realised too that he could not judge Thornton Bassett in two days of a mellow October week-end.

The winter would be the testing time. If he could survive the rigours of the life—both within the community and on the moors, in pursuit of his professional duties, he would be well set up for any vicissitudes. And he would make his own discreet private enquiries on any other matters which might catch his interest. But that there was something wrong in Thornton Bassett he had no doubt.

The half hour passed all too soon and the two men walked back along the façade of the house.

As though conscious that he had spoken too warmly and at too great length, the Rev. Sennen stood in front of the great wooden studded door of the Rectory. He put out his hand with a flourish.

"I hope you see me as your friend, Mr. Carter. If you ever have any problems, if you are in trouble of any kind, you have only to come to this door. It is open day and night to those in need."

The two men shook hands solemnly.

"I will remember, sir," said Carter slowly. "I think we shall be friends indeed."

SIX
Evening at the Inn

1

HANDS HAD NOT returned by supper-time. Carter guessed that he would be having dinner at the young lady's house. He envied him. Already, Carter was infected by a faint boredom with the somnolence and languor of Thornton Bassett. He realised he was being unfair; that it was Sunday night in a small town and that he knew few people here. All the same he was looking forward to the bustle of the office on the Monday morning and his first grasping at the threads of a career.

There would be new friends too; and doubtless interesting acquaintances, among them clients who would one day become friends also. For some reason tonight Mrs. Tregorran had vacated her table by the fireplace and the young man dined alone, accompanied only by the sonorous ticking of a great cased clock that stood in a corner of the dining room and measured out the hours with tinny condescension.

The girl Pauline seemed changed also. She went to and fro quickly, with downcast eyes and none of her former coquetry. It was as if she had received certain secret instructions from the landlady that she was not to dawdle or engage in conversation with the guest, for she replied to Carter's muttered questions with monosyllabic answers and was obviously pleased to get away from the dining room into her own quarters in the rear.

Normally Carter would have welcomed this attitude on the girl's part but tonight, without any tangible cause, he felt lonely and depressed. He would have welcomed company—almost any company—and once again he saw in his mind's eye the two solemn processions to the graveyard, and remembered the two separate warnings he had received from Mrs. Tregorran and from the Rector. There had been three warnings if Carter recollected accurately, for Slade had hinted at something on similar lines. And Carter had not forgotten Hand's hunched, strained position below the parapet of the bridge and his strange sentence about another funeral. There was something outre and twisted here, far beyond some unexplained accidents or the epidemics of Carter's imaginings.

Some secret sorrow had stamped itself into the faces of the people; even the phlegmatic Slade had not been immune to it. And Carter could not cast from his memory the recollection of that terrible sobbing he had heard the night before.

He finished his supper in an awkward silence, the girl clattering about as though anxious to be rid of him. It was nine o'clock when he walked back down the path and turned his footsteps in the direction of the inn in the main square.

His mind was much concerned with the astonishing outburst of the Rector. It was obvious that that kindly man was suffering from some sort of inward strain. But as Carter had already heard from so many sources, Dartmoor was a strange place, particularly in the winter-time. There might well be some mundane explanation for the things that he had experienced and the confidences he had been given.

He was a newcomer, someone likely to be long in these parts, and such people formed the immediate focus of attention when they arrived in an unfamiliar place. The architect had noticed that in London; for even a city is divided into a vast number of territories or villages and people in these enclaves tended to confide in some new person, rather than old acquaintances long resident in the area.

Carter carried these and other conflicting thoughts with him into the brightly lit bar of the hotel. He was conscious that he had missed the name graven in gold lettering on the board along the façade, but was immediately reassured by the cheerful, friendly atmosphere and the great bustle and clatter that hit him with almost physical force once he had opened the street-door.

He walked through into the parlour where there was a bright fire glowing in the great stone chimney piece and ordered a glass of sherry. His arrival had not passed unnoticed but Carter feigned to be unconscious of this as he examined a pair of brightly coloured sporting prints that were hanging on the fireplace wall near his end of the bar. The potman in here, a skinny youth with prominent neck-muscles and a green baize apron tied round his diminutive waist, did not seem inclined to talk, and once his order had been filled Carter found it impossible to draw him out. He had seen the look given his employee by the landlord, an enormous bald-headed man whose waist-line almost equalled his height, and guessed that the newcomer was being given the traditional welcome by the locals.

He had heard, before he left London, that one had to earn the respect and friendship of the ordinary people; others, like his landlady, his future colleagues, Slade and the Rector were in a different category. Carter was content to leave things to local custom and whiled away a pleasant half-hour in the inglenook, sitting quietly and absorbing the atmosphere.

He hardly noticed that Jeremy Hands had taken the polished oaken bench opposite.

2

"You seem abstracted, Mr. Carter."

The young man recollected himself in some embarrassment.

"I am sorry. I did not see you come in."

"On the contrary, I have been here all the time," the other went on coolly. "Have you been receiving the usual Thornton Bassett treatment?"

Carter came to consciousness of his surroundings, noting the studied indifference of the people in the bar, the covert stare of the fat landlord.

He smiled.

"Warnings about the moor, you mean."

"Something of the sort," Hands went on. "Would you care for another sherry?"

He got up quickly to replenish their glasses, leaving the architect staring into the depths of the glowing fire. Hands returned almost at once, re-seating himself with fresh glasses.

"I should not take it too gloomily, Mr. Carter. As I indicated earlier, their hearts are in the right places. But I must admit it could sound sinister to a newcomer. I know it did in my case."

"Let us talk of it tomorrow," Carter replied.

Somehow he shrank from speaking to his fellow-lodger of the Rector's vehement expressions of concern. It has been a corner of a man's tortured soul revealed for a few seconds. Incredible that he had chosen to unburden himself to a complete stranger. Earlier, if Hands had returned, he might have spoken of it. But the moment had passed.

His companion regarded him for a second or two from beneath half-closed eyelids. Then he shrugged.

"As you wish," he said easily. "What shall we talk about?"

Carter was immediately warmed by his companion's seeming ingenuousness and by the sharp sense of humour which underlay it.

"Your day, perhaps. I trust you had a pleasant visit."

Hands lowered his eyelids completely as he took another sip at his sherry. His sandy hair looked fiery red in the firelight as he sat across from Carter with his strong hands clasped about the stem of his glass.

"An excellent day, Mr. Carter. Patricia is a most delightful girl. I hope to introduce you to her at some future date."

"I shall look forward to it," Carter said.

He had not thought it wise to mention Hand's presence at the funeral; it was obvious that his companion had not seen him in the press of people on the bridge. His curious remarks still echoed in Carter's inner ear. If Hands wished to confide in him on some later occasion, that would be time enough. Carter already felt as though he had spent a lifetime in this remote Dartmoor town though he had not yet completed a whole day here.

The conversation turned to the trivialities of London life as opposed to those of the country and after the newcomer had purchased a glass of sherry for Hands in his turn, an hour had passed and it was time for them to return to their lodgings.

There was an odd quietness as the two young men quitted the bar and Carter sensed more than one pair of eyes fixed on their retreating backs. Perhaps the landlord felt it too because he came forward with an outward show of joviality and wished them a gruff goodnight.

It had long been dark. The stream made an agreeable plashing noise in the distance as they walked back down beneath the mellow glow of the few street lamps.

"The people here seem strange and reserved," Carter observed. "I am astonished that they were not more cordial with you this evening."

Hands laughed, the sound echoing from the granite façades of the buildings about them.

"They are pleasant enough," he said. "It is just that the landlord of The Bassett Arms is rather strict about church-going. Though a publican he believes that one should go to church on Sundays at least once. He has managed to instill his disapproval into his clientele."

Carter joined the other's reiterated laugh.

"They are curious folk, though," added the latter, as they came off the bridge.

"Half the people at the inn would have a cheery word for me if they met me in the street tomorrow. But it is something, after all, which you must meet and settle in your own fashion."

Carter gave him a shrewd look as they walked up the path to Mrs. Tregorran's welcoming front door.

"At least you seem to have developed a gift for friendship."

Hands' white teeth gleamed in the semi-darkness.

"It took me a year before I could engineer a suitable introduction to the young lady. And a further six months before I first set my knees under the family dining table."

"I shall be an old man before I find such fortune," Carter laughed.

Once in his own room he went across to the desk and opened the window. He sat there for a long time, listening to the distant fret of water, but the strained, wild sobbing of the previous night was not repeated.

SEVEN
Pollard, Bassett

1

"WELCOME, MR CARTER! I trust your long journey to this remote corner of Dartmoor has not dampened your enthusiasm for Pollard, Bassett?"

Mr. Pollard's beaming features came into sharp focus from among a blur of the faces in the spacious entrance hall of the family firm as Carter stepped through into the cool interior with its solid wood panelling reflected in the gleaming parapet. He felt, rather than saw, Jeremy Hands melt away from his side.

Carter smiled.

"Not at all, sir. But I must confess I had not expected such a welcome."

"Nonsense, my boy! The firm desires to do justice to its new member. You know my fellow partner, Mr. Bassett, by repute of course. Thornton Bassett is named after his family."

Carter shook hands with an enormously tall, cadaverous-looking man with deeply rutted cheeks and long grey sideboards. But his grey eyes were humorous and he muttered amiably, "Delighted to make the acquaintance of a fellow martyr."

The third of the four partners—Carter, of course making up the quartet—was a Mr. Charles Innsley, a man of about forty-five with a grave, reflective manner who nevertheless made himself out to be agreeable. Carter was soon lost in a sea of faces as the members of the drawing-office staff, who nominally included Hands, were separately introduced to him.

There was also a Miss Harkness, a small, mousy woman who kept the accounts, and two or three other men, including Slade, who had been held back from his outside duties to greet the new member of the firm. Carter was impressed and even touched by the thoroughness and warmth of the welcome and a number of differing impressions flooded his brain as Pollard gave him a rapid tour of the spacious ground-floor offices, rattling out information with a bullet-like precision, before ascending to display the light and airy drawing-offices on the first floor.

What was somewhat grandiloquently called the board-room, together with separate offices for each of the partners, was reserved for the second floor, set at the top of the rather fine mahogany staircase.

"We designed the building ourselves," said Pollard jovially. "Which is why it is so splendid."

The wry smile Bassett gave Carter revealed that this was a standard joke with the senior partner. Pollard led the way over to a series of framed drawings and water-colours which included plans of the firm's own offices, a few of their more notable commissions, and some fine water-colours featuring Dartmoor views, which Pollard had executed himself.

After Carter had been shown the magnificently panelled board-room where the partners met, both formally and informally, and entertained important clients, he was given a brief tour of the individual offices which, as might have been expected, were equally impressive. The attic floor, he gathered, was reserved for storage space, mainly plans, files and ledgers.

As Carter realised, his own office, as the most junior member of the partnership, was the smallest and most sparsely fitted but it nevertheless represented the finest quarters he had ever occupied in the course of his professional career and he was much gratified as Pollard continued his exposition.

The four men were alone now, the others having dispersed to their duties on various floors with suitable expressions of esteem. Carter listened carefully as his duties were explained. He learned he would not find things very strenuous for the first week or two but that the partners would take him about with them on their commissions and introduce him to clients and important people in the neighbourhood.

"I am most grateful, gentlemen," Carter said when the tour was ended.

Bassett closed one heavy-lidded eye in a knowing wink.

"I will remind you of this on the same date next year, young man," he said jocularly as he went out, taking Innsley with him.

"I will leave you alone for a while, Mr. Carter," said Pollard. "You will no doubt wish to settle in. Join us for coffee in the board-room at eleven when I will explain something of the workings of the practice to you."

He glanced at the cases Carter had placed on his green leather-topped desk.

"I see you have brought your instruments and I fancy the drawing-board yonder will suffice for most of your requirements."

He pointed to a brass bell-pull set in the panelled wall behind the desk.

"If there is anything you require you have only to ring and Slade or some other member of the staff will look after your wants."

He looked shrewdly at Carter. With his gold pince-nez on which the sunshine, spilling in through the two elegant circular windows, shone; his rumpled and immensely thick grey hair; his ruddy complexion; and fleshy, humorous lips; he looked more like a friendly uncle concerned for a nephew's welfare than the head of an impressive firm like Pollard, Bassett.

His well-cut grey suit made him an immaculate figure, and his highly polished boots had obviously been made by a first-class London boot-maker. Carter was fascinated to see that they had exceptionally thick soles and extremely high heels; no doubt Mr. Pollard also wore them for heavy walking on the moors whenever his professional duties took him there.

"I am most grateful to you, sir," said Carter.

Pollard shook his head.

"I am an excellent judge of character, young man. I never make a mistake. And I fancy the firm of Pollard, Bassett will be grateful to you as the years go by."

The eyes gleamed behind the gold pince-nez as he rubbed his hands together, going out quickly before Carter could say another word.

2

When he had gone the young man crossed to the desk and sat down in the heavy leather chair that reposed there, between the two circular windows. He ran his hands along the arms, savouring the rich, luxurious feel of the leather. The light gleamed on the sombre panelling, on the green surface of the desk, and on the heavy leather chairs that stood about the room for the use of clients and other visitors.

Life seemed to stretch endlessly before him; remote, affluent, exciting; the yeast of extreme youth had not yet ceased fermenting within Carter and he felt almost dizzy for a moment or two, leaning back on the padded rest of the chair, thinking that he had come to harbour at last in this small Devon town.

Then his practical side reasserted itself. Even though he had nothing to do, it would not be seemly for anyone to come in and find him idling there. He got up quickly, noting the finely carved mantel that stood a couple of yards behind his chair and enclosed the fireplace that would give plentiful warmth in the winter months.

It was equidistant between the two windows; everything about Mr. Pollard and his institutions seemed to be symmetrical; he appeared to have gone back to an eighteenth-century style of architectural tradition. Carter felt it was none the worse for that.

He moved to the windows, pleased to see that he had a fine view from both; the roof-tops of Thornton Bassett, of course; the stream winding its way along; and the high, frowning moorland to the westward with, in the blue distance, just a hint of the strange crag-like tors.

The nights were drawing in now but he would explore them at the week-end; he would ask Hands to accompany him, though he had not forgotten Mrs. Tregorran's advice. No doubt he would cross the moors frequently in the weeks to come in one of Mr. Pollard's vehicles, but there was nothing like walking and making one's own tours of exploration.

And despite local fears, he could not see what danger there could be in the warmth and brilliance of such golden October afternoons as they had been experiencing.

He turned away. There were other drawings on the walls, nicely framed in dark woods, together with some more of Pollard's water-colours. Carter went round slowly, savouring them in turn. One set of drawings was a meticulously executed series of elevations of almshouses in Plymouth; the work was exquisite and Carter was interested to see that it had been done by Pollard only some five years previously.

This was Carter's *mètier* and he lingered long over the studies, relishing the fine pen-strokes in the drawings and the elegant brush-work in the water colours. The man was a minor master in his own way; no wonder that his firm was so distinguished and his practice so wide-spread.

When he had finished there he put up the drawing-board and brought it out a little farther into the room, adjusting the angle by the big wooden wing-nuts, bringing over the stool to get the best position. The light was excellent here, as he might have imagined, and he finished his adjustments knowing that he would work well under these conditions.

Then he went down the drawers of the big plans chest against the far wall. There was everything he would need here, including the blank drawing sheets. With a precision born of long habit he went over and set up a sheet against the backing on the board, securing it with the clips until all was to his satisfaction. Lastly he got his delicate drawing instruments and set out those he might need, together with pencils and a rubber on the wide margin.

There was something almost absurd about the gesture, because he had as yet no commission of any sort; but it would at least show Pollard that he intended to pull his weight, if the principal looked back. He consulted his watch at that point and was astonished to see how quickly the time had fled. It was often so when one was engaged agreeably, as now.

He was about to replace the timepiece in his pocket when a sudden tap at the door disturbed his calm. It was Slade, who thrust his head in with a friendly greeting:

"Hope I'm not disturbing you, sir, but I just wanted you to know I was available if you had any messages to deliver."

He grinned then, looking keenly at Carter's preparations.

"Well, of course, you wouldn't have yet, sir, but I thought I'd show myself willing."

"I'm most grateful," Carter said. "I'll certainly let you know if there is anything."

Slade nodded, his eyes shrewd and appraising above his beard.

"All ready to start, sir. That's no bad axiom for a professional life such as yours. My best wishes for your success."

Then he was gone before Carter could make any rejoinder. The latter was still standing there when the shrill ringing of a bell from a corner of the room jangled his nerves for a moment. Then he smiled, realising its import.

He took a last, slow look round the office and then went out to join his colleagues for coffee in the board-room.

Eight
The Man on the Mound

1

"WHAT DO YOU think of that for a view, Mr. Carter?"

As they paused on the brow of the steep hill Slade reined in the pony and pointed with his whip. It was indeed spectacular. From where they had halted the land shelved steeply away into the silent fastnesses of the moor; in the distance blue weird eruptions of rock thrust upward toward the sky, crowned with yellow, brown, and purple gorse; while here and there the rocky, jagged masses of the tors stood out like some gigantic cemetery of pagan gods against the haze.

"Magnificent," Carter agreed.

He did not know whether he was becoming blasé about Dartmoor but he had seen so many similar views in the past two days that their images were becoming blurred in his mind.

Mr. Pollard had been true to his word. After the tranquillity of the first morning, the commissions and inspections necessitating Carter to go here and there upon the face of that steep and jagged countryside had occupied all his daylight hours.

He did not mind that, of course; and he was grateful to Pollard. He knew that the senior man was making sure he knew the district and the moor. He had been out with Hands once; Pollard once; and Slade several times.

The visits had been apparently purposeless in some cases, with the young man merely keeping a watching brief as Pollard examined some moorland bridge which the county authorities deemed needed strengthening or replacing; or perhaps visited some remote farm where the prosperous owner needed a new barn or byre.

But the geography of the fringes of the moor was slowly becoming established in Carter's mind and he knew that Pollard was training him for the more important and difficult visits in winter when the weather would be inclement and he would be on his own. There was only one regret in Carter's mind; he was a very poor horse-rider and it would obviously be better if he could ride a pony across the moor—when he was sufficiently acquainted with the terrain—which would cut off miles over having to take the moorland roads.

He had expressed as much to Pollard but the older man merely sat impassive at the reins, his kindly eyes gleaming behind the pince-nez and had shaken his head.

"It is no good trying to run before you can walk, Mr. Carter. Time enough to be thinking of riding lessons when you have been in the practice a year or two."

He patted the patient back of the powerful cob which he used for his own excursions.

"It is better and safer sticking to the moorland roads. And mists can come down very suddenly in the winter."

Carter had said no more and the subject had been dropped. Now, he gazed at the rugged terrain before them and once again realised the sense of the principal's words.

Slade had been regarding him from beneath his hard hat as though he could read the other's thoughts. He flicked the pony gently and they started on their downward course.

"You have some reservations about the landscape, Mr. Carter?"

"It is not that," the young architect confessed, "but everything tends to look the same out here."

Slade grinned strangely to himself, the grey hair making a marked contrast to the black beneath the brim of his headgear.

"That is good, Mr. Carter. You have already learned an important lesson."

"How so?" Carter wanted to know.

Slade shrugged.

"You have just said it yourself, sir. Because, if you cannot tell one part of the moor from another when you are upon the road in summer, then what chance would there be for you afoot and on your own out there in winter?"

Carter had no answer to that and was relieved a few minutes later when Slade again reined in the pony.

"Here we are, sir. This is Mr. Bonallack's place."

2

The fat, broad-faced farmer with the heavy tweed suit had a disappointed look upon his red face.

"So you think it cannot be managed before the spring, Mr. Carter?"

The architect shook his head. The two stood at the top of the windswept hill, the sun falling mellow and golden on the great flint-floored yard. Farm buildings stood on three sides and farther back, on the fourth, on a higher ridge of ground stood the farmhouse itself, snugly built of granite and with heavy wooden doors.

"You want the two barns, Mr. Bonallack. There is nothing simpler from my point of view. I have taken the measurements and I will see that the drawings are in your hands within a few days. Our office will do the costing. There is no problem there. But I understand from Mr. Pollard that all the available building firms for miles around are fully engaged at present. He asked me to tell you that the end of March would be the earliest "

The big man bit back his disappointment, screwing up his eyes against the sun.

"Aye, that's true, Mr. Carter," he said gloomily. "Mr. Pollard did warn me to have the work done this summer when a Pentarth firm could have managed it. However, it's evidently too late now."

"I will speak to Mr. Pollard on my return," said Carter briskly. "But we should be able to supervise those repairs to your labourer's cottages before the winter sets in."

Bonallack smiled unexpectedly.

"Well, that's something at any rate. And I'm obliged to you for your trouble, Mr. Carter. You're quite good for a London man."

Carter concealed his inner amusement as the other took him by the arm.

"There will be time enough for that after lunch, sir. Come along into the house before the food gets cold."

Carter looked back toward the main road where Slade had sat patiently with the pony and trap, but there was no sign of the equipage now. He followed his host into the house wondering what Slade intended to do about lunch. Perhaps he had something with him. Carter had earlier glimpsed a wicker hamper on the floor of the trap at his feet. Slade was a resourceful man and would not have come for a day upon the moor unprepared.

Bonallack proved an unexpectedly gracious host; his wife was pretty and welcoming, and the food was excellent. Carter suddenly realised with a start that almost two hours had passed since they had sat down at table. He excused himself quickly, surprised at the laughter of his host and hostess.

"You mustn't mind us, Mr. Carter," said the former. "Though we might not be outgoing to strangers, it's a lonely life upon the moor, and when we do have a visitor like yourself, we try to be hospitable."

And he added shrewdly.

"I've no doubt Mr. Pollard will put the time down on your expenses."

There was another burst of laughter, and Carter had just a brief moment to thank Mrs. Bonallack before he was ushered outside again. He got up into a substantial cart beside his host, looking around for Slade. There was no sign of him but before they had gone half a mile along the moor road there was a pony and trap like a shadow on the highway behind them.

Bonallack smiled at Carter's expression.

"A good man, Slade," he observed. "If a strange one."

Though curious, Carter cautiously forebore rising to the opportunity in case the two men were friendly and his remarks might get back to Slade. They were within view of Dartmoor Forest now and soon came to the cottages the client was concerned about. Carter spent more than an hour here; examining, testing, calculating and entering the details down in a heavy leather notebook he carried.

He had various surveying instruments with him in a small portable leather case, and he enjoyed the work, quite forgetting the time. At the end he was able to give Bonallack a rough verbal estimate which seemed to please the farmer. He murmured assent and Carter told him he would issue orders for the work to be put in hand on his return.

By this time there were deep shadows on the moor and the pony was obviously as anxious as Slade to return to the comforts of Thornton Bassett. The two men said goodbye to Bonallack and Slade urged the pony on. The sun was sinking now, the shadows deep purple in the hollows and in the places on the moor where shoulders of hill blocked the light.

There was mist in the hollows and an indefinable melancholy, underlined by the solitary echoes of the pony's hooves upon the flinty road which wound between the dark mounds of the hills.

Presently they came to a place much steeper than the others and Slade suggested they dismount. The two men walked in silence for some minutes, both somewhat awed and silenced by the sunset. All the sky seemed steeped in blood which stained the tips of the hills and spilled over into the valleys, which remained a dusky purple.

Apparently they had skirted round a good way to the east, because the same ruins Carter had noted on his first visit were now to the west of them. They stood out as a jagged silhouette against the sky, the ancient stones seeming on fire with the dying of the day.

Carter remained still for a minute or two, his soul awed and chastened by that stupendous sight. It was then he noticed a solitary human figure, black against the sunset, standing on a low knoll or mound some way to the side of the ruins. The castle or whatever it was, must have been a mile or two distant but Carter could see the silhouette clearly.

The figure was that of a tall, broad-shouldered man, who was slightly hunched forward. He appeared to be leaning on a crook or staff which was planted in the ground in front of him. For some reason the image aroused unease in Carter's mind, and he looked round to draw Slade's attention to it but the latter was already a hundred yards away, leading the pony.

When Carter again directed his attention to the scene the knoll was bare and blank, the jagged ruins sinking from sight in fire and shadow.

NINE
Pollard Speaks

1

IT WAS WITH considerable thoughtfulness that Carter went into his supper that evening. He had said nothing to Slade of the figure on the hilltop; it would have done no good, and it was obvious that the man had not seen it. If he had, he would probably have put it down to some shepherd surveying his flocks in the valley below, preparatory to calling them in for the night.

Carter was content to leave it at that but his mind was much exercised with that solitary, brooding apparition on the long drive back. It had seemed like the spirit of the moor, and though there was probably some mundane explanation for its presence, its appearance still brought a faint thrill to his spine.

He had had Slade drop him off at the office; the public reception rooms had long been closed but Carter had his own key now and went straight up to his office to put his things away; to glance over his notes; and to make a start on his report on Bonallack's requirements.

He had noticed lights from the corridor farther down and had guessed that one or other of the partners was still engaged on some late business; though Carter had not been thrown much in their company of late—he had been so much abroad on the firm's account—he knew they regarded his activities for the practice with some approval. It gave him a warm feeling to know that the oldest partner worked just as hard, or possibly harder, than the youngest.

He had not been there more than ten minutes or so when there came the vibration of footsteps in the passage and a tapping on the door. It was Pollard, still in his immaculate grey suit, keen and interested, to get Carter's first-hand views on Bonallack's commission. He sank down into the client's chair on the other side of the young man's desk, his fragrant cigar smoke hovering like a luxurious halo about his head.

He nodded approvingly at Carter's verbal report, his eyes wide and absorbed.

"Excellent," he said finally, glancing across at his partner's detailed notes. "I could not have handled things better myself. You are obviously destined to be the diplomat of the firm."

He smiled again at Carter's patent discomfiture, guessing that he had not been used to overmuch praise in his London billet.

"It was sincerely meant, my boy. Nevertheless, I will try to advance this major building scheme for Bonallack. The man owns a number of houses in the neighbourhood, as well as a small factory in Plymouth, and has been a valued client."

He waited patiently while Carter completed his dispositions for the evening. Then he consulted his watch anxiously.

"Will you join me in a quick glass at The Bassett Arms? It will be a not unagreeable prelude to your supper."

Carter was flattered. It was not only that Pollard was the senior partner and his employer. The man was genuinely convivial and the more time he spent in his company, the more valuable information about his profession, the practice, and the ways of Dartmoor people he gained. When they had put out the lamps and locked their offices the two men descended the stairs in silence, guided by the street lights shining in through the big windows which faced the square.

They walked across together to the inn and into the bar where Carter had last sat with Hands. This time the landlord was much more amiable and came to serve the two men in person, though Carter was not deceived by his attentions. He did not like the man, and in the manner of many frank young men of his class he did not bother to hide the fact; though he took care to observe the civilities for the sake of Pollard, Bassett.

It was early in the evening and many people were probably at table so there were few customers. Pollard waited until they were alone and toasted the young architect over the rim of his pewter mug.

"And how are you finding your way about the moor?"

"Well enough," said Carter easily. "Thanks to you and Slade and Mr. Hands."

Pollard nodded with satisfaction.

"I hope they have been looking after you?"

He chuckled.

"I meant Hands and Slade, of course"

Carter nodded.

"Excellently, sir. They have given me all the standard warnings about the moor."

Pollard's face had clouded a little at the last sentence.

"I hope you have taken heed, Mr. Carter."

The latter made haste to agree.

"I could not see it at first, Mr. Pollard, but a few days about the moor brings things home to one. The reservations you and the others have expressed begin to make sense."

Pollard's face cleared and he took another appreciative sip at his mug.

"The advice is well-meant, Mr. Carter. For instance, have you noticed how all those blue distances out there seem to blend and merge into one; and that each tor looks like another. If you are lost out there in summer it is difficult enough. But you are sure to strike a road eventually if you guide yourself by the sun."

He put the tankard down with a dull thud on the surface of the table and Carter saw the landlord look across curiously.

"But in winter-time, when it gets dark soon after three o'clock in the afternoon and the rain comes down and then the mist . . ."

He made a loud smacking noise with his lips, quite uncharacteristic of him.

"It is dangerous, young man!"

2

There was a long silence between them. Carter knew the elder partner had his interests at heart and he was emboldened by this.

"I have been studying the maps, Mr. Pollard, but they are remarkably reticent about the old castle out there, toward the edge of Dartmoor Forest."

A veil seemed to have sunk across Mr. Pollard's eyes and he started at his companion blandly.

"That place, Mr. Carter? Strictly speaking it's not so much a castle as an eighteenth-century folly, so far as we can make out. There are a number of confused stories about it in the neighbourhood."

He chuckled drily.

"Some of the Thornton Bassett people call it Rats' Castle, for some reason I've never been able to fathom. But its correct name is Temple Ruins."

He shrugged expansively.

"Though what temple and of what religious denomination I know not. It's my impression it's a good deal older than eighteenth-century but nowhere near as old as some people would have us think. If you look at our up-to-date maps you'll find the site carries a symbol, with the legend in the margin."

His eyes were clear and open again now.

"If you've a taste for history, young man, why not consult the Rector? He's our local antiquarian and has written a monograph or two on the curiosities of these parts."

Carter nodded, his mind revolving this new information. Mention of the Rector reminded him of something else.

"The night I came here, Mr. Pollard, there was a funeral. And again, on the Sunday morning, another. The people of Thornton Bassett seemed most affected. Any death, of course, is the subject of mourning but there seemed something quite extraordinary in their reactions."

Pollard nodded thoughtfully, sipping at his mug.

"You're right there, Mr. Carter. Perhaps the people here did not want to discuss their griefs with a stranger. The bodies of the two young men were found out on the moors, some miles away from the village. They were employed by the county highway authorities on road mending and the maintenance of walls."

He leaned forward, lowering his voice, his eyes steady on the other's.

"There are a number of wild stories going the rounds, Mr. Carter," he said grimly. "Best to ignore them. They range from accidental death to suicide and murder."

He compressed his usually amiable mouth into a grim line.

"It smacks of mob hysteria to me. The truth remains that two healthy young men died and their bodies were found by searchers in a badly mutilated condition."

Carter felt a strange compression round his heart.

"That is terrible, Mr. Pollard."

They grey-haired man nodded, his eyes gentle and abstracted now.

"It is indeed, Mr. Carter, and I would be the last person to deny it. But the police have the matter in hand, and they are best suited to such things. I read the newspapers and I keep my eyes and ears open, but I remain impervious to the wilder imaginings of the local folk."

He gave the other a wry smile.

"We are architects, Mr. Carter, and the firm of Pollard, Bassett sticks to its own business."

He laid his hand upon the other's arm.

"But we also are human beings. And we feel as human beings. These two young men were out on the moors at night. They were not engaged on the affairs of the county highway authorities. Who knows why they were killed or exactly how they met their end?"

He drained his tankard fiercely.

"I am horrified, of course, as all right-thinking men must be. But that is what the police are for. They are bringing in high-ranking officers from the city forces. And I hear a squadron of dragoons is due in Thornton Bassett to comb the moors."

He shrugged.

"Though what they expect to find is beyond me."

Carter sat still, his mind a mass of conflicting emotions. Jeremy Hands's words came back vividly to mind.

"You mean some wild beast?"

Pollard shook his head.

"I did not say, Mr. Carter. Who knows? Who knows what is out there at the best of times? And that is why I always advise my staff to keep to the roads."

His features relaxed, the corners of his mouth expanding into a slight smile.

"Fatherly advice, Mr. Carter. I value my staff and my partners. That is why I always try to act the heavy father. Some of them resent it but, I hope, they realise my heart is in the right place."

"I am sure of it, sir," Carter said warmly.

Pollard glanced quickly at the big cased clock that stood behind the bar.

"Well, I must not keep you from your supper any longer. Thank you, no; I will forgo the pleasure of you buying me some refreshment until some other evening."

The two men were back in the street before Pollard spoke again.

"You must come to dinner some time before the winter sets in. Mrs. Pollard keeps a fine table."

He chuckled agreeably.

"Well, goodnight, young man. And remember, my advice is given in the proper spirit."

"I'll not forget, sir."

Carter had much to think about as he walked across the bridge in the direction of Mrs. Tregorran's.

Ten
Night Visitor

1

HANDS WAS LATE to supper this evening or perhaps the architect was early, for there was no sign of the articled pupil as Carter took his seat at the customary table. Mrs. Tregorran was presiding as usual by the fireplace and greeted him with a slow, enigmatic smile.

It was a little colder tonight, and the fire had been well-banked and threw out a warm glow on the flag-stones of the beamed dining room. The girl Pauline did not put in an appearance. He was served instead by an even younger girl whom he supposed normally worked in the kitchen.

But she was pleasant and willing enough, flushing agreeably at his muted praise of the service and the courses. As was his custom when he dined alone, Carter read over his notes or technical works propped by the side of his plate; and he quite forgot the passage of time.

Coffee had long been served when he came to himself to find that he was the solitary occupant of the dining room; the other lamps, except for that directly above his table having been extinguished. He made haste to collect his material and left the room with rather more noise than he had intended.

It was obvious that Hands was going to be late this evening. Carter had understood there was a small room in which the lodgers were encouraged to sit and smoke after supper, particularly in the winter months; but he did not know where it was and he did not wish to disturb Mrs. Tregorran to ask.

There was a possibility that Hands had already returned and gone to his room. Carter ascended to the first floor of the house, conscious of the quietness which reigned here, broken only by the faint creak of beams—almost as though the old house was alive and breathing in the night.

He looked over his shoulder almost guiltily as he gained the stairhead; he was beginning to be infected a little by the talk about Thornton Bassett and the various friendly warnings he had received. Carter smiled wryly to himself and crossed to the door of Hand's room.

He knocked gently but received no reply. He stood there for a minute or two, his ear close to the panel, hearing nothing but the dull thumping of his own heart. He knocked again, this time a little more imperatively. Hands could have gone to bed, of course. He did not wish to wake him for something as frivolous as a few guarded queries.

He need not have worried. It was obvious after a few more moments that Hands was not there. He remembered then some vague remark by Jeremy early in the day about him dining at the young lady's home—in which case he might be back very late indeed. Carter crept across the passage to his own room with an absurd sense of disappointment upon him. Without mentioning to Hands anything about seeing him when the funeral cortege passed on Sunday morning, it would have been quite in order for Carter to have asked his opinion on Mr. Pollard's revelations this evening.

Obviously, it would have to wait until tomorrow now. The lamp on the table outside the bathroom was burning steadily in the distance, and by its light Carter inserted the key in his own door. Having trimmed his own lamp, he placed it on the desk between the windows and set to work for an hour or so, revising and checking his notes of the day.

He was not at all tired, and it still wanted an hour of midnight. As though on cue the church clock chimed melodiously, the sharp notes vibrating in the heavy silence and falling trembling across the houses and gardens of the little town.

Tonight Carter did not bother to open the window; he had been out of doors all day in any case and now he relished a quiet period in the silence of his room, working on at the notes and the detailed problems they presented, with the patience and the dedicated pleasure of the expert professional.

He was so absorbed that it was almost one o'clock before he closed the book, tiredness suddenly descending like a cloak. He quickly undressed, turned out the lamp and sought his bed.

2

Carter was awakened by a low, insistent tapping. At first he thought it was some faint noise from the street. He was fully conscious now, lifting his ear from the pillow, trying to distinguish the sounds from those made by his suddenly racing heart. He eased back on the bed, thinking he must have been mistaken.

It was incredibly quiet, and only moonlight penetrated the windows, the street lights having been extinguished hours before. The slight tremble of a board from the corridor outside was the only thing that disturbed the velvet silence. Carter could now see the outline of the door; he supposed it was distinguishable by the dim light from the lamp burning in the corridor.

He put his head back on the pillow, ready for sleep again, when once more there sounded the infinitely furtive knocking. There was no mistaking the imperative urgency of the summons, despite the delicacy and care of the soft application of knuckles to the door panel.

Carter felt a sudden drenching fear which he bit back angrily. It was absurd and to be resisted at all costs. He jumped out of bed, blundering into the chair on which he had placed his clothes. But his hands were steady now, and he struck the match first time, lit the green-shaded desk lamp. Sanity came back with the mellow light.

The sound of tapping stopped then, as though the person outside the door had seen the glow beneath. Carter stumbled around, still half asleep. His eye, lighting on his watch on the desk, saw that it was half-past three. It must be something serious for him to be aroused at this hour. He shrugged into his robe, went across to the door in his bare feet.

"Who's there?"

The urgent, quavering whisper came back.

"Hands. I must speak to you."

Carter was astonished. It seemed as though his colleague had the same idea which had come to him earlier. He wondered, though, why his business could not wait until morning.

"Just a moment."

Cautiously, he turned the key, trying not to make any noise. The door gaped a crack as he slowly opened it. The hinges had a tendency to creak, and he had no desire to arouse the landlady.

Hands' face appeared in the opening between the door panel and the jamb. He looked white and tired, his hair awry as though just risen from his bed. But Carter could see that he was fully dressed, and there appeared to be a black smear of dirt on his right cheekbone.

"I must talk to you, Mr. Carter, on a matter of the utmost urgency."

Though he whispered the words, it seemed to Carter in his half-awake state that their conversation must arouse the whole house. He hesitated, still standing with the door knob in his hand.

"Can it not wait until morning? I am half-stupefied with sleep."

Hands bit his lip.

"I am sorry indeed, Mr. Carter, at the untimeliness of the hour. But I would not have sought you out if I had not thought it necessary."

Still Carter hesitated. He sensed a faint vibration from somewhere within the house.

"You had better come in, then."

He held the door wide when there came the click of a lock from somewhere in the corridor beyond them. Light began to grow, spreading great sweeping swathes of black and yellow across the passage.

Hands' face expressed alarm.

"It is Mrs. Tregorran," he whispered hastily. "I shall try to make opportunity to speak to you tomorrow. Forgive me."

He fled, a fugitive shadow on the opposite wall as Carter gently re-closed the door, locked it and swiftly extinguished his lamp. With beating heart he went back to the door, hearing Hands' own door close gently in the furtive silence.

Heavy footsteps sounded now, and beams of light penetrated beneath the door. The person with the lamp stood outside for a moment or two as though listening for the breathing of the occupant. It was an unpleasant thought, and Carter felt a thin bead of perspiration trickle down his cheek. Then the footsteps went heavily away in the direction of the bathroom. A door slammed in the distance and the house resumed its silence. Carter went back to bed but not to sleep.

Eleven
A Message from Jeremy

1

HANDS APPEARED STRAINED and ill at ease at breakfast. He said nothing of his nocturnal visit—and indeed he had no opportunity, for Mrs. Tregorran presided smilingly at the coffee pot and the girl Pauline was tripping in and out all the time. The landlady cast a benevolent eye on the two young men as she passed their table on her way to her own.

"You were late last night, Mr. Hands," she said softly. "I thought I heard you come in."

Hands flushed.

"Yes, indeed, Mrs. Tregorran," he mumbled. "I hope I did not disturb you."

The landlady smiled again.

"It was nothing, Mr. Hands. That is why you young gentlemen have your keys. You obviously had a pleasant evening."

"Oh, yes indeed, Mrs. Tregorran."

Hands looked most uncomfortable, and Carter felt sorry for him. He hastened to change the subject to some more innocuous topic, and Mrs. Tregorran eventually passed on to her accustomed place by the mantel. The sun of the Indian summer burned on and though it did not directly illuminate the interior of the dining room, Carter could see it though the nearest window, gilding the roofs of the town and uplands beyond.

The two young men ate in silence and presently Hands rose with a muffled excuse, saying that he had to be at the office a little earlier than usual that morning as Mr. Bassett had some special instructions for him. He gave Carter an enigmatic, warning look and then went out. A few moments later Carter heard the slam of the hall door and the footsteps of his colleague hastening down the street toward the bridge.

He finished his leisurely breakfast, still only half-awake from his disturbed night, aware of the benevolent gleam of the landlady's eyes from the corner. He ordered extra coffee in order to combat his fatigue and felt a little more alert when he eventually rose from the table.

He went back up to his room to retrieve his notebook and certain instruments he might need for his day's activities and slowly walked down through the town to his offices. Already, after only a few days, the place was becoming familiar to him; now and again as he progressed through the streets he saw a face he vaguely recalled, and there were a number of salutations from people who obviously remembered him more clearly than he did them.

Arrived at his desk he sat for some time staring with a heavy frown at Pollard's drawing of the almshouses on the opposite wall. When he looked at his watch he realised with a start that it was already 9:40 A.M. This would not do. He almost flung himself at his drawing board and in an hour had made up his arrears. Both Bassett and Innsley looked in with cheery good-mornings during that time but there was no sign of Pollard.

It was almost eleven when Carter strolled downstairs to the busy hubbub of the drawing-office, where he was now accepted on easy terms. To his disappointment Hands was not there, and he learned that he had gone out on a survey across the moor which was likely to keep him all day.

He went back upstairs as the bell for coffee rang; the board-room was empty except for Bassett, and he had to endure the latter's lugubrious jokes while he drank the black brew and pondered during cracks in the conversation just exactly what Hands' urgent business could have been.

2

But Carter's routine was to be thrown off balance today. Just before lunch he was called into Bassett's office to be told that the new partner was invited to an informal gathering in a private dining room at The Bassett Arms to be introduced to some important clients.

Carter had just time to make a quick toilet in the partner's top-floor cloak-room when he was whisked away by Bassett, talking easily and agreeably, across the square to what he felt might be a considerable ordeal.

He was surprised. He was ushered into a long, panelled room filled with the reek of smoke and conversation. Despite the warmth of the day a great wood fire burned in the stone hearth, and the landlord bustled pompously about supervising the arrangements at the enormous table which glittered with cutlery and glass. Carter hoped there would be no speeches; certainly that he would not be expected to respond.

Instead, Pollard, who was flushed and in good humour introduced him to a number of people—none of whose names he was able to catch properly—and a glass of sherry from a silver tray was pressed into his hand by an obsequious waiter in a black cutaway coat.

Innsley was there, of course; he had been preparing things with the senior partner, Carter realised; and shortly after the company sat down; Carter at the end of the table with Bassett to his left and a small, excitable, red-faced, bald-headed man, on his right. But all seemed extremely affable, both partners and clients; and more than one congratulated the young architect on his new appointment.

After a few minutes Carter realised that he would not be playing a very great part in the proceedings; indeed, most of those present seemed to have forgotten him and were concentrating on an important-looking personage in a black suit who sat on Pollard's right as the guest of honour at the head of the table.

He had long hair tinged with silver, a ready laugh; and the lamplight gleamed on his gold-rimmed spectacles, which gave him the aspect of Mr. Pickwick, Carter thought. But Bassett was gradually drawing him into the conversation, with skilfully directed questions of a professional nature, and Carter soon realised that the little man on his right was listening with rapt attention.

He turned out to be the managing director of a major West Country building concern, whose head offices were at Plymouth, and he drank in Carter's discourse on modern architectural problems with an awed respect which Carter would have found comical under other circumstances in another situation.

But he realised he had made a good impression and, sensibly, did not seek to enlarge the subject into areas which were beyond his own knowledge. He quickly led the conversation back to Bassett and the stranger and sensed the approval in the former's eyes as he took over the reins again.

"Have you been long upon the moor, sir?" the little bald merchant on his right was asking now.

Bassett laughed, before the young man could reply.

"He has been here only a few days and has had enough warnings about the moors and its dangers to last him a lifetime, I should think."

The bald man looked indignant for a moment, and then a halting smile crossed his face.

"I meant merely to speak of the weather, Mr. Bassett."

He turned back to Carter.

"We have appalling winters here, sir. The blizzards are particularly bad upon the moor. The snow sometimes lies ten feet deep."

Bassett pursed his lips, replacing his sherry glass upon the table by his place. He had a job to make himself heard above the babble of voices.

"We do not emphasise those aspects of Dartmoor to our new partners, sir. Else they might not arrive to take up their appointments."

The bald man smiled delightedly. Carter joined in.

"It would have made no difference, sir," he told Bassett. "The extremes of weather are one of the great imponderables of our profession. Three years on Dartmoor are worth a dozen in London, so far as practical experience is concerned."

"Well said, my boy!" chimed in Mr. Pollard, who had caught this sliver of conversation from his end of the table.

He beamed at the company.

"And if an aged person like me can survive upon the moors, I am sure that a young man like you will flourish!"

Carter joined in the general laughter and rather unwisely allowed his neighbour to re-charge his glass. Unwisely, in the sense that he had a great deal of meticulous drawing to do after lunch, for which he particularly needed a clear head. He noticed that the distinguished-looking gentleman who sat in the place of honour was looking approvingly at him, and when he again glanced across a few moments later he saw that the guest of honour and Pollard were deep in conversation. Carter was obviously the subject under discussion.

The rest of the occasion passed in an agreeable blur so far as Carter was concerned. Not that he drank injudiciously, but there were so many people in the room; the conversation was so highly-charged and lively; and the atmosphere so convivial that the ever-changing impressions of the people around him shifted every minute and left his brain tired, and his concentration exhausted.

The fire had burned low in the hearth, and the daylight too was declining at the window when Carter finished the last course and gratefully turned to the *café noir*. He was aware of renewed congratulations; of many people shaking his hand; and when he eventually found himself outside in the square again with the other three partners, the church clock showed half-past four.

Carter was not used to this sort of treatment, and he wondered perhaps whether he might be expected to make up the missed hours in the evening, but Pollard seemed highly amused at his suggestion, though he spoke highly of the new partner's attitude.

"We have been oiling the wheels, Mr. Carter," he said jovially. "The office will profit by it, mark my words. It is an occasional diplomatic gesture which sometimes bears fruit; perhaps months, even years afterwards."

He put his hand familiarly across the young man's shoulder.

"It should not, of course, be considered in a purely pecuniary light. Lasting friendships grow from these original business associations. Take my advice, Mr. Carter. Cultivate the people of Thornton Bassett. Cultivate also the people of the moors. They are a deal more approachable than perhaps they seem."

Carter nodded.

"I'll remember what you say, sir."

They were at the office now and the members of the staff not employed on outside commissions were at great pains to restrain their curiosity regarding the business lunch. Carter found Miss Harkness at his side as he crossed the entrance hall.

"This is for you, Mr. Carter. It was left on my desk earlier in the afternoon."

The young man nodded and put the thick envelope into the breast pocket of his jacket, its contents unread. He went up to his office in an euphoric haze. He made a pretence of setting up his drawing board and then, struck by a sudden thought, started downstairs again. He met Pollard in the elegant hallway outside.

"Ah, I had a message for you, Mr. Carter. It quite slipped my mind at lunch. I have had to send young Hands to Plymouth on a commission and he is like to be away a few days. I believe he intended some words with you and asked me to give you his excuses. I must apologise for my tardiness, but he had already caught the train while we were at lunch. He has apprised Mrs. Tregorran of his absence so there is nothing to do in that direction."

"Thank you, sir," said Carter.

He had been on his way down to the drawing-office to seek his fellow-lodger and felt frustration at not receiving Hands' confidences over the urgent business which had impelled him to Carter's room the previous night. That it was important he had no doubt; now it would have to wait perhaps a week. It could not be helped, of course; Pollard was staring at him as though his expression were strange. He thanked the senior partner again and went back to his office.

Here he attempted to throw off the doubts and surmises which surrounded the affair and set to work on his set of drawings. Slade poked his head round the door just before six o'clock, and Carter sent him for a pint of coffee and some sandwiches. He worked on by the light of the powerful lamp, his pen scratching soothingly over the virgin surfaces of the expensive white paper. He ate the sandwiches when he became hungry and drank the coffee with them and felt better.

He was vaguely aware of closing doors and departing footsteps, but still he worked on, and eventually all was still. He found the last cup he poured was cold, but the drawings were finished and they represented some of his best work. He was satisfied then, but drooping with fatigue. He was astonished, on glancing at his watch, to see that it was past eleven o'clock at night.

He walked back across the town quickly, feeling the night air fresh and cool upon his heated face.

It was not until he was within the privacy of his room and had lit the lamp that the full extent of his tiredness struck him. He removed his jacket, preparatory to placing it over the back of a chair, when he heard the faint crackle of paper. He remembered then the letter that Miss Harkness had given him in the afternoon.

It was from Hands. Smoothing it out beneath the lamp on his desk he sat down to read it.

Twelve
The Rector is Reticent

1

IT WAS SHORT, almost curt in its brevity. Apart from the customary courtesy greeting, it read: I much regret I am called away by Mr. Pollard for several days on the firm's business. I may refer to our conversation of last night on my return. Forgive me for disturbing your rest. With every regard, Jeremy Hands.

Carter read it and re-read it with puzzlement; not to say rising irritation. Hands had appeared at the door of his room in the dead hours of the night; agitated, almost distraught one might say; and had intimated to his colleague that he had something of the utmost urgency to impart. Now, less than twelve hours later—Carter was here going on the actual time the note must have been written—he was saying he might take the latter into his confidence. Not that he would.

Carter was more annoyed than cast-down with the contents of the envelope. He replaced it and put it to one side of his desk, before starting to undress. But he had no sooner removed his jacket than he returned to the note, scrutinising both sides of the paper beneath the lamp as though somehow Hands might have left some cryptic message in cipher on the reverse side.

There was nothing, of course; neither had Carter expected there to be but he found himself mightily put out, as though Hands had been about to impart some tremendous and highly important secret when he had appeared so strangely at Carter's door. The architect was perhaps reading far too much into all this and when Hands did eventually unburden himself it might turn out to be something relatively mundane in absolute terms.

Yet Carter felt there was something badly wrong with the situation. A series of outwardly trivial events had prevented him and Hands from conversing together, initially by someone coming along the passage in the night, then by Mrs. Tregorran's inhibiting presence at breakfast, and finally by Pollard's lunch and the commission for Hands to go to Plymouth.

The truth was that Carter was inordinately intrigued, not only at the possible object of Hands' interview with him, but the circumstances which had led up to it; particularly by the Rector's strange outburst on his first Sunday in Thornton Bassett, and by Hands' own odd behaviour at the funeral.

He was certain that there was a common factor linking these disparate events and even though it might eventually turn out to have little import, it continued to twist and weave in the far recesses of his mind, like the sinuous movements of some exotic dancer, obliquely glimpsed from the corners of one's eyes when passing by a fairground booth.

Carter sat for a long time at his desk, his head resting on his hands, seeing little of the homely room but turning these matters back and forth in his troubled mind. It was past midnight when he reached his bed.

2

Carter breakfasted early in the morning. Contrary to expectation he had passed an excellent night, and it was only just turned eight when he descended the stairs. It was another brilliant day and all the dining room windows were open, bringing into the beamed room the fragrant odour of cut grass and the perfume of late garden flowers.

Early as he was Mrs. Tregorran was already in her accustomed place, reading some weighty volume with a leather cover whose gold-leaf title he was unable to make out. She rose quickly to greet him, and, after watching sharply to see that the girl Pauline served him promptly and efficiently, returned to her reading.

Carter had finished his breakfast by half-past eight and after briefly ascending to his room quit the house a few minutes later. It still wanted twenty minutes to nine when he was raising the big iron knocker at the door of the Rectory. The Rector was pacing in his garden, a sheaf of papers under his arm, and he came immediately round the corner of the building before his housekeeper could answer the tattoo.

His face lightened.

"Why, Mr. Carter! A pleasure and an honour, sir."

"I hope I have not called at an inopportune moment, Rector. And that I do not interrupt your breakfast."

The black-haired man shook his head.

"By no means, Mr. Carter. I breakfasted at seven and have been wrestling with parish accounts ever since. I should be glad of the interruption, to tell the truth."

He smiled benevolently at the sourness on the face of the woman who opened the door.

"I will attend to it, Josephine."

The woman slammed the heavy portal imperatively, the Rector apparently oblivious to her displeasure. Carter was secretly amused but he let nothing of it show on his face as the two men walked back down the side of the trellised building, still holding the gold and cream of a few late roses.

"Will you sit down, Mr. Carter. It is a pleasant spot and I do some of my most intensive thinking here."

It was indeed a cheerful place, being in full sunlight near an old stone sundial, at the junction where two paths met; the oak benches set at right-angles to make a little corner where the Rector's pipe still lay on a slatted table from his after-breakfast smoke. Carter cast a quick glance at the church clock, just visible above the trees and made it a quarter to nine. Pollard would surely not grudge him coming in at quarter-past this morning after his labours last night.

The Rector seemed to have some glimpse of the architect's mission, because a shadow passed across his face.

"The last time we met, Mr. Carter, you must have formed a poor opinion of my ministry here," he began cautiously. "I am not usually so intemperate of language before a complete stranger, I can assure you."

Carter shook his head.

"That was the last thing on my mind, sir. But I was interested in your remarks. And that was one of the reasons I called this morning."

An expression Carter found difficult to read traversed the Rev. Sennen's furrowed face beneath the thick hair flecked with grey. He took up his stubby black pipe from the table-top and turned it over in his hands as though he found the movement soothing.

"There was another reason too, sir," said Carter, more to give the churchman time to recover his thoughts than anything.

He drew the thick brown envelope from the case he had carried with him from his room.

"There are some drawings and rough estimates for the work we discussed relating to the church. They are purely informal, you understand. But I thought it best to let you have them and you can study them at your leisure before we go into it more fully."

"That is extremely kind of you, Mr. Carter," Sennen said warmly, sliding his thick, capable fingers into the envelope. He drew out the drawings and other material quickly, scanning them with relish.

"You will forgive me if I do not peruse them now. They appear excellent, but I could not possibly do them justice in a few minutes."

Carter shook his head.

"Let me have your observations later in the week, Mr. Sennen. There is no hurry, I assure you."

Carter nervously flicked his eyes to the lofty church tower and then back to the dusty ground at their feet.

"You mentioned something about people with warped desires and perverted minds, if I remember correctly. I wondered if you would care to be more specific?"

Sennen looked at him sharply.

"I am afraid I was rather indiscreet on Sunday, Mr. Carter. You must forgive an overworked and sometimes explosive personality."

Carter shook his head doggedly.

"Pardon me, sir, but I think it was something a little more than that. I seemed to sense some very real and secret sorrow in your face. And you so spoke so passionately..."

He broke off, conscious that he may have said too much. But the Rector did not seem to take offence at his words. Instead, he had a smile of singular sweetness on his face, though the other fancied that his features were somewhat pale.

"It is good of you to bother yourself about my affairs, Mr. Carter. It is normally my task to comfort. But you are unusually perceptive and sensitive to the problems of others, for such a young man."

He put out his hand fleetingly and laid it gently on the other's sleeve, before moving it restlessly back toward the pipe again.

"It was true, Mr. Carter. I spoke of vengeance and murder. And I have been much affected by those deaths of which I spoke. Those two young men, whose funerals I had conducted a few short hours earlier."

Carter nodded.

"It was of those accidents, sir, that I wished to speak."

The paleness was back on Sennen's face again.

"You have not seen or heard of any specific incident since last we met, Mr. Carter?"

It was a curious question, and it was a somewhat startled face that Carter turned to the cleric.

"I am not quite sure what you mean, sir."

Sennen shrugged, still turning over the stubby black pipe in his thick, patient hands.

"I meant merely had you heard some rumour; some specific incident of the past," he said carefully.

Carter shook his head.

"No, sir. I was referring back to our previous conversation."

The Rector opened his mouth as if to reply, but the two were interrupted at that moment by the chiming of the church bell, marking nine o'clock. Time was short. He really should be leaving. He bit his lip, rising to his feet. The Rector must have read the disappointment on his face, for he gave another of his sad smiles, rising in his turn.

"We seem doomed to have our interviews cut short, Mr. Carter."

He fell into step beside the other as they walked round to the front of the Rectory, where Carter could take the driveway that led beside the river. He saw the curtains twitch in the Vicar's study and guessed that the housekeeper was watching them from the shadow.

"Let me counsel patience, Mr. Carter. Patience is usually not a virtue of the young, but I do urge you earnestly to cultivate it."

Carter gave the other a wary smile.

"What is that supposed to mean, sir?"

Sennen favoured him with a frank, open countenance this time.

"I am not being Machiavellian, Mr. Carter, I can assure you. I am your true friend, and I hope you will see me in that light. As I said before, you know where to find me if you need help and advice."

"As before, I am grateful, sir."

There was a brief pause between them as they reached the front gate. Carter looked unseeingly at the brown, turbid mass of the river foaming over the boulders tumbled in the stream bed.

"I will speak of these matters again, Mr. Carter," the Rector assured him firmly. "I will tell you something of what troubles me. But the time is not yet."

He drew himself up and looked the young man squarely in the eyes.

"When that time does come you may be sure we shall have things to say and actions to take that will aid each the other."

Carter nodded slowly. He took the cleric's hand.

"I am glad to hear you say so, sir. Because there are matters beginning to trouble me also. I am a man who likes to run at a situation head-on. Your advice would be invaluable."

The Rector nodded. He stuck the pipe in a corner of his mouth, which gave him a slightly nautical appearance, like that of some middle-aged, thickset barge captain.

"Go slowly, Mr. Carter," he advised.

"I will remember, Rector," Carter said.

The short, powerful figure remained staring in the direction the young man had taken a long time after his physical presence had disappeared into the bustling streets of Thornton Bassett.

Thirteen
An Unexpected Meeting

1

IT WAS THE first time Carter had been alone upon the moor. Or at least upon the moorland road. Hands was still detained in Plymouth, though the office had received an express letter from him, with a private enclosure for Mr. Pollard which that gentleman had seemed to find eminently satisfactory. There was no personal message for Carter and no separate letter addressed care of Mrs. Tregorran.

It was as though Hands' problem, whatever it was, had never existed. Almost as if Hands had volunteered for this expedition to Plymouth, though Carter knew he was being unfair here. Pollard had told him of the specific circumstances under which he had dispatched young Hands. There had never been any question of sending anyone else; Jeremy's talents had uniquely qualified him for the commission involved, and Carter was satisfied in his own mind that there was no ulterior motive there.

Today he had been given his first independent commission at a large house on the outskirts of Thornton Bassett; one said the outskirts as though it had been a city with sprawling suburbs, but in point of fact the mansion involved was in a hamlet about two miles from the town, along the moorland road.

Slade, who was forbidden to accompany him, had offered the use of the pony and trap, but Carter had smilingly declined; he did not feel up to it today. It was still swelteringly hot as the golden weather continued, and he did not relish leading the pony up the interminably steep roads in the heat.

He knew he would have to master such conveyances in due time, but he had explained the dilemma to Mr. Pollard, who had concurred. Instead, Carter had chosen to walk, but had been given permission to quit the road and go across country, where he could see the curve of the highway ahead.

In this way he hoped to cut at least a mile off the journey and he had been given specific instructions by both Pollard and Slade as to what landmarks to look for, and both men were confident he could not fail to find the hamlet or the house which it concealed.

The house bore the mundane name The Priory, but Carter, used to late eighteenth-century villas in St. John's Wood and similar districts of London, knew he would find something very different here. He was far from confident that he would find his way across a mile or more of broken ground, even in broad daylight and in such clear, sunny conditions, but he had not dared mention that to any of his colleagues at the office.

He wore his lightest suit this afternoon, with a letter of introduction to the client in his breast pocket, and carried a small case of drawing instruments. Before he had left the environs of Thornton Bassett and a mere quarter of an hour had passed, he realised he had made the right choice. It was unconscionably hot, and very hard work indeed even for young muscles breasting the precipitous slopes of the road which looped and rose and twisted until the roofs of Thornton Bassett below looked like child's toys jumbled about and discarded after play.

On the far slopes the moorland rose, dark green; then flecked with the gold and brown and mauve of the gorse; and finally a deep, mysterious blue which dwindled into the haze. The sun shone on benevolently, but to Carter it was beginning to strike heavily on his shoulder blades and the back of his neck.

He had now gained the highest point, where the road commenced to loop away from the town and an ancient inscribed stone at the side of the highway gave the name and distance to the small hamlet he sought.

This was the point where he must quit the road and Carter looked anxiously ahead to an even higher ridge where this very same road, making an enormous curve, ran parallel, possibly some hundred feet higher up. He stepped down from the flint surface and almost immediately ran into unyielding rubble beneath the short, withered grass.

He soon realised that his shoes were most unsuitable for such terrain, and that with so much loose scree, pebbles, and granite boulders lying about, he would have to keep his wits if he were to avoid turning his ankle on this bleak slope.

He went down very cautiously, the road and the uplands sinking rapidly from sight until all that remained were the slopes above him and the great blue mass of the sky. He could now imagine something of what the moor might be like in winter. With a dark sky and no sun to guide one, it would be incredibly easy to get lost, pinned like an insect at the bottom of one of these vast, bowl-like depressions, in which it was impossible to see one's way forward.

He was breathing heavily and perspiring before he had gone a hundred yards, and he paused awhile to shed his jacket, carrying it carefully over one arm, making sure his precious letter of introduction was safe. His inside pocket had a buttoning flap and he first secured this before pressing on. He felt captive in the airless hollow and longed to rise again at the other side.

The moorland reared before him, seemingly as steep as the side of a house, and it needed little imagination to picture the conditions when thick ice and snow would cloak the moors. Carter's respect for the local people increased considerably. Survival here, even for a young man, would be difficult under blizzard conditions, for example, when one would not be able to see a hand's breadth before one's face.

He was already feeling blown by the time he had reached the jumbled bottom of the valley, where a ragged thread of stream ran among the boulders, not more than a foot across; the thin ribbon of liquid, brilliant where the sun briefly touched it, looked as sharp and bright as metal for a moment as he jumped awkwardly across.

He was rising from the valley now, his face set resolutely upon the opposite slopes, his muscles straining as he wound between the boulders, seeking the line of least resistance. Even so it was stiff work and every now and then the furtive pattering of small rocks and scree marked his passage, sliding and skittering into the depths below.

He looked back. Already, twenty feet higher, the almost imperceptible passage of the water was invisible, so seamed and pitted was the harsh surface of the moor. It was almost a lunar landscape, despite the superficial cloaking of green; composed of thin, scrubby grass, mosses, lichen, and weeds. The cattle and sheep must be hardy indeed to draw any nourishment from this, though Carter realised the verdure would be richer in the rainy months.

He paused again, his heart thudding in his throat, before going on, his path describing a zig-zag pattern across the facing slope. He was almost at the top; it had been a good lesson, and he knew now why Pollard had suggested the exercise. A morning of such ascents and descents, under ideal, summer-like conditions was worth a day spent in idle lectures. Carter drew his lips together in a wry smile as he plunged on, conscious of the damp, sticky patch of perspiration on the back of his shirt.

Once his foot skidded on loose rock, and he almost pitched back the way he had come; his heart was thumping wildly now and he halted in the shadow of a boulder to rest. He drew out his watch during the interval, saw that it wanted a few minutes to eleven. He was due to lunch at the client's house at one o'clock. Pollard had timed things to a nicety.

He moved with caution once he had quit the boulder. He was almost at the rim of the down, making for the stunted tree he had noted from the lower road. He could see the latter, a thin steel ring burnished and beaten from the undulating terrain. With a final scrabble and clatter of pebbles and rocks Carter had regained the road. The lesson had been well learnt.

He smiled grimly as he consulted his watch again. He was dishevelled, out of sorts, hot and inordinately tired for such a young man. He had gained perhaps half a mile of roadway and lost half an hour in time.

The road looped onward and upward. Carter waited until his racing heart had stopped its violent beating. Then he resumed his jacket, checked his instrument case. He carefully dusted the toe-caps of his shoes with his handkerchief. Then, still smiling, he set out to mount the looping curve of the road, ignoring the tempting short-cut of the purple valley below.

2

There was a cooling breeze now on the uplands and Carter's spirits rose as he mounted higher into this lighter, more ethereal world. He had met no-one and had seen no sign of life except for the occasional sheep grazing in the far distance and once, the flight of a great bird whose shadow, startling on the dusty road before him, had flapped heavily onward to the south.

Thornton Bassett was invisible, hidden in the crinkled curves of the terrain, and Carter realised he was penetrating the fringes of the moor itself. To the east he could faintly see the dark mass of Dartmoor Forest, though the ruins of the castle were hidden in the haze. In the middle distance the sinister granite stacks of the tors themselves were beginning to rear, like some ancient temples of a pagan cult.

The hollows of the moors were purple with shadow, and the tumbled boulders now represented to the young architect a pedestrian calvary where a man might spend hours climbing painfully from gully to gully. He was content to keep to the road which he knew must take him to his destination at The Priory where Pollard's client, Simon Hemmings, awaited him with lunch, hospitality, and a new commission.

Carter knew little about him except that he was an important man in the neighbourhood; a collector of books and such-like; rich, of course; a local magistrate; and a person of consequence in the county. It was obvious Carter now had Pollard's trust; he would not have sent him on such a prestigious mission otherwise.

Pollard had told him Hemmings required some extensions planned for his already extensive abode to house his ever-growing collections, Pollard supposed, though he had not particularised in his initial letter, and the senior partner had omitted to ask him at subsequent meetings. Carter had already learned that this apparent casualness held sway in the higher reaches of the business; but no doubt Hemmings would apprise him of everything once he was on the spot.

He glanced again at his silver-cased watch. It was almost twelve; he had nearly an hour yet and not quite a mile to cover, though the walk would still be trying in this heat and mostly uphill. It was a great pity that the railway only skirted the moor, though Carter's commonsense told him that what he desired was an engineering impossibility as it would be quite impracticable to drive vast cuttings into the heart of Dartmoor to serve such small hamlets and scattered communities as existed there.

He shrugged off the conceit and mounted the next curve, his feet gritting on the granite chippings of the road surface. He could hear the faint sound of hooves and an equipage now. He shaded his eyes, peering upward toward the next ridge. Another road apparently ran at right angles to this because the young man saw the silhouette of a barouche or similar vehicle with a pair of spirited horses in the shafts pass across his field of vision, from right to left, before sinking slowly from sight among the brownish-purple folds of moorland.

This was the only thing which broke the monotony on the last part of Carter's walk. He had carried a large-scale map of the area with him, and a short while later he stopped to study it and to orientate himself. If he had not missed his way entirely, Tor Bridge should be only some half mile ahead of him and probably to the right.

A tiny thread on Carter's map indicated a road bisecting the main highway on which he was embarked and the side lane on which the carriage was travelling, connecting the hamlet which was his destination to another small community in the next valley.

Carter did not know whether he was employing the correct terms; they were certainly his own, and the vast undulations of the moorland wastes indicated to him valleys and hills and lanes as understood in other parts of England.

He put the map back in his inner pocket and plodded on. In rather less than a quarter of an hour he had covered the remaining ground and had arrived at the point where the two roads intersected. He was pleased to see that his professional instincts had not led him awry, for here was a large stone column at the top of which was an addition of newer date; a sturdy wooden finger-post whose incised inscriptions indicated an illegible village to the left and, he could just make out, Tor Bridge to the right.

He turned briskly on to the level, the folds of the moor marching in low, undulating swathes to the horizon now; it was just half-past twelve and the sun, bland and glaring, was almost overhead. A thin dust attested his progress and hung like a pall in the air behind him, it was so still, even up here.

The road ahead rose a little and at the end of it he could make out the grey humped groupings of buildings; here were hedges, even stunted trees and what looked like symmetrical stone walls; in short, all the civilising evidence of a settled community in what Carter was coming to recognise as a somewhat barbaric place.

His shadow was almost beneath his feet on the dusty roadway and the echo of his progress must have been heard from a long way off. He could hear the creak of a cart and presently a farmer's wagon passed him, the patient horses covered in flies. The carter himself, though obviously curious, contained his curiosity and raised his wide-brimmed straw hat in courteous greeting.

Carter stopped to ask him the way to The Priory and was told that he couldn't miss it; it was the biggest residence in the village, at the far end of the main street. Carter thanked the man for his directions and gave him some small coins he found in his pocket.

He went on considerably refreshed in his mind, if not in body. A few minutes more took him to the entrance of the village where he paused in the welcome shade; there was a small green here, with a trough for carter's horses; and an ancient stone cross with what looked like Runic inscriptions.

The solid granite houses were closed and blank against the sunshine though the doorways of a few shops and commercial premises gaped blackly upon the road. Carter resisted their blandishments and went on, conscious of eyes watching him from behind half-raised blinds and thin muslin curtains.

Then he had turned the bend in the road, into the cooling shadow of a vast hedge, and the huge bulk of The Priory was before him. At the same moment there was a thunder of hooves on the gravelled drive and a pony and trap was upon him as he stepped out into the sunlight.

The animal reared with a scream and Carter had a brief glimpse of a tall, fair-haired girl with steady eyes who tugged impotently at the reins.

Then he was rolling over in the sunlight with the taste of dust in his mouth before darkness descended.

Fourteen
Fiona

1

THE GIRL'S FACE was anxious and concerned as Carter focused on it with difficulty. He tried to get up, found himself pressed back by a small but determined hand.

"You must rest a moment. You have had a nasty shock."

Carter felt his cheeks burn but it was not due to the sun as he was sitting in the shade, his back to a granite boulder. Two or three people with rustic dress were staring down at him too as the girl held his hand, kneeling at the roadside.

Remembrance flooded back as he saw the pony and trap. He started to scramble up.

"I am not hurt, thank you. But I must not be late for lunch with Mr. Hemmings."

The girl smiled a sweet smile which Carter remembered for a long time.

"It is I who should apologise, sir. I live at The Priory and my guardian had sent me to see where you had got to!"

She stared at Carter with parted lips.

"You are obviously Mr. John Carter."

Carter smiled.

"Obviously. But you have the advantage of me. Miss . . ."

The girl helped him to his feet and brushed down his dusty clothing. Someone handed the young man his leather case.

"Fiona Hammond."

Carter took her small, cool hand in his own, conscious that he must cut a sorry figure.

"I do not usually become unconscious at such a mild shock as a horse and trap passing," he said by way of explanation. "I think I must have had too much sun."

The girl nodded seriously.

"You have been across the moors on foot, sir, without anything on your head. It can be dangerous in this heat."

Absurdly, Carter thought, this unusual girl was merely repeating a warning which everyone seemed to have expressed ever since the moment of his arrival on the moor. But he kept his own counsel.

"You are doubtless right, Miss Hammond."

"You had best get in, Mr. Carter. Your indisposition lasted a mere two or three minutes. Thank goodness you do not seem to be hurt. And my apologies again."

Carter shook his head.

"Not at all. It was my fault for stepping out of the shadow and so frightening your horse."

"You had best get up alongside. I have to take her back to the stables in any case and it will be quicker."

The small knot of people dispersed with relieved expressions as Carter got up into the trap. The mare was still snorting and shivering and the girl calmed her with a few soothing words. Expertly, she turned the trap and they went clopping up toward the great façade of The Priory, which rose to receive them.

2

Though somewhat confused and bewildered, Carter had yet enough of his senses about him to see that the girl was dressed informally, in a grey riding costume, the lightweight jacket cut with square lapels and held at her trim waist by one large silver button.

She was hatless, her fair, tawny hair tumbling about her soft oval face with that careless art that denotes careful effort. Her hands were bare and devoid of rings, the only jewellery she wore being a small gold brooch on the breast of her jacket. She wore a white silk shirt, open at the neck, exposing the creamy pillars of her throat.

As though conscious of her passenger's careful scrutiny she gave him a slow lazy smile, regarding him circumspectly from the corners of her eyes. They were brown so far as he could see. Altogether, Carter had not been so much taken with a young lady for as long as he could remember.

She would have been about twenty-two or twenty-four years of age, and her firm, though delicate jaw, indicated a good deal of determination, not to say stubbornness. Her mouth was finely moulded with a full, sensual underlip, and there were two small lines of humour at the corners. Her teeth were white and strong in the dappled sunlight as she manoeuvered the trap expertly between the massive pillars of the main gates of The Priory, which carried the legend in wrought iron in a great curved arabesque that straddled the columns.

They were running along the façade of the building now, its mellow granite showing alternate bands of gold and black where the sun's rays were interrupted by great banks of foliage. To his astonishment Carter saw that the building was just what its name indicated; though obviously restored, it must have been a priory at one time for long, arcaded cloisters ran the length of the front, looking cool and inviting in this weather.

Beyond there came the flash and glitter of glass which showed where the modern additions of the house had been skilfully blended with the ancient cloisters to make an enormous mansion, the extent of which he could not yet comprehend; for the fretted buttresses of the ancient building ran up to an enormous height and had been cleverly merged with the modern roof of the new building.

The girl smiled at his expression.

"Extraordinary, is it not? But, of course, sir, as an architect no-one would appreciate that better than yourself."

"I must admit my professional instincts are aroused, Miss Hammond," said Carter enthusiastically. "This new commission of your guardian's should be interesting indeed."

"I hope you will find it so," said the girl drily, turning the mare round the corner of the building.

They were going downhill fast now, the terraced garden sinking from view, giving Carter just time to see a glittering façade of hot-houses and southward facing windows which reflected back the sunlight in a great brazen glare.

The pony's hooves were clattering on setts and as they descended beneath a broad stone copy of an eighteenth-century bridge which linked the gardens and a ridge which lay the far side of the stable buildings, Carter had a final impression of a large sheet of water in the distance, which resembled an ornamental lake. Then they were under the bridge, in a sort of tunnel paved, floored and walled in granite before this shadowy space opened out into a huge cobbled stableyard, where the mellow old buildings either side were hung with baskets of flowers and the stroke of one was just sounding from the gilded turret of the main stable block which faced them.

Carter was astonished at the splendour and size of the estate, but it was obvious that any such impression it may have once given Miss Hammond had long since worn off, for she paid little attention to her surroundings, throwing the reins to a strong, sandy-haired man who hurried out from an archway beneath the clock-tower and saluted her respectfully.

Her eyes were grave and concerned as she gave Carter her hand to assist him from the trap, as though he were some elderly invalid. He felt confused and embarrassed, and the girl smiled impishly, as though she had read his thoughts.

"You have had a great shock, Mr. Carter. I know you are a strong young man who is used to scrambling about dangerous places in the exercise of his profession, but fatigue and slight sunstroke are not to be tampered with. I insist on being your nurse, if only for a day."

Carter decided to enter into the spirit of her mood.

"If you were my nurse, Miss Hammond, I fancy I could bear quite a long convalescence."

They were down and the groom or stable-manager—Carter was not sure of his function—was staring from one to the other with a half-smile on his lips. The girl had a slightly heightened colour and her eyes were fixed on the toes of her smartly polished shoes which she seemed to find infinitely absorbing.

Carter examined his leather case to make sure it had not been damaged in his fall and brushed himself down surreptitiously as he followed the girl back along the yard, beneath the bridge. She was silent as she walked and Carter soon felt the energy and strength surging back. It was obvious he had merely suffered a momentary giddiness with the shock and surprise of the trap running at him; as the girl had observed, the sun may have had something to do with it, for he had been close on two hours upon the moor.

He had almost caught Miss Hammond up and she paused, still with her back to him.

"Is there no other way of getting about the moor except by foot or horseback, Miss Hammond?" he asked, more to break the silence than anything else.

She carried a small riding whip and she tapped with the handle on very white teeth as she stared at him.

"There are a number of horse conveyances which take people about the moor for pre-arranged fees, Mr. Carter. But I daresay you would find that a cumbersome method."

She put her head on one side and surveyed him gravely.

"The railways do circulate about the fringes of the moor. But you will still need some sort of transport to penetrate to any great distance."

She gave him her slow, lazy smile again.

"I take it you are not a great rider, Mr. Carter?"

The architect shook his head.

"Horses and I have never been very great friends, Miss Hammond, as you may have already gathered."

They were standing beneath the shade of the arch, stray beams of sunlight piercing the gloom and she gave a tinkling laugh which echoed beneath the stonework.

"Well, you are honest at any rate, Mr. Carter. You would find it best to use a pony and trap, and stick to the roads. But I am afraid that is a problem you will have to solve for yourself if you are to remain long upon the moor."

Carter looked at her steadily.

"I hope to remain upon the moor, as you put it, Miss Hammond, for a very long time," he said softly.

She did not answer that. He was unable to read her expression as they had fallen into stride again and she had her face averted. A few moments later she took a path that led to large ornamental steps mounting the bank at the left.

"The carriage entrance is up on this side," she offered gratuitously, taking the steps with long, graceful strides.

Carter followed, content to observe the almost Palladian splendour of the house that began to rise about them.

FIFTEEN
Simon Hemmings

1

CARTER NOTICED, as they got up on to a stone-flagged pathway leading straight as a rule across the close-cropped turf of the lawn, that another small driveway led off and up in a gentle slope to the great stone entrance porch of the house. He had not noticed it before as he had been sitting on the girl's left in the trap and the lane had been blocked from his view.

He noted with keen professional interest the detail of the crisply carved stonework and the incised armorial bearings above the main façade of the porch. The girl glanced at him quickly as they walked across.

"Please don't be overawed by my guardian and his house, Mr. Carter," she said. "You will soon get used to it if you come here often."

Her words were innocuous enough but Carter perhaps read more into them than the girl had intended and he felt his pulse begin to race a little. He looked at her sharply, but she had her gaze averted again.

"I will try not to," he said in as normal a tone as he could muster. "But the whole estate is rather awe-inspiring at first glance."

She smiled briefly, still leading the way at the same decisive pace. Carter realised it was just a few minutes after one, and it might be that her guardian was a stickler for punctuality. He had not thought of that; he hoped his late arrival would not reflect badly on Pollard, Bassett.

"Indeed," the girl said gravely. "It had the same effect when I first came here. But, as I said, one gets used to such things."

"How long ago was that?" Carter asked.

The girl gave a careless shake of her head.

"A little over six years, Mr. Carter. Both my parents were killed in a railway accident, and I was left an orphan. I have no other living relatives, you see, and my guardian immediately assumed his duties."

"I am so sorry," Carter said, realising his trite phrase was clumsy and badly expressed. "I was referring to your parents, of course."

The girl had come to a stand just outside the porch. Her eyes met his in a way that was difficult to read.

"Thank you, Mr. Carter. It seems a long time ago now. I was only fifteen at the time. One is more resilient at that age than one becomes later with increased sensitivity and understanding, do you not think?"

Carter nodded.

"Quite."

They were descending another shallow flight of steps now which brought them out within the shadow of the great porch. The flagstones carried on along the frontage of the house and disappeared at right-angles. Carter supposed, correctly, that the walk ran within the cloisters he had already seen as they drove up. It was an extremely clever application of the old to the new, and he sensed Pollard's hand in it.

The girl agreed with his supposition, when he voiced it.

"Certainly. They are old friends. I understand Mr. Pollard thinks very highly of you. And my guardian has every confidence in your abilities or he would not have commissioned you."

Carter shrugged.

"I hope you are right, Miss Hammond."

The two were still standing within the cool shade of the porch; farther on, where the vast lawn curved round, he could see the sun glittering on the conservatories.

"Is that the side on which the extensions are required?"

The girl smiled.

"I am sure my guardian will convey all the necessary information after lunch, Mr. Carter. Do you not think we ought to go in?"

"Forgive me, Miss Hammond."

Carter quickly crossed the porch toward the big glass double doors that gave on to a lobby, but before he had reached them one wing was opened and a middle-aged, smiling woman with dark hair was standing in the entry.

"Mr. Hemmings was getting quite worried about the young man, Miss."

"It is quite all right, Mrs. Arkwright. There has been a slight mishap, but Mr. Carter is uninjured. This is our invaluable housekeeper, Mrs. Arkwright."

Carter nodded acknowledgements of that lady's bobbed courtesies and followed the two women across the handsome parquet floor to a second set of doors which were opened to reveal an even richer interior.

He had time to notice much elaborate panelling, cream coloured walls, flowers set about in copper jugs and pans, and several exceptionally fine oil paintings.

The housekeeper stood patiently waiting at the end of the vast hall where a finely carved staircase ascended to a domed ceiling with the sun throwing down a many-coloured halo through the stained glass of the dome. Perhaps it was his exertions of the morning, or the unexpected presence of the girl, or the combination of both, but Carter again experienced a momentary dizziness. The girl was at his side in an instant.

"If you would care to wash your hands, Mr. Carter, Mrs. Arkwright will show you the cloakroom. It is just a step here. I will re-join you in a few minutes."

When Carter had refreshed himself and regained the hall, the housekeeper had disappeared somewhere, and the girl was nowhere in sight. An unbroken silence reigned. Carter recovered his leather case from the corner of the great carved chest on which he had placed it and examined a huge oil painting which depicted some primitive hunting scene.

It obviously took place on Dartmoor because here were the tumbled moors rolling to the horizon and the jagged cairns and tors that reared to the darkening sky. It was a sinister, winter scene and Carter was astonished to see, in the background, a solitary figure leaning on a staff, such as he had himself seen near the old ruins not two days since.

Then he heard the girl's footsteps, young and vibrant, on the parquet and she re-appeared at the foot of the stairs. She had changed into a simple white dress which clung to every line of her figure as she advanced toward him. He thought he had never seen anything so fine and graceful. She regarded him a little breathlessly.

"Shall we go in?"

"I think it is about time," said a deep voice drily.

The couple turned to find a familiar face regarding them at the entrance of the hall. A shaft of sunlight glinted benevolently on the gold spectacles as the elegant figure of Simon Hemmings advanced across the parquet to meet them.

2

"I am honoured, sir," Carter stammered. "You must forgive my lateness. A minor accident..."

The girl interrupted smoothly, linking her arm through that of the tall man in the grey suit.

"It was entirely my fault, uncle. I am afraid I almost ran Mr. Carter down in the dog-cart. He had walked across the moor."

She smiled up at her silver-haired guardian.

"A touch of the sun plus the shock of seeing me and Mr. Carter was lying unconscious upon the grass."

The man in the gold spectacles turned a little pale. He looked at the girl in amazement.

"Goodness me. I am so sorry, Mr. Carter. I did not dream of such an unfortunate event. Might I summon the village doctor?"

Carter smilingly declined the offer.

"It is very good of you, sir, but I am perfectly all right now."

The host became brisk.

"Very well, then. A glass of sherry before lunch is a capital remedy for minor ailments. And Mrs. Arkwright has prepared something special."

The three walked across the echoing hall toward the double-doors of the dining room which were already open. Carter was dazzled by another magnificent interior; he was conscious of Elizabethan furniture, fine tapestries on the walls and a great beamed ceiling which had been skilfully designed to blend in with the general atmosphere of the Priory. He gazed at Pollard's work with increasing fascination.

"You will realise, of course, Mr. Carter, that this room is a copy. But I think your friend Pollard rather excelled himself on this occasion."

"I should think so, sir," said Carter warmly. "It is superb."

Hemmings flushed with pleasure, and Carter knew that he had found a fellow enthusiast. The host excused himself and went over to a side table where the housekeeper was busying herself with glasses and a decanter. He came back with three filled goblets and handed them round.

"Let us drink to the success of your commission here and to your new career upon the moor, Mr. Carter."

The three glasses made an agreeable tinkling sound and Hemmings smiled encouragingly at the two young people as they took their first sips.

"Superlative, is it not? I have it specially shipped through a merchant friend in Bristol."

"I have never tasted better, sir."

They moved to a long settle with padded cushions which stood at right-angles to the massive stone fireplace; the latter was empty now and banked with scarlet flowers, arranged with careful art by either the girl or Mrs. Arkwright. Carter was quietly observing his surroundings and now had time to study his host. He realised the latter was staring at him in an anticipatory manner.

"You have not recognised me, Mr. Carter. Do you not remember we met at lunch the other day?"

Again Carter felt embarrassment flood through him. Of course! Now they were at closer quarters he recognised the guest of honour at The Bassett Arms, who had sat on Mr. Pollard's right and had smiled so benevolently on him. No doubt the two were discussing Carter's commission here when he had noticed them whispering together.

Carter smiled wryly at the girl, transferred his glance to his host.

"I am afraid I have a created a very bad impression, sir."

The older man mildly disclaimed any such thing, shaking his head from side to side, his spectacles catching the light, while the girl looked amused.

"You are incorrigible, uncle," she said.

She glanced quickly at the guest.

"Mr. Hemmings is not really my uncle, but my guardian, as I have explained, Mr. Carter; but he has been more than any relative to me."

The Magistrate gazed at her fondly.

"And she has been the finest niece a crusty bachelor ever had, Mr. Carter. Fiona is as straight and warm and frank as any man could hope to be."

The faint pink was back on the girl's cheeks now. She picked up her glass with a quick, decisive movement.

"Come now, uncle," she said sharply. "You will frighten Mr. Carter with such praise. I am sure he has no wish to be associated with such a paragon."

The Magistrate dissolved into hearty laughter, which brought a curious glance from Mrs. Arkwright at the other side of the dining room. Carter saw that the table was fully laid for three.

"You see what I mean, Mr. Carter. Franker and more unexpected than any man. I can do nothing with her."

He got up with a surprisingly swift movement for a man of his middle years.

"Another sherry, Mr. Carter. Fiona? It will give one an appetite for lunch."

The housekeeper was already at the decanter before he reached it and Carter, aware by that invisible, subtle network of intelligence that binds young people together, saw that Fiona Hammond had no wish to continue the conversation for the moment, and so had time to study his host.

He was exquisitely dressed, his perfectly fitting grey suit obviously tailored in Savile Row; the only touch of colour about him being the red silk handkerchief which peered from his breast pocket. His long, well-barbered hair, sprinkled with grey, hung low upon his collar; and his face had that smooth pinkness men get when out and about in the open air while at the same time resisting being burned by the sun, which turns the skin to leather.

In fact, Carter realised he was nowhere near so old as he had originally supposed; not much past sixty at the most. His jaw was strong and solid, and his well-kept yellow teeth were certainly his own. Carter felt now that his original assessment of Mr. Pickwick had been superficial.

Though the long hair; ready laugh; pink cheeks; and gold spectacles gave that initial impression, he soon realised that here was a well-educated, deeply cultured and erudite man whose library; collection of esoteric objects; and paintings stamped him as one who had unusual and surprising interests which set him aside from other bibliophiles and art collectors of his own taste and station. Of course, all this did not come to Carter at once but emerged during the course of the day and during subsequent weeks. His host was aware of his scrutiny and asked, as he brought the glasses back, "What do you think of my estate?"

"It is superb, sir," said Carter warmly. "I did not realise that the property was literally a priory."

Hemmings gave another of his ready laughs.

"The original building was believed to have been built by the Benedictine Order, though records are scarce."

He glanced at the girl, laughing again.

"Unfortunately, no trace of that Order's incomparable liqueur was found in the cellars. Eh, Fiona?"

The girl nodded, rising easily to her feet.

"Ought we not to begin, uncle? Mrs. Arkwright has been waiting long enough, and you know how she worries about the food."

"Eigh?"

Hemmings stared at the architect and the girl as though the notion had come to him as a surprise.

"By all means," he said kindly.

He moved forward.

"Come to the table, my boy."

Sixteen
The Commission

1

"A LITTLE MORE cognac, Mr. Carter?"

Carter smilingly shook his head, conscious that he had just partaken of one of the finest meals of his life.

"I would prefer another cup of coffee if I may. I must keep my wits about me for the more serious part of my day, sir. Would you prefer to discuss the matter now or later?"

He glanced at the girl's intent face.

"Although it might be boring for Miss Hammond."

She went on stirring her coffee, her eyes fixed on his face.

"I can assure you, Mr. Carter, it would not bore me. I do not engage myself in boring matters. My uncle has taught me that much."

Carter was impressed. Hemmings looked round benevolently.

"Let us just take things as they come. In the meantime let us all have more coffee."

Mrs. Arkwright came forward to pour, and a brief silence descended upon the table.

Hemmings raised his large porcelain cup to his lips, made a contented face.

"Did Mr. Pollard acquaint you with my requirements, Mr. Carter?"

"We had considerable discussion, of course, sir. Apart from routine matters of maintenance, I gather the major commission concerns two further large rooms to house your collections."

The young man flung out his hands as if to embrace the vast house and, by implication, the great estate. The housekeeper shifted uneasily in the background as Hemmings' chuckle broke the silence.

"You are wondering, Mr. Carter, why a man of my obvious wealth, who inhabits an enormous house, should require extra space."

Carter bit his lip.

"I hope I have not given offence, sir. It did occur to me . . ."

Hemmings shook his head. He was still smiling.

"It is a perfectly natural reaction, Mr. Carter. And I'm sure Fiona would agree with you."

He made an inquiring face at the two other people at the table and lit a cigar, Mrs. Arkwright coming forward to place a silver table lighter at his elbow.

"Your colleague Pollard made the same observation. In fact, it was his first objection."

He chuckled again.

"One would think that he was not interested in such a commission."

"I'm sure Mr. Pollard had your concerns at heart," Carter put in quickly.

Hemmings studied the glowing end of his cigar.

"I have no doubt of it, Mr. Carter. We have been friends for years. But when you have seen something of my collection, you will realise the problem. I have a miniature museum here. And I wish to display my items in a way which pleases my friends and fellow collectors and does not require them to tramp for miles through dusty cellars."

He tapped out the ash from his cigar into an elaborately chased tray at his elbow.

"It is true, I have vast space in my cellars, surplus to my requirements. I have my workshops there where I repair and renovate my exhibits."

He smiled as he saw the puzzlement in Carter's eyes.

"I am not talking about paintings, porcelain, objets d'art of the normal sort, Mr. Carter. What I have here is something unique, original and extraordinary. Things of beauty, nevertheless, that will one day be worth a good deal of money. I think Fiona would agree with me in all respects."

The girl nodded, putting down her coffee cup with a faint chink in the silence.

"That is undoubtedly why Mr. Pollard did not acquaint Mr. Carter with the nature of the collection. Preferring surprise. It is magnificent, Mr. Carter—and unique."

A faint shiver seemed to pass through her frame.

"If a little disturbing."

Carter sensed an undercurrent.

He turned in his chair.

"Disturbing? I do not quite understand."

Hemmings smiled, the sunlight glinting on his gold spectacles.

"I respect your feelings, my dear," he said soothingly to the girl. "There is that aspect of it, Mr. Carter."

He rubbed his hands and became brisk on the instant.

"Let us leave that for the moment. As Pollard has told you, I want two new galleries here. What are your ideas?"

Carter was equal to the occasion.

"Allow me, sir. I have my case to hand. Mr. Pollard showed me the designs of the existing galleries. I have my tentative plans here."

Hemmings smiled benevolently across at Fiona.

"Excellent. Your choice of architect has been fully justified, it appears, my dear."

2

The air was full of cigar smoke and the three sat in a semi-circle up at one end of the table, Mrs. Arkwright hovering like some benevolent deity in the middle distance.

"Of course, this is only a very rough idea, sir."

Carter sketched in a new design swiftly, with one of his shading pencils, pushing aside his preliminary studies.

"By utilising the orangerie as a vestibule to gain entrance to the new galleries, you would save enormous expense by obviating the building of two new main walls at the end of the house. Of course I would have to see the existing structures in situ to check if my plan is feasible, but I have seen all the specifications and drawings at the office, and there should be no problem at all."

Hemmings blew out a wreath of aromatic smoke and looked at Carter admiringly.

"What do you think, Fiona?"

The girl gave Carter a glance in which brightness was mingled with approval.

"As you said earlier, uncle, it seems as though I made the right choice."

"I do not understand, sir."

Hemmings smiled again, looking at his ward affectionately.

"I left the choice of architect to Fiona, Mr. Carter. She, being young, of course, came down on the side of the new. I, being older, waited to see. Now I thoroughly agree with her choice. It is a plan brilliant in its simplicity and would not, I fear, have occurred either to Pollard or myself."

"It is simple enough, sir. The new galleries will be free- standing and will have no overhead load on them. It merely means piercing two new sets of doors to give access to the glasshouses. I am sure the quotation will meet with your approval."

He turned to the girl.

"But how on earth . . ."

Hemmings blew out another plume of smoke.

"Fiona has had her eyes on you from afar, Mr. Carter," he said blandly.

The girl smiled and interrupted swiftly.

"What my uncle means, Mr. Carter, is that I knew you were coming to join the firm. I saw you in the street the evening you arrived, quite by accident. And so I made a simple suggestion to my uncle."

Carter was dazzled by the expression in this young girl's eyes. He felt a strange conflict of emotion within him. But he kept his expression non-committal.

"Let us hope neither of you have cause to regret your decision, Miss Hammond."

His smile was broad now.

"If the galleries should collapse beneath the weight of my revolutionary ideas!"

Hemmings joined in the general laughter.

"I do not think there will be much danger of that, Mr. Carter."

He rose from the table, bringing the light-hearted banter to an abrupt end.

"And now it is time, I think, to see something of the exhibition and to put your theories into practice."

Carter hastened to draw back the chair for his hostess. He was again conscious of some faint, heady perfume emanating from her hair. The girl was aware of his reaction also because he saw the slow, lazy smile begin. He hurried to follow Hemmings who was standing somewhat impatiently at the door of the dining room.

They went first to the orangerie he had already glimpsed from outside; the warmth was incredibly cloying, the heat of the sun through the glass multiplied a thousand times. But Carter had no time for the splendour of the foliage, or the immensity of the great green growths that writhed their way upward toward the huge iron trusses that supported the span of the roof.

He was the professional now, almost forgetting the presence of the girl who went to stand, a dazzling white figure in the shade by a cast-iron water-tank at one end of the immense structure. Hemmings had seated himself in a white metal chair in the shade also, consulting the rough sketches Carter had made at lunch.

Carter put down his instruments, selecting those he needed from time to time as he went about his calculations, completely absorbed. He was soon finished, two pages of his notebook filled with facts and figures. They filed outside now and while the girl paced the lawn, glad of the breeze which had sprung up, Carter turned his back on the magnificence of the view and explained to his patron how he would construct the two new galleries, taking advantage of the overlap here where the orangerie ran out at right angles to the main building.

It was obvious that Hemmings followed even his most abstruse calculations with ease and Carter wondered whether he himself might have some professional qualifications in that line. Hemmings was busy with his own notebook and his own calculations, as absorbed as Carter in his fashion and the young man did not dare to interrupt him. Instead, he glanced across quickly at the girl, who stood with feet apart some way back from the great façade, her dancing eyes upon his face.

Hemmings had finished at last. He put the notebook back in his pocket and came across to the young architect, his face blank and anonymous beneath the sun-dazzle reflected from his glasses.

"Excellent, Mr. Carter! I think you have hit upon the crux of the problem. And solved it at the same time. If you will proceed with your drawings and specifications I will instruct my builder to hold himself in readiness."

"Very good, sir," said Carter. "And now, if you would oblige me by pointing out those defects you wish put in hand before winter, I will prepare a schedule for them at the same time."

Hemmings gave a mysterious little smile, glancing across at the immobile figure of his ward.

"As always, you are right, my dear," he murmured. "This young man is a glutton for work."

He led the way back across the lawn.

"You will stay to tea, of course, Mr. Carter. We are counting on it. And Fiona will drive you back to Thornton Bassett. You have done enough walking for one day."

"It is extremely good of you both," Carter began.

The tall man in the immaculate grey suit cut off his protestations.

"Nonsense, young man!" he said kindly. "You are here at my behest, and at some inconvenience to yourself. It is the least we can do."

The next hour passed in a dazzle of fragmentary impressions as Carter passed from one part of the mansion to another; Hemmings giving him staccato statements, while the accumulated notes in his book grew to several pages.

It was late in the afternoon before they again emerged into the sunlight. A circular table had been laid beneath a striped awning on the terrace, and the girl awaited them, still standing in the same position as though she had been there all the time they had been touring the house.

Mrs. Arkwright also stood by an open glass door on the terrace, ignoring the magnificent view across the moors as she awaited her master's convenience. From this airy platform Carter realised they could see far to the eastward, where the blur of Dartmoor Forest began. The faint silhouette on the horizon could only be Rats' Castle, of which Pollard had already spoken.

Hemmings held up his hand. He did not actually snap his fingers but Mrs. Arkwright stiffened as though he had.

"Give us twenty minutes, Mrs. Arkwright," he said gently.

He turned back to his young guest.

"You have not yet seen the collection, Mr. Carter. Something unusual! Automata!"

And with a chuckle for Fiona he led the way at a cracking pace along the façade of the great house.

Seventeen
The Collection

1

CARTER SAW THE girl's shadow at the corner of his eye, waited for her to catch up. They walked together in unspoken intimacy in the wake of the energetic figure of her guardian.

"Do not be too put out, Mr. Carter," she whispered. "It is a somewhat bizarre pursuit, though not without great interest."

"I am sure," Carter said politely, though he was far from certain what his host had meant.

"You have not yet gone into the detail of the interiors of these two great rooms you propose constructing," she explained patiently. "Uncle will want exhibition cases of certain dimensions. The whole place must be laid out to match the existing chambers."

"I see," said Carter, though in fact he did not see at all. He wondered if he had heard his host aright. Hemmings waited politely for the other two to catch up, before closing the big glass door behind them.

They walked down the polished parquet of a corridor where absolute silence reigned. Carter felt he ought to whisper as though they were in the interior of a church, but the host felt no such inhibitions. He had dropped back a little until the three were walking abreast.

"What do you know about automata, Mr. Carter?"

The young architect shook his head.

"Precious little, sir. I have seen animated figures at fairgrounds, like most people, of course."

Hemmings shook his head, smiling. He glanced at the girl benevolently.

"Crude stuff, my dear young sir. You are about to be initiated into another world. Eh, Fiona?"

"It will certainly be that," said the girl, smiling in turn. "Only do not frighten Mr. Carter away, or he may not want to return. Start off with something gay and cheerful."

Carter listened to the conversation with increasing bewilderment, glancing from one to the other. Hemmings caught the query in his eyes.

"Patience, Mr. Carter," he said gently. "You have only a moment or two more and you will see what I have in mind."

He was fumbling in his pocket for a bunch of keys and had stopped in front of another massive set of double doors. From the internal geography of the house Carter realised that the room, or rooms, which his host proposed showing him, ran along the same side as the orangerie; his new structures would complement them, and he would expect to see the overlapping wing of the great glasshouse from these museum chambers.

So it turned out, but he had little time to note it as Hemmings threw open wide the doors. The windows in here were high up and the light showed green and aqueous through tinted blinds. There were banks of green-shaded oil lamps hanging from fittings in the ceiling, and Carter saw at once the system of wires and pulleys on which they could be raised and lowered for cleaning, lighting and trimming.

The floor seemed to be made of polished marble tiling and their footsteps echoed as though they were in some great public art gallery. The chamber, which must have been at least sixty feet long, was divided up into aisles by large glass cases set out on high wooden bases which brought up the contents to eye level.

At the right, to the far end of the gallery, was another set of doors which led, Carter guessed, to the next exhibition room. Hemmings rubbed his hands and smiled blandly as though he were some benevolent magician.

"I will explain more in my study after tea, Mr. Carter," he said. "I keep all my books on the subject in there, and I want you to design me bookcases for the new rooms so that I can house all the relevant material in these galleries."

He was busy with a small metal wheel as he spoke. There was a barely audible rumble as two of the ceiling blinds unrolled, letting in the sunlight high up. The room was now reasonably illuminated, though the glass cases were still partly shrouded in white dust-sheets which came down three-quarters of the way each side.

"Does the name of Baron von Kempelen mean anything to you, Mr. Carter?"

The young man shook his head, conscious that the girl had walked away toward the far end of the gallery.

"I am sorry sir, but this is not my subject."

Hemmings inclined his head, the light flashing from his golden spectacles.

"Quite so," he said. "There is no reason why you should know him. For those who, like myself, study the subject, the Baron is a great man. He virtually invented automata—ingenious mechanical figures which simulate life-like activities, usually through the most incredibly delicate clockwork."

He looked round the vast chamber, a faint sigh escaping his lips.

"I flatter myself I have one of the finest collections in the world in these rooms, Mr. Carter. Parochial as we are here, people come from all over the globe to see it. And my correspondence on the subject occupies almost four cabinets."

He flung up arms in a mock gesture of despair.

"So you can see why even I am beginning to run out of space."

"I think I follow you, sir."

"Good."

Hemmings became brisk again.

"I feel the brief history is apposite before I show you some of the exhibits. There is another aspect, you see. To reconstruct, re-build and even reconstitute such figures in their infinite complexity, one must become a clock-maker; a mechanic; a blacksmith; a costumer; an inventor; and a general mountebank!"

He clapped his hands and roared with laughter. Only Fiona Hammond seemed unmoved by his display of histrionics. Carter guessed that she had seen her uncle's fits of enthusiasm many times before.

"Fiona designs and makes the costumes, working from old books and catalogues," Hemmings went on, "while I have elaborate workshops deep beneath the Priory where the work of reconstruction goes on. I already have enough completed material there to three-quarters fill one of the new galleries."

"It seems an incredibly fascinating hobby, sir," Carter observed cautiously.

The eyes gleamed enthusiastically behind the spectacles again.
"Not a hobby, Mr. Carter. A passion, sir! A religion almost. Come, let me show what I mean!"

2

He pressed a button and at the same time removed the dust sheet from the nearest case. Carter gasped as a fairground tune, sweet and tinny, sounded through the great room. He caught the girl's smile as she stood in a shaft of sunlight at the far end of the exhibition hall. He walked closer to the case, aware of Hemmings' absorbed eyes on him. It was indeed astonishing. There was a polished wooden platform within the case, on which stood three small monkeys dressed in red, white, and blue military uniforms. Their accoutrements flashed and sparkled in the subdued lighting. One played the drums, another the cymbals, the third a trumpet.

From the eyes which opened and closed, to the simulated breathing which animated the chests of each animal and vibrated the muscles of the leathery throats, Carter could have sworn the little beasts were alive. As Fiona Hammond had hinted it was bizarre—uncanny even. As he walked this way and that to get a better view of the strange little trio he felt the eyes of the animals were watching him.

"What do you think, Mr. Carter?"

Carter was breathless.

"It is amazing, sir. It is almost witchcraft!"

Hemmings was smiling; he looked approvingly at the girl, who was now approaching over the marble with long, easy strides.

"You see, Fiona! He is as captivated as anyone else who has ever been here."

He looked at Carter again, his eyes half-closed as he followed the vibrating rhythm of the tinny little fairground tune.

"Believe it or not, Mr. Carter, it took me almost three hundred hours of work to restore this piece to working order. And Fiona put in a deal of time on the costumes."

"It is magnificent," said Carter, going closer to look at the detail of the extraordinary group.

The girl was not so impressed.

"Do you realise, uncle, that we shall be here at dinner-time if you propose to show Mr. Carter the whole museum? The twenty minutes is almost up."

Hemmings' eyes followed her absently.

"A hard taskmaster, is she not?" he observed casually. And then, quite unexpectedly, "You are not married, Mr. Carter?"

The young man felt nonplussed. He could feel Hemmings' eyes on his face.

"I, sir? No, of course not."

He turned toward their smiling faces, hastened to make amends. "I am sorry. I did not mean to give the impression that I am a misogynist."

Hemmings held his hand up deprecatingly.

"Never try to make impressions in front of young ladies, sir. You will always be doomed to failure."

He turned to the girl.

"I think we have time for the quick tour, Fiona."

Eighteen
Baron von Kempelen

1

"YOU WILL FORGIVE the little lecture, I'm sure, Mr. Carter," Hemmings said smoothly. "The next time you come things will not be so formal. And Fiona can show you the exhibits when you are on your own."

The girl's eyes were expressionless now as Carter glanced over his shoulder. She was following on behind as Hemmings stopped first before one case, then another.

The tour was definitely fascinating, Carter felt; he was truly astonished at his host's ingenuity. He had not known that such artefacts existed. He had seen a manikin on a donkey, galloping in a most life-like manner; more groups of monkeys; animals that performed dazzling tricks; and even a group of doves which appeared to fly around a fountain on invisible wires.

The man was a genius—the term was not too strong to describe him. Carter's respect for his ingenuity was increasing by the minute. The girl too had carried out exquisite work in clothing and furbishing the miniature figures; particularly that of a pianist in velvet and lace who played a minuet upon a grand piano.

Hemmings had explained something of the systems of pulleys and wires and levers, and cogs and ratchets, each set animated by clockwork which brought the automata to life, but even now Carter was not quite sure he had grasped all the principles.

"Von Kempelen was an Austrian who lived from 1734 until 1804," Hemmings was explaining. "He more or less invented the whole world of mechanical figures. His chef d'oeuvre was a mechanical chess-player which unfortunately perished in a fire in America about 40 years ago."

He threw up his hands in dismay.

"Alas! What secrets perished with that amazing piece of work. In this field might also be mentioned Pierre Jaquet-Droz, who manufactured life-size automata; the Swiss master, Johann Maelzel, whose Turkish chess-player was taken over and developed by von Kempelen; and Louis Rochat."

He looked at Carter shrewdly.

"But I bore you sir."

Carter shook his had vehemently.

"On the contrary. It is just that I find so much information, on a theme which is entirely new to me, utterly bewildering."

The girl had stopped opposite the latest exhibit, a golden swan which glided up and down a lake of black glass with silvered edges, dipping its neck occasionally out of sight as it dragged up miniature fish. Carter was almost stupefied with the technical virtuosity displayed.

He could have stayed here a long time, but he knew the girl was becoming impatient from the faint tapping of her toe on the tiling, though her face was still blank and expressionless for the moment.

Hemmings saw the situation in an instant and easily resumed his role as diplomatic host. He switched off the mechanism and dropped the dust sheet over the case almost in one movement.

"You are quite right, Fiona," he said cheerily. "We are overdue for tea. And we must not get in Mrs. Arkwright's bad books."

He led the way down the echoing gallery. Carter followed in the wake of the girl, feeling that he had never had such an absorbing day in his life.

2

"That is better, Mr. Carter, is it not?"

Hemmings put his spoon back in his saucer with a tinny clattering sound, looking round at the debris on the tea-table with vast satisfaction. A cool breeze animated the awning, and from here Carter could see bars of red falling like fire across the distant undulations of the moor.

It was a fabulous view from this terrace but Carter was conscious at the same time of the small, but almost unnoticed army who toiled about the great estate to make and maintain this beauty. There was a subdued, metallic activity from the stables; the subtle echo of footsteps from the great house beyond as Mrs. Arkwright and her staff went about their domestic tasks; while Carter could see at least three gardeners grooming the grass and tending the glasshouses from where he sat.

The girl looked cool and relaxed as she sat opposite Carter, her gaze apparently fixed on the distant purple of the moor.

"A penny for them, Mr. Carter."

He smilingly shook his head.

"My thoughts are worth a good deal more than that this afternoon, Miss Hammond."

A glance passed between the girl and her guardian, and then the latter had become brisk again.

"I hate to mention business after such a delightful day as we have spent, but when do you think I might have your proposals?"

Carter was on sure ground here.

"Certainly, my informal suggestions, before the end of the week, sir. I hope to make a start on the detailed drawings for the extensions by tomorrow. I have all the data in my notebooks."

"Capital!"

Hemmings slapped his thigh with his right hand with an explosive cracking sound. He was like a child with his enthusiasms, Carter thought. For of course he realised that this man was not concerned with the renovations, as important as they might be to the structure of the house. He was thinking only of the new galleries and of the marvellous toys he would be able to display there.

A shadow fell across the terrace and Carter was aware of the housekeeper's return. A tall man in black with dark hair stood at a respectful distance. Mrs. Arkwright's face looked worried.

"I am sorry to bother you, sir, but the gentleman insisted. It is court business..."

Hemmings bit his lip. He glanced quickly down the terrace to where the dark man hovered uncomfortably. He gave him a brief gesture of recognition with his hand.

He looked at Carter with regret.

"It looks as though our little chat in my study has gone by the board, Mr. Carter. I had hoped to show you something of my collection of books. But there it is. I have the misfortune to be Chief Magistrate in these parts, and it looks as though these rascals on the moor will be taking up my attention for the next hour or two. Please forgive me."

He got up and offered the young man his hand to shake, waving off the latter's proffered thanks.

"Fiona will take you back."

He turned to the girl.

"Will it not be dangerous for Miss Hammond to be alone on the moor after dark, sir?" Carter asked. "You said something about rascals . . ."

A shadow passed across the Magistrate's face.

"An audacious set of fellows, apparently. The superstitious locals round about attribute some supernatural agency to them."

He smiled grimly.

"I fancy a few stiff sentences would disperse their supernatural aura. Fiona will tell you all about it, Mr. Carter."

He was addressing the girl again now.

"You stay with the Trevithicks tonight, do you not?"

The girl nodded.

"Mr. Carter will see me to my destination, I am sure. And we shall be there before dusk if we leave soon. I will be back in time for lunch tomorrow."

"Goodnight then, my dear. And again, my apologies, Mr. Carter."

The girl rose from her chair and kissed her guardian affectionately. Then he had turned on his heel and was striding down the terrace toward the man in black.

"More tea, sir?"

Mrs. Arkwright was leaning forward, her figure stiff and black against the sunset.

Carter looked across at the girl.

"I think we have time," she said softly.

3

They were halfway to Thornton Bassett and the pony was ambling quietly at its own pace before Carter and the girl broke the silence that had fallen between them. The sun was still strong, but there were purple shadows and faint mist rising in the hollows and from where they breasted the rise, Carter could see a stream as cold and glittering as a scimitar which cut an irregular line through the landscape.

The tors leaned awry, the tumbled granite boulders looking like fallen chess-men. It was a stupendous spectacle, and there was little sound except for the progress of the dog-cart and the faint, lonely cry of a bird now and then. They had met no-one on the road, and eventually he had asked whether she did not find the life solitary and trying.

She shook her head, handling the reins expertly, her small hands sheathed in leather gloves. On the seat at her side reposed her overnight case in a smart shade of pigskin. Carter felt that he could have sat at her side and gone clopping through the dusky lanes like this for ever.

"Why should I, Mr. Carter? I have plenty of friends on and around the moor. And I have much to do about the estate."

"I am sure," he ventured. "It was just that I found the moor so different from London. Have you ever lived there?"

"For a while," she said carelessly. "It can be just as lonely as Dartmoor. It depends upon one's personality."

There was a good deal in what she said, Carter felt, but he chose not to reply, just kept his eyes fixed upon the glow in the west that stained the road behind them. He changed the subject abruptly.

"What did your guardian mean? About a band of people upon the moors?"

Fiona Hammond smiled, raising her eyes from the road to his.

"It sounds like superstitious nonsense. People have been talking about Satan and His Hounds. A body of horsemen upon the moor, they say, riding down innocent people during the night."

She gave him a mocking smile.

"Have you ever heard the like?"

Carter felt the smile freezing on his face. Something dark and sinister surfaced in his unconscious for a moment; then passed off in the gaiety of the girl's features.

"No," he said. "But all the same, could there not be something bad involved? I saw two funerals in Thornton Bassett. People spoke of accidents on the moor . . ."

There was a shadow in the girl's eyes now, which had not been there before.

"I have not heard the hounds and riders blamed for that, Mr. Carter. Though I do not live in Thornton Bassett, of course. The people my guardian is after are more likely to be drunken hooligans riding about after dark and frightening honest folk. I do not know all the ins and outs, and I do not care to listen to gossip."

She smiled again.

"But next time you come to The Priory ask my guardian. He will keep you up to all hours talking about it."

Carter again remembered the figure he had seen upon the mound. Satan and His Hounds. The gossip certainly left an unpleasant impression upon his mind. And he recalled the great oil painting he had seen in the hall of The Priory only a few hours before.

"Might there not be some truth in old superstitions, Miss Hammond?" he said gently. "I saw a painting in your own house only a few hours since that might have served as a model for such a scene as you describe. There were huntsmen and hounds; the venue was certainly Dartmoor; and even an old man leaning on a stick who looked like Satan himself!"

The girl stared at him incredulously, her eyes dancing.

"You surely do not mean it, Mr. Carter? That was something my guardian inherited with the property. We had always taken it for a meet of a local hunt."

She was laughing openly now.

"I can see we must carry out much deeper research into our local customs in future!"

Carter felt warmth on his cheeks.

"Please do not laugh at me, Miss Hammond. It is just that a stranger may see things which are not quite so obvious to people who have lived in a place for years."

The girl had drawn the trap to a halt now, to rest the pony. Her eyes were cool and appraising.

"Indeed they may, Mr. Carter," she said gently. "And you must forgive my rudeness."

Carter shook his head.

"That would be the last trait I would attribute to you, Miss Hammond. But do think about it. I have seen and heard things in my few days in Thornton Bassett which have given me pause."

The girl looked at him steadily, the declining sun staining her frank, open face a deep bronze colour. She looked very captivating like that, and Carter could have studied her features for some considerable time.

But she suddenly broke the spell and then the pony had roused himself, and they were trotting gently down into the hollow where Thornton Bassett lay, the purple and gold of the landscape turning dusky now as the evening advanced. It was almost dark as they gained the streets which Carter was beginning to find so familiar.

The pony seemed to know his own way and trotted willingly across the two bridges, rapidly leaving the little town behind until he eased back halfway up the hill beyond, both Carter and the girl descending to give the little beast a chance to breathe. The two walked alongside the dog-cart in thought, the deepening twilight throwing long tendrils about them.

"I am sorry to have taken you so far out of your way, Mr. Carter," she said eventually, as the willing animal turned the cart into the entrance drive of a large mansion to the left of the lane, flanked by stone pillars of baronial proportions.

"A pleasure, Miss Hammond," Carter mumbled.

The girl held out her hand hesitantly.

"Will you not come in and meet my hosts?"

Carter shook his head regretfully.

"I would not put them out. And my supper will be waiting."

He tapped the leather case which contained his instruments and notebooks.

"Besides, I must work on your guardian's commission before I seek my bed."

The girl smiled gravely.

"You must not overdo things, Mr. Carter. Remember the sun this afternoon."

The young man's smile echoed her own.

"I am not likely to forget it. And even you are giving me warnings now."

The girl's eyes were dancing with amusement.

"At least you cannot say the people of Thornton Bassett are not concerned with your welfare."

"Indeed," Carter returned reflectively. "I must say that I find the people hereabouts extremely pleasant. When one gets to know them."

The girl was drawing a little pattern in the dust at her feet with the toe of her shoe, while the pony contentedly nibbled the grass of the hedgerow.

"Does that include the inhabitants of The Priory?" she asked softly.

Despite himself Carter again felt the old embarrassment envelop him. He put out his hand to stroke the pony to cover the emotion.

"I would say the term was far too conservative to encompass the situation, Miss Hammond."

The girl's face was lowered to the ground, and as it was almost dusk, he could not read her expression clearly.

"When may we see you again?" she asked.

"I will be up shortly," Carter replied. "Within two or three days at the outside, as soon as I have some satisfactory drawings."

Miss Hammond raised her face and smiled one of her long lazy smiles.

"I wish all speed to your pen, Mr. Carter!"

Then she had jumped briskly to the driving seat, urged on the little pony, and had disappeared along the driveway in a cloud of dust.

Carter was left staring after her with a mass of conflicting impressions in his mind.

Nineteen
Hands is Fearful

1

IT WAS QUITE dark when Carter arrived back at his lodgings, but he hardly noticed his surroundings. He went quickly to his room and set out his instruments, notes, and rough drawings on his desk. He sat there for some while staring at them and trying to distill the scattered recollections of the day. He gave it up in the end, realising that the time was getting on.

He made a quick toilet in the bathroom and descended to the dining room as the cased clock was chiming the hour of nine. To his relief, Hands was in his familiar place, and two young men occupied another table in the far corner. Carter took his seat as Mrs. Tregorran bustled in, followed by Pauline and the second girl, both bearing steaming trays. Hands looked a little haggard, Carter thought, but his mood was ebullient.

"Full house tonight!" he said, rubbing his hands. "I will introduce you to our fellow-guests tomorrow. They are pleasant enough."

He nodded familiarly to the young men in the far corner as would a grand seigneur acknowledge the presence of his subjects. He waited until the first course had been laid before them. Then he spoke quietly, below the general level of conversation, his eyes half-closed.

"I must speak with you after supper, Mr. Carter. It is extremely important. May I come to your room?"

Carter was startled by the sudden confidence but he kept his features blank as the girls passed and re-passed among the tables.

"Of course, Mr. Hands. Is it about the same subject as before?"

He was referring to Hands' nocturnal visit, and the latter nodded.

"I cannot speak here," he continued in a low voice. "And I must confide in someone."

"How was Plymouth?" said Carter in a loud voice as Mrs. Tregorran smilingly progressed toward the far table, no doubt to engage the two young men in talk about their recent holiday.

"Exhausting," Hands returned in the same tones. "I have enough work in my satchel to last me for several evenings in addition to my normal commitments."

Carter gave the other a sympathetic look.

"I have been busy too. A major commission for Mr. Hemmings."

Hands glanced swiftly into the far corner, where their landlady was engrossed in conversation. The two young girls had momentarily left the room.

"The Magistrate?"

Carter nodded.

"He is much concerned about a group of horsemen who have apparently been wreaking havoc among the locals on the moor. His ward referred to Satan and His Hounds."

It may have been Carter's imagination, but he thought his companion grew a little pale. He continued in a low voice before the other could answer.

"Is it the same business upon which you wished to consult me?"

Hands swallowed, his eyes wide and somewhat fearful.

"It may be, Mr. Carter," he said in low tones. "Perhaps we are talking of the same thing."

He glanced round quickly, almost furtively.

"There is talk that Mr. Hemmings is sending to the county town for a troop of dragoons."

He put his hand toward Carter's on the table top.

"There is something damnable going on upon the moor," he said with terrible emphasis, the sentence being underlined by the very low tones in which he was obliged to enunciate it.

"I would be glad if you would share my knowledge, Mr. Carter."

He smiled absurdly and raised his voice again.

"Excellent soup, do you not agree?"

Carter assented, aware that the girl Pauline's shadow had fallen across the table.

Hands waited until she had moved away again. His eyes were haunted as he stared at his companion across the mundane supper things.

"I would like you to know something of the truth, Mr. Carter."
He lowered his voice again.
"Just in case something happens to me."

2

Carter sat in his room for a long time waiting for Hands' arrival. He had begun some desultory work at the drawing board upon Simon Hemmings' commission, but he had soon realised that his mind was too agitated for the moment to admit of expert application to his task.

He glanced at his watch for the fifteenth time. It wanted a quarter to eleven now. Surely Hands would come soon.

As if in answer to his thought, there came a low, repetitive tapping at the door panel. Carter opened it, to find Hands, a somewhat diminished, uneasy figure in the opening. He put his finger to his lips to enjoin caution and slipped inside the room while Carter softly locked the door behind him. He sat down in a chair by Carter's desk as though physically and mentally exhausted. "You must think I am a very strange and impressionable creature, Mr. Carter."

Carter smiled wryly.

"Not at all. I have heard some stories of the moor, though I have been here only a few days. Your own hints have merely strengthened what I was already beginning to fathom for myself."

Hands' eyes lit up. He leaned forward on his chair, his brown eyes below the thick, sandy hair, fixed steadily on his companion.

"You are a shrewd man, Mr. Carter. It took me more than a year to give credence to the old wives' tales the locals muttered over their winter fires."

He shuddered, putting the twitching fingers of his hands together as though rent by some sudden paroxysm of fear. It made a dreadful impression on Carter, like some savage scene suddenly revealed by the glare of lightning and convinced him of Hands' sincerity more than half an hour's verbal protestation would have done.

"Can I get you something?" he asked gently. "I have some whisky in the desk here."

Hands shook his head.

"Thank you, no. That would do little good. I am getting to the heart of the mystery, Mr. Carter. I am sorry to involve you, but you are a newcomer, and there is no-one else I can trust. It has taken me two years of patient investigation. What I am going to tell you must remain within these four walls until I give you permission to speak. I want that solemn promise before I continue."

"You have it."

Hands nodded with satisfaction.

"I make the point, dear Mr. Carter, because my life may be in danger."

He put up his hand to forestall the other's questions.

"I am perfectly serious, sir. And perfectly sane."

He shuddered again.

"There are dark things out there on the moor, Mr. Carter. Even in summer. Even in broad daylight, in smiling sunshine."

He put his hand across his mouth as though to stop his sudden trembling.

"Have you noticed, Mr. Carter, how the countryside can somehow be far more terrible than the town? One expects crime and greediness and evil deeds in a great city. What one does not expect is such things carried out when nature smiles, while the sun shines and the birds sing."

Carter was astonished. He had a job to keep his voice low and steady as he replied.

"It is extraordinary, Mr. Hands. The Rector, Mr. Sennen, said something almost on the same lines when I spoke to him a few days ago."

Hands turned a startled face to his.

"Ah, Mr. Sennen. Just so, Mr. Carter. It does not really surprise me. He must know many of the secrets of Thornton Bassett. In his capacity as a confessor, do you see. I know he carries the marks of grave sorrows upon his face. I wish I had confided in him, but I felt I had to keep things to myself. Until you came."

His eyes widened.

"You have not spoken to Mr. Sennen of your own suspicions? This place has far too many ears. You might be in danger yourself."

Carter felt a quick thrill of fear which he instantly suppressed.

After all, Hands was expressing verbally only what he had himself already felt.

"I have not said anything compromising. I know nothing. Merely suspect that all is not well."

He was determined to be frank.

"Those two funerals on Saturday and Sunday, for example. There was something badly wrong there, which even a newcomer might read. Even you yourself said something strange and cryptic when I saw you standing below the parapet of the bridge."

Hands gave a hissing inhalation of the breath and put his hand up to his face.

"Ah! So you were there? And you saw me?"

Carter's face was grave.

"What I read upon your face, so could another. Had you not better unburden yourself?"

Twenty
The Black Death

1

"You are right. And perhaps I will have that drink after all."

Carter found the bottle in his desk but there was no glass. He poured out a liberal measure of the spirit in the metal cap. Hands took it quickly, put it to his lips and drained it as though it had been water. Carter gave him another. When he had finished the second the colour was returning to his cheeks and he seemed more like himself.

"It must seem incredible to you, Mr. Carter, that a man who is almost a stranger should confide in you this way."

He gave a long shuddering gasp.

"Most people would suspect my sanity."

Carter shook his head.

"I have learned that few things are impossible in this world, Mr. Hands."

He looked round the quiet room, remembering the harsh, dry sobbing he had heard in the night; the sad, almost sullen look of the people at the two funerals he had glimpsed; the fierce, passionate declamation of the Rector.

He remembered too, the grim look on Simon Hemmings' face when the man in black had called for him. The recollection compelled him to his next sentence.

"I was at Mr. Hemmings' house most of the day, on a commission for Mr. Pollard. Hemmings seemed to take these moor-riders seriously enough. A man in black called to see him while I was there this afternoon."

Hands nodded, his face expressing his interest.

"That would be Pommeroy, the magistrates' clerk. If anyone can put down this thing it will be Hemmings. He is a strong, not to say extraordinary character."

He shot his companion a look compounded of curiosity and slyness.

"You met his ward, Miss Hammond, I take it?"

Carter cut back his momentary discomfiture.

"I did. A most remarkable young lady. She drove me home earlier this evening."

Hands raised his eyebrows with comic effect. He seemed almost himself again.

"You are richly favoured, Mr. Carter. And I must say the young lady shows excellent taste."

A humorous glance passed between the two young men. Normally they would have expressed their amusement openly; and though the comments had momentarily lightened the atmosphere the moment was too solemn in the semi-darkness of this secret meeting so late at night.

"I have been through much, Mr. Carter." Hands went on. "And I digress."

He leaned forward, fixing his companion with compelling eyes, pitching his voice low.

"There is something terrible going on upon the moor, Mr. Carter. I do not know what it is. As I have said, I have been carrying out my own inquiries, but it is an almost impossible task. These people that use the moor can see a man afoot coming from miles away in summer-time."

He shrugged bitterly.

"And in winter it is incredibly difficult to get about the moor, anyway. It is my opinion that the legend of Satan and His Hounds has been deliberately spread."

"But for what reason?" Carter asked.

"To keep people off the moor," said Hands simply. "So that whatever is going on there can be kept secret."

He saw the impatience in Carter's eyes.

"It is too long a story to go into now, Mr. Carter, as to how I stumbled on this thing. There is a large body of horsemen abroad upon the moor at night sometimes. I have established that as a definite fact."

Carter gave a puzzled little shrug.

"But for what purpose, Mr. Hands? Not smuggling, surely?"

The other gave him a crooked smile.

"Hardly. I first thought of that. Bristol and suchlike ports would be the places. And it would need a large organisation to evade the Excise. They would not come upon such a remote place as the moor."

He looked at Carter grimly.

"There have been six deaths upon the moors during the past three years, Mr. Carter. Of people who either saw too much after dark, or who suspected something and tried to find out what was going on."

"But what about the police?" Carter asked.

Hands shrugged.

"The police know something about it, Mr. Carter. They have been powerless so far. They watch and wait, and hope for an opportunity. But the men behind this are clever. They watch the police too. And, as I said, it is difficult to move upon the moor without one's movements being observed."

"You seem to have managed it," Carter said.

Hands shook his head.

"At great risk to my own life, Mr. Carter. But I want you to know these few facts in case anything happens to remove me from the scene. For I am determined to discover this secret which has evaded so many others. The only reason I am sitting here talking to you tonight is because I have confided in no-one—until now."

Carter put his hand out impulsively and clasped the other's.

"It is still a secret, Jeremy, so far as I am concerned."

The young man gave him a tight smile.

"I am putting your own life in danger by confiding in you, John, so do not thank me for something you may regret."

He leaned forward, lowering his voice.

"The police know all about these murders. They have done their best to hush things up. But it is difficult to prevent rumours flying from village to village. They use a terrible term for a terrible and quite inexplicable form of murder."

Carter bent forward to catch what his companion was saying as he reduced his voice to the merest breath.

"They call it The Black Death!"

2

There was a long and deep silence in the bedroom, broken only by the faint creaking of a board in the passage outside. Carter could feel a pulse beating somewhere raggedly in his throat. He looked at his watch in order to disperse the tension. It was almost a quarter to twelve.

"The Black Death?" he repeated somewhat uncertainly.

Hands nodded, his eyes fixed watchfully on the other's face. The green-shaded lamp was turned low, so that it was difficult to read expressions in here. Carter had thought it best to dim the lamp so that anyone passing in the corridor outside would not see the light beneath the door and realise that he was still up. Hands' own watchfulness and barely concealed terror seemed to have affected his own nerves.

"I was there when the police brought one of the bodies in last year," his companion went on. "The surgeon looked sick, and I have never seen such faces as those of the police officers who carried the stretcher on which the corpse reposed. It was all covered with canvas and strapped around so that no-one should see it."

"But why The Black Death?" Carter repeated.

"This is the story which got about among the village people," Hands returned. "It is obviously to someone's advantage to spread terror among these simple villagers. The educated people do not talk about it. But you can see why Magistrate Hemmings is so worried, and why the dragoons are being sent for."

"The two young people whose funerals I saw died of The Black Death?" said Carter.

He knew the answer before the other spoke.

"Most certainly," Hands replied. "And I could not help being affected. I could see on the Rector's face and on those of the persons who found the bodies that the thing had struck again."

"Is it a disease, then?" Carter persisted. "The Rector said not."

"I am sorry," Hands went on. "I am telling it badly. I will come to that in a moment. I just want to spread the facts before you, so that you will have an idea of this terrible thing that menaces the people of this part of Dartmoor."

Again, he laid his hand on the other's arm, and once more the young architect was impressed with the fear and terror in his eyes.

"But please, as you value your life, do not commit anything to paper. Any suppositions, any mention of this thing, of my name, or of our interview. For if such a document fell into the wrong hands we should be lost."

Despite the other's earnest manner Carter was becoming a little exasperated with the air of mystery and doom that surrounded his companion.

"But whom do you suspect?"

Hands gave him a twisted smile.

"That is just it, John. The principal problem in this business. Everyone and no-one. I do not know who the leader of these people is. No-one does, outside their organisation. I should not be here if I did."

He lowered his voice again, as his tones had risen in his agitation.

"All I know is that a band of horsemen do ride upon the moor on certain nights. They have been heard and seen at distances, both winter and summer. Any people who got close to them have died. Those are facts."

He looked at Carter grimly.

"What they do upon the moor and why they ride there no-one knows. The matter had been taken up with the judiciary long before there were any deaths. Nothing came of it. Nothing has come of it since the series of murders. That is why the Rector is so concerned. He suspects also, but he can do nothing, poor man."

"He spoke something of his thoughts to me on Sunday," Carter said.

Hands shook his head.

"He was very unwise, John. You have not told anyone of this?"

"No. Only you."

"That is good."

A deep silence fell between the two friends. It was eventually broken by Hands.

"Here is how things stand at present. The local people keep clear of this part of Dartmoor at night. They do not make it their business to pry too closely even during daylight hours. One of the young men whose funeral you saw last week-end, was a confidential agent of the police, who had been employed to make inquiries about this matter."

Carter turned a startled face to his companion.

"How could you possibly know that, Jeremy?"

"I was walking upon the moorland road last week when they brought his body in. It was wrapped and strapped around in the manner of the others. I followed at a respectful distance. No-one took any notice of me. A piece of paper fluttered to the ground, unnoticed by the stretcher-party. I put my foot on it and retrieved it when no-one was looking."

His eyes seemed like holes burned into his face as he stared at Carter.

"I have that paper still, to my danger, locked in a cupboard in my bedroom, of which I hold the only key. It identified the unfortunate young man as a police official. And there were notes in some sort of code."

He mumbled something which Carter could not catch.

"How it escaped I do not know, though the edges were charred and blackened."

He paused, and Carter silently passed him another small measure of whisky. He took a draught himself and felt better then. The atmosphere of darkness and conspiratorial danger was beginning to infect him.

"I hoped we could work together," Hands went on. "To bring about some light in a dark place. Without standing ourselves in too much peril. By watching; by patiently waiting; by piecing together small scraps of information. Even these people must make a mistake some time . . ."

"But what can we do where the police have apparently failed?" Carter asked. "And surely the dragoons will put a stop to this and bring the murderers to justice?"

Hands spread his arms wide on the desk.

"I do not know exactly, John," he said frankly. "I only understand something must be done to rid Thornton Bassett and the neighbourhood of this terrible plague which has settled upon it. These creatures will laugh at the dragoons, as they have at the police."

His eyes looked pleadingly at Carter.

"Will you help me, John?"

"Of course, Jeremy. But what is this plague of which you speak?"

"The Black Death!"

The other leaned forward until his mouth was almost up against the young architect's ear.

"I do not blame the local people for invoking Satan and His Hounds, for the fires of the pit could have done no worse upon these unfortunate victims." His throat worked convulsively, and his eyes rolled in his head. "Winter or summer, it is always the same. In the depths of January with the temperature below freezing, in sunshine, or in rain, the corpses have been scorched and blasted until their charred remains are beyond recognition!"

TWENTY-ONE
Carter is Troubled

1

CARTER COULD NOT sleep that night. Three times he woke from a broken doze, on the third occasion crying out in the darkness as though the fearful images painted on his imagination by Jeremy Hands' jumbled sentences were actually present within the room. Drenched with perspiration, he lay staring into the darkness until dawn began to streak the sky.

There was a possibility, of course, that his colleague suffered from some sort of hallucination. He had been down in this small town and upon the moor for a long time. Yet even as he conceived the notion Carter dismissed the idea as nonsense. Hands was too solid and sensible a personality to be the prey to delusion.

There was another thing that struck Carter also, and he had a conscience about it too. Hands had blurted out his confessions so precipitously that Carter had had no time for deep consideration. He had told his colleague he had voiced his opinions to no-one but he had, of course, made his anxieties plain to Miss Hammond during their drive back to Thornton Bassett the previous night.

Though he had known her for only a few hours he had formed various opinions about her; he was almost certain she would not speak of their conversation to anyone. She had seemed eminently sensible, if not cool, about such matters and had frankly chaffed him for entertaining such possibilities as the Hounds of Satan.

Carter's only worry was that she might confide the gist of their conversation to her guardian, with the best of intentions, of course. Yet what harm could there be in that? Hemmings himself was the Chief Magistrate hereabouts, and had himself openly voiced his anger at the band of horsemen and their riotous behaviour in the neighbourhood. According to Hands the Magistrate was calling in a troop of dragoons to ride the moors in search of these people; and Carter himself had seen the girls's guardian hurry off to confer with the magistrates' clerk on the very same subject. Hands' urgent entreaties to secrecy did not quite square with what Carter had already seen and heard in his own travels about the moor.

There was another, even darker suspicion in his mind, now that he had some hours to consider Hands's whispered conversation. How did Hands himself know of the condition of the corpses if the authorities had taken such pains to conceal them from the general public?

Combined with all these tangled thoughts, which kept Carter awake through the dawn as hour followed hour, was a rising anger against Hands for making him the receptacle of his confidences. Yet he knew he was being unfair to his young colleague. The man had obviously gone through a great deal and he was showing immense public spirit in trying to track down the source of these atrocities.

At this point, haggard and sleepless, Carter consulted his watch. He knew that he had to be fresh and at his best for the long labours that awaited him, not only on Hemmings' major commissions; but on all the tasks that were beginning to accumulate for other clients upon the moor, including the work for the hill-farmer which he had recently undertaken.

Somehow, wretched as he felt, Carter forced himself into a leaden sleep and was only aroused from it by Mrs. Tregorran's repeated tappings upon his door with the news that it was a few minutes past eight o'clock and breakfast awaited him below.

2

He was finding it difficult to concentrate. Twice he had spoiled a section of his drawing and had to rub it out and begin again. He was pleased when the bell summoned him to coffee in the partners' board-room. He had not seen Jeremy this morning. He had arrived at breakfast so late that his colleague had already left for the office, the two young clerks who shared the dining-room just on the point of leaving.

Now he was glad to take his place at the long table and sip gratefully at the thick, strong brew, unconscious of the frowning portraits in oils that stared down at him from the walls. Mr. Pollard seemed a little abstracted this morning but had greeted Carter effusively enough.

He chatted intently with Bassett at the head of the table, leaving Innsley and Carter to their coffee and their thoughts halfway down. It was a pleasant enough silence though, because Carter had by now summed up his colleagues and knew a little more of their habits; their methods; and their preferences. Slowly, day by day, he was slipping into the comfortable routine of Pollard, Bassett, and despite the pressures of the work which weighed upon him a little from time to time, as it was bound to do, he knew it was a life which would involve and satisfy him as the weeks went by.

Now he listened as Innsley, hesitantly at first, and then with more confidence, proceeded to tell him a little of his family circumstances and his likes and dislikes in the small world of Thornton Bassett. As the talk went on, Carter was tempted to draw him out; to sound him on the topic which was beginning to absorb him; but little warning bells were reverberating in the back of his mind, and Jeremy's urgent entreaties to caution reasserted themselves.

He understood something of the strain under which that young man had been living. Self-imposed strain, it was true; but if he suspected such monstrous things as he had detailed last night then it was his duty as a law-abiding citizen to assist the authorities to the full extent of his power.

Though Hands had been frank to the point of recklessness the previous evening, there still remained a few points on which Carter was not clear; he would seek out his colleague at a more appropriate moment later in the day for enlightenment. Though even that might not do; if Hands, as he himself hinted, were under suspicion by these mysterious and lethal beings who apparently prowled the moor, his continued discussions with Carter might point an unwelcome finger in his direction.

Not that Carter was afraid for himself; not at the moment. And in broad daylight it was easy to brush away such imaginings. But he could not rid his mind of their discussion last night, by the dim light of the green-shaded lamp, in the dead hours, when all things seemed possible.

Carter knew he would never again be able to look at those innocent-seeming rounded hills, the sunlight skimming their tips, and the tors tilted at crazy angles, without thinking of the dark, sinister secrets that might be hidden behind that smiling face. He had missed the thread of his neighbour's discourse now, and had to ask him to repeat the question. A moment's clear reflection on last night's problems, however, disabused him on one major point. Surely, there would be nothing suspicious in him and Hands frequenting the inn together, in taking walks, and engaging in long conversations.

After all, they were fellow lodgers and were both engaged by the same firm. What more natural? Yet Carter, his mind clouded with his young colleague's imaginings, was resolved to take greater care; to observe all that went on in Thornton Bassett and off and on the moor; and, above all to cultivate discretion, even in his talks with the delightful Miss Hammond.

Pollard was asking him a question now, and Carter's mind snapped back abruptly to the present.

"Yes, sir. There are no problems, so far as I can see. I pointed out to Mr. Hemmings the size of the undertaking and the necessity of starting well before winter sets in. As I understand it the gentleman has his own building contractor."

Pollard nodded affably.

"Oh, yes indeed. Fortunately, that will not concern us."

He laughed musically, and spread out his hands on the big board-room table, at the head of which he naturally sat.

"Otherwise we might run into difficulties, gentlemen, as widely committed as we are."

There was a general murmur of approval among the partners. Pollard nodded benignly.

"I would appreciate a word or two with you, Mr. Carter, before we again disperse to our various duties."

So Carter drank another cup of coffee, and when the others had withdrawn, walked up to the head of the table where Pollard sat in solitary splendour, a little apprehension at the back of his mind. He need not have worried. Pollard's thoughts were far from censure.

The older man put his carefully manicured hands together on the polished mahogany in front of him, his eyes smiling beneath the mane of thick grey hair.

"I have heard very good reports of you, Mr. Carter. Very good reports indeed," he said in a low, precise voice.

He nodded ponderously.

"You are very well spoken of in Thornton Bassett. I am deeply gratified to find my trust in your abilities has not been misplaced."

Carter felt an inward glow at the warmth of the man's words.

"I am delighted, sir. As you know, it is my considered aim to give satisfaction in my new sphere."

Pollard nodded blandly.

"Quite so, quite so."

He shot the young man an amused glance from the corners of his eyes.

"I am impressed too, with your ideas and your draughtsmanship. I should think you would have a very good future with us, Mr. Carter, if you so wish."

"I do wish," said Carter simply.

Pollard nodded again and rose from the table.

"That is most gratifying, and I am glad to know it, young man. And now, I must not keep you from your duties any longer."

Carter went back to his own office with the clear feeling in his mind that all was well at Pollard, Bassett, at least. And therefore the odds were that things were equally well in Thornton Bassett.

He was thinking of Hands' confidences, of course. The Rector had been indiscreet in his talk with him but then he was at the heart of this tragedy; and must obviously have seen the state of those charred and disfigured bodies as they were brought in. Carter did not lay any undue significance on the other warnings he had been given.

He had paused at the head of the gracious staircase that led to the ground floor of the firm's offices. From here he could see though the great square windows that fronted the street and some way along the principal thoroughfare. As he stood there he saw the fair hair of Miss Fiona Hammond as she urged her pony-cart over the imposing bridge that led into the heart of the town.

Two seconds later Carter was hurrying down the staircase and out into the sunlight of the open square.

TWENTY-TWO
An Invitation

1

HE CAUGHT UP with the vehicle as the pony was putting its forehooves on the approach to the smaller bridge at the far side of the square, where the stream looped round to bisect the little town for the second time.

The girl was hatless and appeared a little out of breath as she caught sight of him over her shoulder. She flung him a muttered apology and ran the pony on across the bridge before drawing to a halt.

"Forgive me, sir. I did not wish to cause an obstruction in the roadway. My guardian is a magistrate, remember!"

Her eyes were dancing with mischief as Carter smilingly hurried up to take her hand.

"I saw you passing, Miss Hammond, and could not resist the temptation of saying good-morning."

She put her head on one side, looking at him appraisingly, oblivious of the curiosity of the people passing.

"It is a beautiful day, is it not? And is it such a temptation when a rising young architect sees a humble pony and trap passing his window?"

"You are teasing me again, Miss Hammond."

Carter joined in her own laughter. The girl hesitated and then said softly,

"It is a beautiful day. Will you not accompany me a short way on my journey?"

"With pleasure."

He took his place at her side, and the little pony trotted gamely up the long slope outside the town, the jumbled contours of the moors, all grey and green and purple and yellow in the sunshine, rising to meet them. At the beginning of the steep incline the girl reined the pony in.

"I fear I must say goodbye here, Miss Hammond. Until our next meeting."

The girl bit her lip quickly as she got down from the driving seat to take his hand.

"I have kept you too long already. Thank you for your company this far."

Carter kept his eyes on hers. The more he saw of this girl the more he liked her. But it would be foolish to allow too great an intimacy to develop. Her guardian was a rich and powerful man, and a girl like this would obviously be setting her sights on some equally wealthy county magnate's son.

"I said some rather foolish things last night," he said without preamble.

"Miss Hammond's eyes were wide and surprised.

"I do not remember any such conversation, Mr. Carter."

"You mistake my purpose, Miss Hammond. I was referring to my remarks about the Hounds of Hell and that painting in the hall of The Priory."

He hesitated and then went on quickly, feeling his courage fail before those frank eyes.

"I would appreciate it if you would not repeat my suppositions to any third party."

He smiled down into her face.

"It might reflect rather fancifully upon the prospect of a rising young architect, as you put it."

The girl's face cleared.

"Your secrets are safe with me, sir," she said softly. "I thought you were referring to other matters."

Again Carter felt a faint wave of confusion sweep across him. Miss Hammond was a very frank and disconcerting girl; not like anyone he had ever met before.

"I shall get in a tangle if I elaborate any further, Miss Hammond," he went on briskly.

The girl was walking on at the head of the pony now, resting the little animal on the steep slope, and Carter walked at her side, the two enjoying a comfortable silence for a couple of minutes. They were at the crest of the hill, where the road curved in large esses about the landscape.

"Come to lunch again in two days' time, sir. I am sure you will have something to show my guardian by then."

Carter felt his heart leap.

"Is that an order?" he asked quickly.

The girl bowed gravely before resuming her seat in the trap.

"Most assuredly," she said softly. "And stick to the road next time!"

Her smile remained with him as her lithe figure urged the pony forward. He stood by the roadside watching the trap out of sight. When its faint image had finally disappeared from view he started back down the hill again.

Though the sun shone as brightly and the birds sang as loudly the moor seemed a dark and dismal place as he descended toward the town.

2

The mousy Miss Harkness met him in the hall on his return. She smiled cheerily on the young man, so he guessed she might have seen his precipitate departure in pursuit of Miss Hammond.

"Mr. Hands was asking after you, Mr. Carter. He is in the drawing-office if you wish to speak to him."

"Thank you, Miss Harkness. I am obliged to you."

The little lady looked at him with shining eyes before gliding back into the sombre chamber where she spent all day working on the firm's accounts. Carter ascended the stairs two at a time, his heart light. He looked through the glass partition into the drawing-office. Hands caught his eye at once and slid down from his stool.

The two men met on the airy landing, where they were out of earshot of the others. Hands looked at him anxiously.

"You did not sleep well?"

Carter shook his head.

"Hardly, after your revelations."

Hands made a wry little grimace.

"I am truly sorry for that, John. I have taken the liberty of cancelling our lunch at Mrs. Tregorran's today. I'd be obliged if you'd join me in a chop in the dining room of The Bassett Arms at one o'clock."

"With pleasure," Carter said. "So long as it has not put Mrs. Tregorran out."

Hands shook his head with a ready smile.

"She is a very equable lady, as no doubt you have noticed. And correct too. She will remove the cost from your monthly bill. She is most meticulous about such matters."

"All the more reason for taking up your invitation," Carter smiled.

The two men hesitated, a shadow crossing Jeremy's face. He had his hands up nervously before him, clasping and unclasping his long, sensitive fingers. Carter noticed for the first time that he had a curious ring set upon the little finger of his left hand. It was of plain gold, but with a twisted mount of the same material into which was set a large ruby.

It was altogether a handsome and unusual piece, and the only reason Carter had noticed it now was because a single ray of sunlight, penetrating the high window of the staircase, had caught the ruby, sending a blood-red glow up into its owner's face.

Carter wondered whether it had been a gift from the young lady, Patricia. He forbore to ask the question at the back of his mind. It was no concern of his, after all. Hands put his ring-hand on Carter's arm with an affectionate pressure.

"Until one o'clock, John. I have booked a corner table. We will be private enough there."

Carter nodded.

"Until one o'clock, then."

He went back up to his office to resume his interrupted drawing with an easy mind. For the moment he had his hands on the levers which controlled his small, individual destiny. Pollard was pleased with his work for the firm; that was a gift not to be taken lightly. He got on well with the other partners; another credit on the book.

The clients, among them one of the most important, Simon Hemmings, thought highly of him. Even more important, from Carter's point of view, so did Miss Fiona Hammond. These were all credits which lay on the upland side of the moor, as it were; where the crests reared to the golden sunlight and everything was high summer.

On the debit side were other, darker matters, in which Carter felt himself becoming inextricably involved. Firstly, there was his colleague Hands with his evil, shocking stories of murder and mutilation on the moor. Carter had himself seen the two funerals and the sorrowful faces of the mourners and the townspeople.

The Rev. Sennen too was burdened with the guilt of this evil. Carter himself could now see that his frenzied outburst to which he had given the outward form of drunkard husbands, domestic problems, and drownings—which, though shocking, were natural enough occurrences—masked his deep horror and revulsion at a series of brutal and inexplicable murders.

On top of all this were the hints of people like Slade and Mrs. Tregorran. The friendly warnings, underlined by his employer Pollard, perhaps reinforced by the knowledge of these darker happenings.

Then there was Hemmings with his grim expression when the clerk brought him news of "these rascals", lawless bands of hooligans on horseback; and finally, not only according to Hands, the country people's talk of Satan and His Hounds.

Carter paused in his drawing and shivered slightly, even though the golden sunlight poured in blandly through the windows. He remembered the dying of the sun and the solitary figure leaning on the staff near the ruins of the Castle, uncannily like the figure in the painting in the hall of The Priory. Carter would have to examine it again the next time he went there. He picked up his leather-bound diary and made a note of the lunch appointment at Hemmings' mansion. He would tell Mr. Pollard this afternoon. He would have no objection, as Carter was due to present his preliminary data to Mr. Hemmings shortly in any case.

It might mean working on in the evenings, but the young architect had no objection to that. He wondered idly what the Castle ruins were like. Perhaps he could get Miss Hammond to take him there on the pretext of an afternoon ramble. It would depend on the time.

He rose from the drawing-board, conscious of a dull ache in his back. He had done a good deal since he had returned from his short expedition with the girl. He grunted with satisfaction. He looked at his watch, astonished to find it a few minutes after one o'clock.

He quit his office hastily, conscious now of the faint pangs of hunger as he hurried toward the big hotel in the square.

TWENTY-THREE
The Dragoons Arrive

1

HANDS HAD CHOSEN the place well. He was seated in a corner of the big, panelled room of The Bassett Arms, in a sort of alcove approached by a fairly narrow entrance. There was only the one table which was already laid for lunch, and Hands gave him a cheery smile as he threaded his way between the other diners.

Carter sank on to the heavy leather banquette next to his friend, conscious that the table commanded almost the entire room. At the very same moment Pollard, accompanied by Innsley, passed across the field of view, the head of the firm giving the two young men a slight bow of recognition as he made his stately progress toward his regular table near the fireplace.

The lunch was a good one as Hands had hinted, and as he sat now, exchanging friendly banter with the young architect, it was difficult to believe that their interview of last night had ever taken place.

Yet every so often Jeremy would lay down his knife and fork and make the same nervous gestures with his hands, in which the fingers of his right continually caressed the ring on the little finger of his left.

He did not seem at all conscious of this nervous habit, and Carter did not think it tactful to draw his attention to it. Neither did Hands say what had impelled him to seek this private interview, and several times during the meal he seemed about to broach the subject before veering off in some other direction.

In the end, the waitress having withdrawn and it being impossible to be overheard in the alcove, Carter himself brought the matter up.

"We were talking last night . . ." he began haltingly. "This business about Satan and the Hounds of Hell. You say it was a legend invented to frighten the country people hereabouts. Might it not have some basis in fact?"

Hands raised a startled face to him, putting down his knife and fork again.

"What do you mean, John?"

His lips were white as Carter could plainly see.

"I saw a strange figure leaning on a staff, soon after I came to the moor. It was at sunset when I was with Slade, our carrier."

Hands stared at him, an incredulous expression on his face. He said nothing, so Carter continued.

"The thing, which did not look like a human being to me, was inexpressibly sinister. It stood quite near the ruins of that old Temple which lies out there on the moors. Slade was ahead of me and did not see it. Mr. Hemmings said the original building's history was lost in time."

A thin bead of sweat ran down Jeremy Hands' forehead. He seemed oblivious of it.

"You did not tell him about the figure?'

Carter shook his head.

"I merely mentioned the Castle. One can hardly avoid seeing it on one's travels about the moor."

Hands nodded. He seemed relieved. He appeared suddenly conscious of his tense appearance and made an effort to relax.

"That is true enough, John. Perhaps it was some shepherd looking across the moor?"

Carter shook his head.

"I am convinced it was not, Jeremy. Besides I have seen the figure again."

This time there was no doubt that Hands was startled. He made such a convulsive movement of his right hand that he upset a little of the contents of his wine-glass on the table cloth. To Carter's somewhat overheated imagination it looked like a large spot of blood there on the crisp white linen.

"What in God's name do you mean?"

Hands stared at the other, white-faced.

"Just this. There was a very curious oil-painting in the hall of The Priory, which I had time to study. It depicted a group of men hunting with horses and hounds."

He put his hand up to still the other's question.

"There was no doubt at all that Dartmoor was depicted because of the distinctive landscape with rocks and tors. I am not even sure that the ruins of the Castle were not included. But that was not the only thing."

Carter leaned forward at the table and lowered his voice, even though he knew it was impossible for anyone to overhear.

"In one corner of the painting, standing on a knoll, was the self-same figure, leaning on a staff and staring across the moors."

Hands forced an uneasy smile.

"Satan, perhaps?"

Carter shook his head.

"I did not say so. I have no theories. I spoke of the matter to Miss Hammond, and she laughed. She said the painting came with The Priory when her guardian bought it. They had taken it merely to be the meet of some local hunt. I wish I had looked more closely. I did not even notice the name of the artist."

Hands stared at Carter for a long moment.

"So you have confided in the young lady," he said slowly.

His hands were definitely shaking now. He looked at his companion sadly.

"It is true, when I asked you here, that I wished to discuss last night's matters further. I have no wish do to so now."

"But why?" Carter asked. "I understand you desired us to work together."

"So I do."

Hands' tones were so faint that Carter could hardly make them out.

"God help you, John. Now you are involved just as deeply as I."

And he shook his head once or twice and refused to say anything further on the subject for the rest of the meal.

2

Carter went back to the office after lunch and worked on mechanically at his drawings, his mind elsewhere. At about half-past three Slade looked in, his face sardonic beneath the brim of his hard hat, which he rarely removed indoors; and presented Carter with a few memoranda and internal documents emanating from Pollard and other members of the firm.

Tea had just been brought on a tray by a tall, sallow girl who seemed to have few other duties at Pollard, Bassett and Carter went to sit by the window with his cup, while he studied the contents of the various missives.

There was nothing of real importance, but he swiftly noted various points in his desk diary. It was incredible how quickly he was slipping into the routine of the firm. Things were very different from his last post in London. Now that he was a partner his wishes were deferred to by junior members of the staff, while the senior partners offered nothing but friendly advice, leaving him to get on with his work in peace.

He put the memoranda down and went back to his drawing board. If it were not for Hands and these dark problems on the moor, life would stretch before him in almost a glittering manner. He did not like to hope in that direction, but the presence of Fiona Hammond on his somewhat limited horizon had changed his outlook completely. He lived from day to day so far as she was concerned, and it would not do to raise his expectations there.

He thrust these and similar thoughts from him and worked on uninterruptedly for another hour. When he had finished he was satisfied that the designs for Simon Hemmings were as good as he could make them. And if the client required a little more strengthening of the ceiling supports, Carter could provide them while at the same time maintaining the graceful curves of the retaining buttresses.

It really depended on the wind strengths on the moor in wintertime. The Priory was quite exposed on its great ledge with its sweeping views across the moor. Carter sat on at the board for a few minutes tapping with his pencil on strong upper teeth. He roused himself when the girl came back for the tray, realising that the time was advancing.

In the end he took the sheaf of drawings along to Mr. Pollard's office. He was alone and looked with great interest as Carter spread the material out on his desk. The young man waited anxiously for the senior partner's verdict. He need not have worried. Pollard turned a smiling face to him.

"Capital! I see you have made some daring innovations without diverging too much from my original design. You display great tact for such a young man!"

And he gave a throaty chuckle.

"I was anxious to get your opinion about wind strength up there," Carter said. "Do you think I ought to strengthen the supports for the side walls a little? After all, Mr. Hemmings may wish to add a second storey at some stage."

Pollard chuckled again.

"You have seen something of his collection?"

Carter nodded.

"It is quite fantastic, sir. And no doubt valuable."

Pollard raised his eyebrows.

"No doubt. Yes, I should strengthen the design a little without making it too obvious. When in doubt always add a third more than the estimated stress. But you know all that, young man."

He flicked the drawings flippantly with the fingers of his right hand.

"I could not have done better myself. And your design is far superior to mine. Those windows and the louvres there are really capital pieces of invention."

Carter mumbled some rejoinder, picked up his drawings and went out, warmed by the senior partner's praise. He took the material back to his office, rubbed out a few lines and drew in slightly thicker supports, making notes on the load and stress in his meticulous and minuscule block capitals.

When he had finished he put all the material carefully in a large leather case which would keep the drawings flat. Most architects rolled their plans, but Carter preferred this method for smaller drawings. Tomorrow he would complete the notes and specifications for Hemmings' approval. When he had that the firm would then take over and produce further working drawings and final specifications before construction was put in hand.

That had nothing to do with Carter. Apart from glancing over the material to see that it was as he had specified, his part in the preliminary stages was finished. Though he would obviously be on site as the work progressed to supervise and see that all was in order. Which reminded him of the girl's invitation to lunch. . . .

He was just turning out his lamp preparatory to quitting the office when he heard the heavy clatter of hooves from outside and an unaccustomed bustle in the street. He gained the square in the fading sunlight just in time to see the dragoons ride by.

TWENTY-FOUR
Signs of Winter

1

CARTER THOUGHT HE had never seen a tougher or more efficient-looking body of men. They sat their jet-black horses as though they had spent all their lives there, and Carter realised they had been specially trained in rough country. They would, no doubt, be able to ride the moors as easily as this band of horsemen of which Hands had spoken.

He remembered what he had heard of their coming and gathered that they would be quartered in the extensive stables at The Priory during their stay in the neighbourhood. Their Captain, a tall, dark-haired young man with a determined chin and a flowing black moustache rode proudly at the head of the troop on a white horse, looking neither left nor right.

There was a small ripple of applause from the crowd which had gathered, somewhat dazzled by the fine turn-out. Carter had to admit that the troop made a splendid sight, the fading sunlight turning cuirasses and brass helmets into molten gold; the tassels of the uniforms, the plumes of the helmets, and the horses' own plumes waved in the wind; while sabres clashed, leather accoutrements creaked, and the hooves made a muffled thunder on the cobbles.

The smatter of applause grew and the Captain, reining in his white horse before the troop reached the second bridge, graciously acknowledged the citizens' salute by making a slight bow. A hoarse-voiced sergeant who rode a little to one side then croaked an order and four buglers in the front rank of the troop split the air with some brazen tune which echoed against the granite façades of the buildings and seemed to roll away across the surrounding moors.

Carter stood still until their glittering and blood-stirring progress had died away on the curving road outside the town, but for a long time the people of Thornton Bassett could hear the sad notes of the bugles as the troop ascended higher into the fastnesses of the moor until even those piercing instruments were lost to distance.

"Let us hope they will have some success," said a low, sad voice from somewhere behind Carter.

With a start Carter noticed that the Rev. Sennen had joined him. The Rector, his face marked with the ravages of the secret sorrow the young man had previously noted, stood a yard or two behind Carter, his eyes shaded against the light as he searched for the last of the troop on its way to its temporary billet.

Remembering Hands' warning, Carter gave the Rector a cheery good evening but remained non-committal about the troop's presence upon the moor.

"I understand the Chief Magistrate has called them in to investigate these mysterious riders, Mr. Sennen."

The Rector nodded, drawing closer. It was obvious his thoughts were a long way off.

"Ah! It is a good idea. But I wonder whether anything will come of it?"

Carter shot him a swift look, but his haunted eyes were still fixed upon the far distance.

"The moor is a big place, I understand."

For the first time the cleric looked at him directly. He nodded slowly, as though only then aware of Carter's presence.

"Hundreds of square miles of nothing but rock and moorland and inclement weather, young man. I would not give much for their chances of success."

"We must hope for the best, Mr. Sennen" said Carter encouragingly.

He kept his eyes on the Rector's face. It was all stained with the rays of the dying sun so that he looked like a study in bronze. Carter was reminded vividly of one of Hemmings' automata: the figure of an oldish man, a musician, who played the piano exquisitely by some ingenious arrangement of clockwork mechanism; and whose carved and painted face, with its moving eyes and lips, flexible neck muscles, and deeply lined features, bore something of the same inner sorrow and melancholy which seemed to animate the Rector.

Carter felt a sudden stab of pity for the worthy churchman; he realised something of the burden he was carrying and longed to help. He had in fact given the Rector his word that he would confide in and assist him in his problems; but he also remembered Jeremy Hands' solemn warnings and he bit back the ready assurances which had been on the point of his tongue.

The Rector had recovered himself now. He turned to face the young architect with blank features.

"In any event I wish Captain Henderson luck. It is no easy task they are undertaking."

He clasped Carter's hand, and the young man returned the pressure for a few seconds as they stared into one another's eyes. Then Carter passed on, realising that the shadowy figure who stood a few yards apart from them was that of Jeremy Hands. Carter turned back as he got to the bridge.

The Rector was standing in the same position, his eyes shaded with his hand from the sun, as though he could still see the dragoons on their long ride across the moor.

2

Hands caught him up as he gained the far side of the bridge. His voice was careless enough but the tone seemed a little anxious to Carter.

"What did he want?"

Carter shrugged.

"The good Rector was just wishing the dragoons well on their hunt across the moor."

Hands twisted his mouth so that for a moment or two he had an ugly expression.

"What can these people do that the police cannot?"

The two men were alone now on this side of the bridge, and they paused here, their low conversation overlaid by the heavy plashing of the stream.

"They are good riders at any event," Carter observed. "Picked men, so I understand. Well able to find their way about the countryside."

Hands shrugged.

"I give you that, friend John. But will Henderson's wits be up to the people—or fiends perhaps—behind these deaths?"

Carter looked at his friend in silence for a moment.

"Your self-imposed task is turning your mind into strange channels, Jeremy."

The other gave him a bitter smile.

"You may be right, John."

Carter pressed on, feeling he had a slight advantage.

"You have not yet told me how you came to know of the state of these bodies when they were found upon the moor? Or why the newspapers have not been full of these murders."

Jeremy Hands bit his lip. He glowered moodily at the dusty ground.

"It is impossible to keep such things secret about the moor. But the police have withheld the true state of affairs from the national press. I have kept my eyes and ears open in the streets and hostelries of Thornton Bassett. What I have told you is the truth."

Carter nodded, digesting the information.

"I am going to lunch with Miss Hammond the day after tomorrow," he said. "Magistrate Hemmings will have conferred with the Captain by then. I may learn some crumbs of information on the matter."

Hands nodded.

"Remembering that tact is the watchword at all times."

"Of course," said Carter quickly. "And I am anxious to examine that old painting again. I am certain that the Castle was depicted. There is a topic of conversation innocent enough."

Hands' face brightened.

"Let us talk of happier things. It seems as though I am turning Thornton Bassett into a fearful place for you."

He glanced at his watch.

"It wants some while to supper. You are not familiar with The Lanes, I think. Let us walk a while."

He drew his companion back across the bridge and so through the square into the tangle of alleys and quaint old byeways that Carter had already glimpsed with the Vicar. Here children wandered, their faces pressed against the rounded glass windows of sweet and toy shops.

Carter felt his spirits rising amid their cheery chatter. He and Hands drifted agreeably in the dying light, watching the street-lamps being coaxed into life by the tall man with the long pole, whose cart, drawn by a patient pony, was filled with strange instruments and the tools of his trade. As he turned the equipage back toward the town centre, the side of the cart gleamed, the light catching the gold lettering and the name and qualifications of the county surveyor.

"And how is the fair Patricia?" Carter asked.

A shadow passed across Hands' face.

"I have not seen her in the last day or two. There is some talk of her going to stay with relatives in Plymouth for a month or so. I think her parents feel we are becoming too close."

He made a strange, deprecating movement of his shoulders.

"And I have little prospects for the moment."

"I am sorry," Carter said quickly, moving aside on the pavement to let an old woman and a large dog go by.

"It cannot be helped," said Hands moodily. "And I should perhaps stick closer to my work in the drawing-office."

He made a savage gesture with the hand which bore the strange ring.

"But these problems of the moor tear at me so!"

He offered a mumbled apology, and was then himself again. Carter and his companion were in a tiny square formed by four sets of terraced cottages, now converted into shops. There were four entrances at the corners and iron posts set in the cobbles to prevent vehicular access, Carter supposed.

Lights gleamed from the shop windows and Hands smiled at Carter's expression.

"Curious, is it not?"

The two young men walked slowly along, glancing in at the familiar wares displayed, conscious of the fading light, while the rays of the sun still stained the tops of the moorland visible from the town.

"I fancy this beats London in some ways," Hands put in, in his drawling manner, stepping out into the roadway to avoid a small platoon of children hurrying to their favourite rendezvous.

"You may have something," Carter agreed, smilingly watching their invasion of the sweet shop.

They had now completed the circuit of the square and paused before retracing their footsteps. They were walking back in the general direction of the main square in the High Street when Carter was startled to hear the sudden clatter of hooves. He had expected the return of the dragoons, but found Hands' eyes on him with amused anticipation.

Instead, some half dozen of the shaggy brown moorland ponies had wandered into the town, and were nosing along these quiet side streets looking for titbits. It was the first time Carter had seen them at close quarters, and he marvelled at their hardiness and tameness.

Children were pressing forward offering them sweets, and an old lady hurried from her cottage, making clucking noises with her withered mouth as she presented them with morsels of sugar. It was a pleasant sight, and Hands and Carter lingered in the dying light, agreeably absorbed in the unusual spectacle.

Carter then recognized the old lady as the one he had noticed with the crate of poultry when he had passed by the same spot with the Vicar on their Sunday walk.

She smiled as though she had recognised Carter in turn and hobbled closer, the ponies milling about her in their greed to reach the sugar.

"It is a sure sign, masters," she observed in a low, country voice.

Hands smiled at her, patting the nearest brown flank abstractedly.

"A sure sign of what, mother?" he asked.

The old woman advanced another piece of sugar to the questing muzzle of the nearest pony, raising her eyes to the dusky light on the moorland that reared up the sky beyond the town.

"When the ponies come down, sir," she said quietly. "Mark my words, it is going to be a hard winter."

Part Two
AUTUMN

Twenty-Five
Hemmings is Enthusiastic

1

THE RAIN HAD COME with a sudden, brutal savagery, as though not autumn but winter had begun at a specified time and place. Carter was astonished at the strength and sheer malignancy of the storm out there on the exposed moors. He and Hands had had to run through the streets, but despite the large umbrella held out by the latter, they were drenched by the time they had reached the office.

Mr. Pollard had chuckled, meeting them in the entrance hall, his pince-nez streaming and shining with moisture.

"What did I tell you, Mr. Carter? Autumn has commenced with a vengeance."

Carter had made some glum rejoinder and had retreated to his office where a coal fire had been lit, there to steam and dry out as best he might. He would not have thought that two days could have made such a difference.

The golden weather of Indian summer had disappeared, to be replaced by black clouds rolling up across the moor, a violent wind which tore at one's clothing, and the driving rain which seemed to penetrate the skin with its biting cold. A thin mist rose from the hollows of the moor, creating milky swathes across the landscape; and the stream, swollen in its course, now roared through the streets of Thornton Bassett, making white froth in its frantic passage against the stone buttresses of the bridges.

Carter had remembered at breakfast that he was due to lunch at The Priory today, but Slade had reassured him, putting his dripping head round the door at ten o'clock.

"Don't worry, sir. I shall have the carriage ready for you at eleven. Mr. Pollard has given me special instructions. And I will come to fetch you at tea-time, unless Miss Hammond has any other orders for me."

He gave a warming, conspiratorial wink at Carter. The latter cast a despairing glance at the window and then at his greatcoat steaming at the fire.

"But we shall be drowned, surely, long before we get there?"

Slade shook flecks of rain from the brim of his hard hat.

"We shall be using one of our closed vehicles, sir. Mr. Pollard was most particular."

He grinned.

"Besides, you do not think I could get about the moor, sir, without some form of shelter in winter-time."

He glanced at the window with a professional eye.

"In any event, these Dartmoor squalls are as swift as to pass as they are to arise. It may well be dry by the time we leave."

Carter went to take coffee with the partners early this morning and to receive instructions from the senior, who gave him a sealed letter for Mr. Hemmings.

At a few minutes past eleven he was leaving Thornton Bassett in light squalls of rain, in a comfortable carriage, rather like a brougham, drawn by two strong black horses, and driven by Slade with a superior air.

In an astonishingly short time, it seemed, and without the two men dismounting, they had risen far above the town, the moors rearing about them, savage and dark now, the tors dimly seen through the mist; while black clouds chased across the sky, driven by the freezing wind.

But Carter was snug enough, and Slade seemed more gregarious than usual and inclined to talk, enlivening their journey with semi-humorous anecdotes of Dartmoor life and the occasional oddities of the architectural profession as seen from his viewpoint.

Carter's spirits had risen considerably, and with every hoofbeat bringing him closer to the girl, he was already thinking of some neutral topic of conversation which would not betray his curiosity about the strange oil painting in the hall of The Priory.

He glanced into the back of the vehicle where the leather case containing his precious drawings and his other data reposed, safe from the wind and the rain.

Slade had caught his concern.

"No worry about that, sir. I'm used to carrying valuable documents for Mr. Pollard in all weathers. We've never yet had any trouble in that line."

"You're fond of Mr. Pollard, aren't you?" Carter asked.

Slade nodded deferentially.

"I am that, Mr. Carter. Mr. Pollard's a fine employer. But I fancy you've already discovered it for yourself."

Carter nodded, removing his gaze from the other and scanning the bleakness of the moor. They were on the high, level ground now, the horses pulling well and in fact could not be more than half a mile or so from Tor Bridge. It was just ten past twelve so Mr. Hemmings could not accuse him of tardiness on this occasion.

Slade looked at him shrewdly from beneath the brim of his hard hat.

"What do you think of the moors now, Mr. Carter?"

The architect gave a rueful laugh.

"I agree with you, Mr. Slade, and all the other Dartmoor people. The moor is a difficult and dangerous place, especially in wintertime."

Slade laughed too, making his whip sing in the air a foot above the patient horses' heads.

"And remembering this is only autumn-time, sir! I knew you'd come around, Mr. Carter. I knew you'd come around!"

And he burst into a high, tuneless whistle that lasted until the village street of Tor Bridge hove into sight through the drifting veils of rain.

2

They were under the shelter of the great Palladian porch before Slade spoke again. He looked anxiously at Carter as the latter got down, handling his leather case with care.

"I'm at your disposal, sir. Regarding your getting back, I mean."

Carter was saved from answering by the arrival of Mrs. Arkwright, whose reassuring and friendly form appeared in the massive doorway beneath the shelter of the porch.

"Good day. Mr. Carter! Mr. Hemmings is expecting you. And you're to lunch with me in my room later, Mr. Slade. Mr. Hemmings insisted upon it."

Slade's eyes lit up as he gave Carter another of his friendly winks. He made a salutation with his whip.

"My compliments and thanks to Mr. Hemmings, ma'am. Another fine gentleman!"

Mrs. Arkwright smiled conspiratorially at Carter.

"You'd best get those horses to the stables and have them rubbed down before you show yourself," she told Slade good-humouredly.

The two watched as the vehicle clattered away down the drive toward the stables.

"Do come in, Mr. Carter. Appalling weather, sir. When you have dried yourself, Mr. Hemmings has asked me to show you to the study."

Carter thanked the housekeeper and followed her through the vestibule into the great hall. He now saw that banked coal fires burned in the fireplaces, a strange contrast to the hot-house flowers that continued to glow in their copper jugs and bowls set about on mantels, on tables, and on the tops of carved wooden chests.

He had hoped to study the painting that was his interest but there was no time for that. Mrs. Arkwright was waiting for him on his return from the cloakroom, and the girl had not appeared. So Carter picked up his leather case and followed the dark-clad form that seemed to glide before him.

She took him to a huge oval room with circular windows overlooking the windswept moor, that must have been somewhere near the museum apartments, so far as Carter could make out. But despite the wild and jagged landscape outside, all was calm within, a leaping fire burning in the huge fireplace with its wooden overmantel; the light from that and the shaded lamps gleaming and glancing along the golden-tooled spines of thousands of leather-bound books that followed the curves of the walls in specially built shelves.

Carter's heart warmed to the good taste and scholarship displayed as he followed the housekeeper down the room to a large desk with a red leather top which almost sagged with the weight of the books and papers on it. Simon Hemmings rose with a gracious smile from behind the desk and came to meet him, the lamplight glinting on his gold-rimmed spectacles.

"Welcome to my sanctum, Mr. Carter. A dreadful day for your journey, I fear, but we will endeavour to make up for it with the warmth of our hospitality."

He shook hands formally with Carter, taking Pollard's letter and muttering something *sotto voce* to the housekeeper, the architect catching the agreeable word, "sherry". Mrs. Arkwright smiled at Carter over her employer's shoulder and glided out.

"I am sure your hospitality would always be warm, sir," Carter replied, putting down his case on the seat of an ornate leather chair that stood near the desk.

"I envy you this room alone."

Hemmings gave another cheerful glance around the chamber.

"You are a scholar too, sir. You will, I am sure, appreciate my collection. Which is why I asked you here."

He took the young man by the arm and led him down the packed shelves to the left-hand side of the fireplace.

"This is the heart of my collection of automata. These volumes are priceless and have taken me almost forty years to collect. I have copies of their contents in longhand, of course, for reference purposes when working on the models, but if anything should happen to these . . ."

He held up his hands in mock despair.

"I am sure they are safe enough, sir," Carter assured him.

He glanced at the spines of the volumes, which were in various European languages, but they meant nothing to him, though he made an outward show of interest.

"Come and warm yourself at the fire", Hemmings invited him. "The sherry will be arriving shortly, and we will be going into lunch almost directly".

Today he wore a dark suit cut on severe lines that was saved from sombreness by the pale blue cravat and handkerchief of the same colour which peeped from his breast pocket. He looked a man at peace with the world, though Carter guessed he would have many worries on his shoulders with his pressing duties as Chief Magistrate.

He would have liked to have questioned Hemmings on the matter closest to his interest at the moment, but he remembered Hands' admonition—though he might introduce the subject of the portrait in the hall, given a suitable opportunity. And it would surely be in order to mention the dragoons' arrival in Thornton Bassett in passing. After all, they were billeted on Hemmings' property, if local gossip were correct.

Carter went over to the fire gratefully. He had not realised how cold the drive had been until then. It was not until he had seated himself that his host broke the silence again.

"You have not yet seen my workshops, Mr. Carter. I think they will really interest you."

Carter nodded.

"You said something about the cellars, sir. Are they extensive?"

Hemmings rubbed his hands together with a dry crackling sound that momentarily eclipsed the low roaring of the fire.

"Enormous, sir. The original mediæval foundations. But admirable for my purposes."

His eyes twinkled mischievously behind the spectacles.

"And we store wine there too, of course."

He turned abruptly.

"Ah, here is Mrs. Arkwright."

The housekeeper was accompanied by a tall, pale girl with a frightened look, wheeling a heavy mahogany trolley. She gave Carter a convulsive half-bow and retired quickly at a murmured order from Mrs. Arkwright.

Hemmings beamed on the latter as she busied herself with the ritual of the decanter.

"I do not really know what I should do without this admirable lady, Mr. Carter. The entire running of the household here depends on her."

Mrs. Arkwright gave a deprecatory shrug at her employer's praise but Carter could see the pleasure his words had given as she turned her smiling face to concentrate on pouring the wine. She brought it over to the two men on a silver tray.

"Lunch in half-an-hour, sir," she said softly, before gliding out.

Hemmings looked after her with affection.

"An excellent woman, Mr. Carter," he said reminiscently. "One might search the length and breadth of the British Isles for such a treasure."

"I am sure," said Carter quietly, getting up from the fireplace. "Your health, sir!"

"Thank you, Mr. Carter. And yours also, of course."

The two men drank appreciatively, the firelight flickering across their faces; the young man's strong and optimistic; the older man's massive and worldly-wise.

"Please help yourself," said Hemmings, going round the desk to re-fill his own glass. "I think you will find it worth the drinking."

"It is first-rate, sir."

Carter put his half-empty glass down on the silver tray and went across to the leather chair to get his case. Hemmings had re-seated himself at the desk but was watching the young man's movements with interest. Carter picked up the case and brought it back to the desk.

Hemmings' eyes were wide as he opened it.

"You do not mean to say you have finished the drawings already?"

He was on his feet, like a child moved by excitement at some unexpected toy.

"Excellent, Mr. Carter. Excellent! This is more than I could ever have imagined."

He ran through Carter's meticulous tracings with trembling fingers, so that the former was moved to smile discreetly at his enthusiasm.

"Really, sir! Pollard, Bassett is honoured by your presence as a partner. Do have another glass of sherry!"

He glanced quickly at the gilded clock over the mantel.

"I fear we may be a little late for lunch today!"

Twenty-Six
The Moor-Riders

1

IN THE EVENT, it was almost half-past one before they quit the study, Hemmings' praises echoing and re-echoing through the great hall as they crossed it. To Carter's relief Hemmings had accepted his plans without demur, his quick brain grasping the more sophisticated points of the design immediately. As Carter had suspected, he was au fait with the latest architectural conceptions, and he might almost have been a professional himself, as he read the drawings with polished ease.

The light from the overhead chandelier in the hall glinted on Hemmings' glasses as they walked toward the dining-room.

"Admirable, Mr. Carter," the host murmured. "Mr. Pollard's eulogies of your abilities have not been exaggerated".

Again Carter felt the old embarrassment pass across him. He made a shrugging, self-deprecatory movement of his shoulders, unable to reply to what he felt to be unwarranted praise. Not that his designs were negligible, far from it. But like many professional men who were also sensitive and artistic, Carter felt an inward shrinking when his own work was discussed; though, on reflection, he was always grateful for the appreciation expressed.

They were in the dining-room, Mrs. Arkwright's deferential figure awaiting them. To Carter's disappointment he saw they were to be joined by a stranger. A young man resplendent in scarlet and gold braid was standing conversing with Fiona Hammond at the end of the table.

The couple were laughing together, and Carter felt an absurd, unwarranted stab of resentment pass through him. Fiona and the soldier had fallen silent now and were awaiting the arrival of Hemmings and Carter across the parquet. The architect recognised the Captain of Dragoons who had led his troops through the square of Thornton Bassett with such dash and panache.

Hemmings had noted the wary glance which had passed between the two young men; had immediately grasped the cause; his lips subtly curved with amusement. But he merely nodded affably, his eyes gleaming behind his spectacles, and took the glasses for himself and Carter from Mrs. Arkwright's proffered tray with muttered thanks.

"To your health and success in your respective careers, gentlemen."

There was an awkward silence, and then the girl and her guardian had raised their glasses in salute, Carter and the Captain responding.

"Forgive me, Mr. Carter," said Hemmings quickly. "I had forgotten that you had not met. This is Captain Michael Henderson, Captain of Dragoons, who has come to rid us of the moor-riders. He is staying here in the house while the troop are billeted in our stables. Mr. John Carter, a distinguished young architect who is designing major additions to my home."

The two men bowed stiffly, studying one another above the rims of their glasses. Carter saw the little impish spark of amusement which passed from Fiona Hammond's eyes to those of her guardian and he made his expression as bland as he could manage.

The patient figure of Mrs. Arkwright acted as a constraint, and the group of four people drank the excellent vintage in a heavy silence, as though not sure how to begin general conversation. Carter used the pause to study the Captain. He now saw that his first impressions had been incorrect.

The man was taller than he had imagined and, in the splendour of his uniform, would be bound to create a favourable impression on such a young lady as Miss Hammond. The uniform became him; it had obviously been tailored to take every advantage of his athletic figure, and the young man wore it with a faint air of arrogance and pride that Carter found offensive.

He realised he was prejudiced and fought to overcome the feeling even as the four of them drank and made low, trivial conversation. Henderson's face was evenly tanned as though he had spent much of the past summer in the open air, and his jet-black hair, which clung closely to his scalp in tight ringlets, gave him something of a Roman aspect.

The military air was emphasised by his strong chin and the flowing black moustache. Though he was otherwise clean-shaven his facial hair was so pronounced it showed as a faint stubble, making for a dark, swarthy complexion. Carter fancied he was a little sensitive about this as he stroked his chin and cheeks with his disengaged hand from time to time, while using the other, that holding the wine-glass, to make little gestures to emphasise the points of his conversation. For some reason this thought gave Carter considerable inner satisfaction, though he was conscious that his attitude toward the young officer was an unworthy one.

"There must be some very fine riding in the neighbourhood," Henderson ventured to the girl, who kept a thoughtful eye on Carter.

Hemmings smiled.

"This is not your part of the country, Henderson", he observed. "You will have to take extreme care, particularly at night. It is easy to break a horse's leg among the boulders. It is no country for gallopers".

Henderson smiled thinly.

"Yet I understand these bands of horsemen ride the countryside unmolested and with apparent ease, Mr. Hemmings. People have been attacked, even killed. The locals have been terrified. You must forgive my observations, but you are Chief Magistrate, and we have been called in to ride these ruffians down, have we not?"

It may have been Carter's imagination but he fancied that a dark flush crossed the host's cheeks. He gave a little impatient movement of his shoulders.

"That is perfectly true, Captain," he said deliberately. "There are places on the moors where it is safe to ride. And some of these areas can be gained by using the roads. But only by using experienced riders, who know the moors as they would their own backyard, both by day and by night."

It was Henderson's turn to flush.

"I see, sir. I hope you will be providing us with useful local guides so that we may use our strength to full effect."

Hemmings nodded absently.

"That will be taken care of, Captain, in due time."

He turned to Mrs. Arkwright.

"And now, I think, we are more than ready for lunch."

2

The meal passed in an uneasy silence, interspersed with short, sporadic bursts of conversation. Carter was ill at ease; an occasion to which he had so greatly looked forward was being marred by the inhibiting presence of Henderson. The Captain himself seemed unaware of this, and his hearty manner and loud laughter at his own sallies were trying to the architect.

The girl herself was conscious of this and put on an unconcerned façade, though more than once Carter caught her eyes on him anxiously. He realised that he himself was becoming childish and boorish. The Captain was a guest under Hemmings' roof; his troop of dragoons was stationed here; and it was obvious that they could not exclude him from the social round merely because another guest had arrived.

Carter was angry with himself because of his irrational resentment against the man, and it showed in his stiff and formal manner. Hemmings had noticed it too, of course, and his graceful conversation and amusing anecdotes were designed to smooth the course of the meal. Henderson appeared oblivious of the other guest's reserve and ate heartily, hardly pausing in his own anecdotal meanderings.

"And where is your troop stationed normally, Mr. Henderson?" Carter found himself saying.

Fiona Hammond was sitting opposite, and he noticed tiny lines around her mouth relaxing, uneasily aware of the dancing laughter in the eyes now lowered toward her plate. Outside the windows the rain seemed to be abating, and a watery sun shone through. Henderson wiped his lips fastidiously with his napkin, silently signalling to Mrs. Arkwright to replenish his plate. He seemed already to be ensconced as one of the family, Carter felt.

"In Plymouth, Mr. Carter," the Captain returned coolly. "Our home barracks are there, but we have spent the summer on manoeuvres in the field before coming here at Mr. Hemmings' request."

"I wish you luck in your endeavours, sir," said Carter, his stiffness momentarily leaving him.

The whiteness of Henderson's teeth gleamed out in his smile beneath the heavy moustache.

"I thank you for your good wishes, sir."

His eyes rested briefly on the girl before passing on to Hemmings.

"We will give these rascals a fright, if nothing else".
The Magistrate shook his head solemnly.
"Do not under-estimate them, Captain."
He glanced across at the windows.
"And the bad weather is settling in. You have undertaken no light task".
The Captain nodded, waiting until Mrs. Arkwright had finished heaping the roast beef upon his plate. He leaned forward to pick up the pot containing the horseradish.
"But you forget one thing," he told his host. "If the conditions are bad for us, then must they not also be the same for these mysterious horsemen of whom you speak?"
Hemmings smiled thinly.
"You may be right, Captain Henderson. But do not under-estimate the moor, especially in winter. I understand you will be here for some two months at least. And I have not seen these creatures personally. We are talking now of official complaints from local citizens. Some of it may be superstitious exaggeration."
"And some of it may not," put in Fiona quietly. "There have been deaths, certainly."
Carter's eyes had never left her face and he sensed rather than saw that she was slightly pale. He suddenly remembered that he had not yet re-examined the painting in the hall outside. He must find an opportunity to do so in a discreet manner, without creating undue attention.
"I do not quite understand that remark, Miss Hammond," Henderson put in politely.
"Like most young people my ward is inclined to use her imagination a good deal," Hemmings interjected smoothly. "And such a romantic background as Dartmoor is a natural focus for legend. But I am concerned merely with temporal things, as a man of the law. The deaths are another matter, which we will not discuss here. The police have them in hand, and the subject is *sub judice*."
Carter felt the conversation was becoming focused on Fiona Hammond, and he sought to lead it in another direction.
"What excuse will you give for your own troop's activities upon the moor?" he asked the Captain directly.
The latter shrugged, sipping fastidiously at the wine in his goblet. He smiled wolfishly beneath the thick moustache.

"Winter manoeuvres, Mr. Carter. It is a standard routine with the Army and covers a great many operations. Besides, the local population must have a very good idea why we are here."

Hemmings coughed warningly and Henderson raised a momentarily startled face.

"We are beginning to bore, my dear Captain," the Magistrate said softly. "And I think the operations of your troop will best be discussed behind closed doors. Is it not so?"

Henderson bit his lip and gave Carter and the girl a fleeting glance.

"You are right, as always, sir." he assured his host. "This wine is really delicious. Might I trouble you for another glass?"

Carter hastened to cover a gap in the conversation.

"And where will you begin, Captain?"

He realised he might be transgressing the Magistrate's expressed intent of privacy and confidence, but the latter gave him a reassuring smile so the architect guessed that Hemmings felt there would be no harm in the Captain answering the question. Henderson himself shot the host a quick glance but evidently saw no stricture there.

"I shall be listening for horses's hooves, sir," he said shortly. "Large bodies of men moving across the moors at night, where there should be no such presence."

He smiled thinly at the girl.

"And I shall also be looking for lights. I feel there is no harm in revealing that much, Mr. Hemmings?"

The Magistrate shrugged but the girl had a puzzled look upon her face.

"Lights, Captain Henderson?"

The Captain nodded, lowering his freshly-filled wine glass to the snowy linen cloth. Shafts of sunlight from the big windows fell across his strong face, emphasising its martial qualities.

"I understand the local people have seen strange lights and flares upon the moors at night. We shall investigate and put a stop to all this nonsense. And also find out what is going on, of course."

The girl slowly inclined her head. Her eyes were on Carter.

"Let us hope that you are right, Captain."

She turned back to the architect.

"It is fine and dry now, Mr. Carter. Perhaps a drive across the moor after lunch would blow such gloomy thoughts from our heads."

Carter warmed to the brightness in the girl's eyes but the Captain's face darkened.

"I shall be delighted, Miss Hammond," Carter said.

Henderson bit his lip again.

"I have matters to discuss with your guardian after lunch, Miss Hammond. But if you would tell me your general direction I will hasten after you when our business is concluded."

The girl smiled, including both young men in her dancing glance.

"We will take the far road from Tor Bridge, Captain. It is at the north end of the village. Take the right-hand fork. You cannot miss it."

She turned back to Carter.

"I believe you have not yet been in that direction, Mr. Carter. I think you will find it of some interest."

Twenty-Seven
Rats' Castle

1

THOUGH THE SUN shone brightly, there was a chill wind which stung their faces as the pony breasted the slight rise out of Tor Bridge, and Carter huddled into his thick overcoat, studying the girl's face as she silently handled the reins. To his disappointment they had quitted the house by a side entrance which lay closer to the stables, so that he had not been able to examine the strange painting in the hall, as he had intended.

They were in a closed carriage in case the rain began again and both had brought waterproof clothing for that eventuality. Carter had not seen this part of the village and he looked about him with interest as they passed the few shops, a shuttered inn of weather-beaten stone, and the venerable mass of a church spire which seemed to have grown from the rocky terrain which surrounded it.

A few moments more and they were at the cross-roads the girl had indicated, and a magnificent view of rolling moors spread before them, the tors half-shrouded in mist. Far to the west the sun was declining though there would be an hour or so of daylight yet, and the dark pillars of Rats' Castle stood out like a fretwork frieze to the eastward.

Every beat of the horse's hooves was taking them in that direction on the lonely, curving, and undulating road. Carter realised that perhaps the girl had some purpose in this apparently casual expedition.

As if *en rapport* with his thoughts she turned her face to him, her eyes studying his own features as though she wished to impress them on her memory.

"You must not mind Captain Henderson, Mr. Carter," she said softly. "He is well enough in his way, but you should remember he is a guest in our house."

The young architect's confusion returned; the girl could not have made her intention plainer but he was in some difficulty over his words in reply. He did not wish the girl to misunderstand his motives; and he certainly did not want her to think him presumptuous regarding their relationship.

There was a wry expression at the corners of his mouth; it was not as though they had any relationship at all. Merely a dim aspiration that was stirring at the edge of his mind. The girl seemed to sense this too, because she suddenly laid the fingers of her left, gloved hand over his own.

"There is no need for you to reply, Mr. Carter," she said gently. "It is just that I do not want any misunderstanding."

Carter smiled.

"There is none, Miss Hammond," he said firmly. "But may I ask you a favour?"

The mischievous expression was back on Fiona Hammond's face.

"You surely would not ask me to lead the Captain to drown in some remote spot on the moor, Mr. Carter?"

Carter's smile broadened. That was exactly what he had been thinking but he had no intention of telling his companion so.

"Nothing of the sort," he said easily.

He pointed over to where the jagged pillars of the ruins stood, half visible in misty vapour.

"Mr. Pollard spoke of Rats' Castle to me the other day. I would like to visit it."

"Now, Mr. Carter?"

The girl's voice was a little startled, Carter thought.

"If we have time," he said apologetically. "And if you are not too tired."

The girl urged the pony on to a brisker pace.

"I am perfectly happy with the suggestion. It is just that we may not get back to The Priory until dusk. And you still have a long way to go to Thornton Bassett."

Carter had his eyes fixed on the distant ruins which were growing sharper and clearer with every minute that passed.

"I am not frightened of moor-goblins, Miss Hammond. And I would be most interested to see the Castle."

Again he gave her an apologetic glance.

"But if you are too tired?"

The girl shook her head, the tawny hair falling across her face.

"When you know me better, Mr. Carter, you will realise it takes a good deal to tire me."

She gave him another of her impish smiles.

"Very well. You had better hold on to the hand-rail there. Rats' Castle it is!"

2

There was still a good deal of light left in the sky when they reached the nearest accessible point to the ruins. Carter was astonished at their size, the gaunt, black arches of stone rearing against the blood-red sky. They had seen or heard nothing of Henderson during their drive, and for this Carter was grateful. He had no wish for the brash, bullock-like figure of his potential rival to break the spell which seemed to have settled over the two of them on their way here.

This afternoon the girl wore a mannish sort of outfit: a tweed jacket with flapped pockets, a long skirt of the same material, and thick brown leather boots that came halfway up her legs; a cape of the same material hung from her shoulders. Altogether she looked like the epitome of a country lady, Carter thought, resembling the drawings of fashionable women he had seen in the London magazines.

Now he helped her down from the cart, conscious of the faint perfume of her hair and the disturbing proximity of her beauty. There was a broken stone stump that projected from the roadside verge like a rotted tooth, and he took the pony's reins and secured them round the rough surface, leaving the animal enough room to graze the wet grass.

The ruins were about a mile from the road and the couple slipped and slid their way into a shadowy valley, the silvery thread of one of the moorland streams, in spate now, menacing in their path. But Fiona Hammond seemed equally at home here as in the more civilised surroundings of The Priory or Thornton Bassett, and she pointed out to Carter some of the peculiarities of the tors as they threaded their way between massive fallen boulders and along undulating surfaces of scree.

"I do not fancy the Captain's chances here," Carter observed as they came at last to the valley bottom. He was amazed at the strength and width of the stream, the water foaming at the bases of great slippery rocks which spanned the flow like stepping stones.

The girl led the way, putting one small gloved hand in his. She waited until they had gained the farther bank, slightly breathless, before replying.

"I imagine the Captain will have a good many surprises before he has finished with the moor," she said calmly.

Carter shot her a swift glance, not sure he had caught her import correctly above the swift rush of the stream, but he was unable to read her expression.

"I am not quite sure I take your meaning," he said politely.

They had paused on top of a worn slab of granite, slightly raised above the bank; the ruins were momentarily hidden by the overhang of tumbled rocks above.

"Take this place for instance," Fiona Hammond went on.

She pointed farther eastward to where the distant road curved, limned against the angry sky.

"By driving or riding round there one would think, from the topography, that Rats' Castle would be just a step from that spot."

She chuckled delightedly.

"But apart from dangerous ravines the distance to cover would be exactly three miles up and down. Whereas the ruins are a mere mile from where we left the carriage."

She led the way forward again, Carter content to follow.

"The apparent steepness of the terrain here, the boulders, and the stream make the casual observer think this route is impossibly difficult for the casual walker. So they go the long way round and find it worse. And, of course, it would be lethal for horses by either route."

She smiled down at her companion.

"So I do not give much for the Captain's chances out here, even with a guide."

"But why did the people who built the place choose a spot so difficult of access?" Carter questioned reasonably.

The girl shrugged.

"Perhaps they wanted to be private," she said softly, "And the track they made has long since been erased by the vagaries of the weather."

The roar of the stream had died now as they moved away from its banks, and he was able to hear every syllable of her conversation without straining his ears. They were ascending again and saved their breath until they had gained the next summit.

Carter glanced back at the course of the stream in the dusk below them. Already it looked remote, insignificant. Yet it would be enough to sweep the strongest man off his feet if one had tried to cross it without the stones. Once again the various warnings he had received came back to him. He followed the girl as she strolled on, across less inhospitable ground now.

"What is this brook called?" he asked.

Fiona Hammond shrugged again.

"It is one of the numerous tributaries of the Dart. It is too insignificant to have a name of its own. I had my pet name for it when I was a child, though."

She bit her lip.

"Or rather, when I first came here. I think of myself as a child when I arrived at The Priory. But I was already a young woman, of course. The stream is visible from my guardian's estate and in fact runs along the border of the grounds."

Carter's eyes searched the girl's face. He was aware of the ruins rising silently and inexorably before them, like great monuments solidified in mist, as the dark red of the setting sun stained the ancient walls and filled in the detail as though a painter were at work with some gigantic colour wash.

"And what did you call it when you were younger?" he asked.

The girl shook her head, her teeth gleaming in the faintness of her smile.

"Perhaps I will tell you one day, Mr. Carter. If and when I get to know you better."

"I shall look forward to it," Carter replied, his pulse suddenly racing a little unsteadily.

Their boots gritted on granite again as they came off the last of the boulders on to a great tableland of paving blocks that were slightly tilted, perhaps with time and erosion; or, thought Carter fancifully, as though the plateau had tired of bearing such an insupportable weight. For the monastic buildings—temple ruins, or whatever structures had once stood here—were of colossal scale and weight. Those walls which were still standing were at least five feet thick at the base, and the window embrasures were on an heroic scale. The early eighteenth century additions had lasted nowhere near so well.

There was something that looked like a copy of a Roman arch in the west wall a little farther down from where they were standing; it had the remains of two small rose windows at its apex and the angry sun gleaming in at the two empty sockets reminded him vividly for one startled moment of two great bloodshot eyes. The same notion may have struck the girl for she shivered suddenly and moved on across the slippery paving.

Despite its exposed position and the coldness and dampness of the day it was extraordinarily warm within the shelter of the ruins; and Carter soon saw that various angles and abutments, evidently of inner partitions that had once divided the building, acted as baffles and stops, making an area of shelter from the winds in the centre.

From here they could see across the grey and green and purple of the moor, all seamed and runnelled with channels and small stream beds and fissures, the whole stained and splashed with heather and lichen, while the baleful glow of the setting sun washed both land and sky in its bloody ochre tints. It was a savage spectacle and Carter, suddenly thinking of Jeremy, marvelled at his colleague's tenacity in venturing out upon that dread place at night and in the face of such primitive superstition on the part of the local inhabitants.

Turning to face the way they had come, he could see clear through one of the great glassless window emplacements; the whole sweep of the road to Tor Bridge was revealed, the pony patiently grazing in the shafts of the carriage, and, a long way off, a solitary figure on a white horse. Carter smiled; it was the gallant Captain and he could not possibly come up with them before they were ready to return.

He said nothing to the girl, and the two wandered on, somewhat overpowered, both by the scale of the ruins and by the stupendous backcloth that lay beyond it.

Moving round one of the buttresses, Carter came upon an area of paving that seemed to be all stained and blackened; the moss and lichen that disfigured the slabs was shrivelled and withered for several yards around. Carter was silent, his eyes stabbing to and fro across the broad nave in which they found themselves. It was sheltered here, and hardly a breath of wind stirred at their level, the window casements being much higher at this point; a long way above their heads, in fact.

"What do you make of that?"

The girl stood with her head lowered, tapping the top of her right boot with the small leather whip she carried.

"Perhaps some tramps have lit a fire here at one time to boil a kettle or cook a meal," she said casually. "We get some strange people upon the moor from time to time, particularly in summer."

"My own thoughts exactly," Carter said.

He looked upward into the shadow; saw a rusty hook and a length of chain. Not dangling as he might have supposed, but tied back against one of the pillars.

"Curious, do you not think?"

The girl followed his glance, her expression clearing.

"Probably left by the contractors. A commercial enterprise came to the moor about two years ago. They proposed lifting stones for some building purpose. As they had no permission and the monument has apparently some historic import, the county authorities sent them packing."

"I see."

Carter moved carelessly on, his mind preoccupied, seeing but not really registering the faint figure of the Captain in the far distance. He had reached the carriage now and had dismounted. If the girl had noticed she gave no sign.

They came to the end of the ruins and gazed from the pillared entrance porch at the darkening spectacle of the distant view. Despite the girl's close proximity Carter felt oppressed and stifled here.

There was a sense of danger and an ominous atmosphere which was not borne out by these simple and rather splendid ruins. Carter remembered the figure he had seen and looked about him quickly, trying to locate the mound.

It had been to the left of Rats' Castle when he had seen it before, which would place it to the west. But the far land was rapidly becoming cloaked in darkness and he could not make it out. The girl had turned away and was walking sure-footedly back down the aisle, beneath the frowning granite walls.

As Carter went to follow his foot kicked against something. There was a great stone slab at his feet, its jointing so flush with the other paving stones that he would not have noticed it had it not been for the massive iron ring which was set into it. Moved by some obscure impulse of curiosity he pulled at it, exerting all his strength.

Despite his youth and his not inconsiderable physique, it was so heavy that it might have taken several men his size to shift it, unless it were mortared in and the ring merely used as an anchoring point for the workmen who had laboured here.

It was a minor mystery and he moved thankfully away, called by the girl, whose clear, cool voice was urging him to hurry before darkness descended.

Twenty-Eight
The Captain is Put Out

1

"I DO THINK, Mr. Carter that you might have had some regard for Miss Hammond in taking her across that very dangerous and difficult ground in the dark."

Captain Henderson spoke evenly enough, but there was no mistaking the smouldering anger beneath the innocuous sentence. The Captain's figure, shifting on his mettlesome white horse, was only half-glimpsed in the dimness of the descending night by the two who emerged from the rough ground at the edge of the roadway. They could see the grim expression on the mouth beneath the dark moustache in the glow from the carriage-lamps which he had apparently lit just before their arrival.

That they had not seen the lights before was because they had been a long way below road level, toiling upward from the stream-bed over boulders and scree. Carter and the girl exchanged glances but before Carter could reply, the girl said coolly: "It is no good you blaming Mr. Carter, Captain. The expedition was my idea entirely."

Carter felt an inward glow spreading, emphasised by the warm and affectionate squeeze the girl's gloved hand gave his in the dusk. Henderson bit back an angry retort, his grim expression relaxing as he realised the anomalous position in which his words had placed him. He gave the young architect a stiff bow.

"My apologies, sir. My concern was entirely for Miss Hammond's safety, as you will understand."

Carter bowed in return, helping the girl up into the driving seat of the carriage. He felt her fingers slightly tremble on his own before she let go and transferred the whip to her right hand.

"Mine also, Captain," said Carter.

The girl smiled sweetly at the disgruntled figure on the white horse.

"I fancy I was in good hands, Captain Henderson," she said levelly.

The big horse was pirouetting now, as though the Captain had made some savage movement with his hands on the reins; and he fought to control the beast. While he was doing so Carter quietly took his place at the girl's side, content to let her fence verbally with the surly officer.

"And now, Captain, I think we have talked enough," she said smoothly. "If you will lead the way I am sure we may rely upon your staunch escort back to The Priory."

She gave a ringing laugh, holding Carter's eyes with her own in the mellow light cast by the carriage-lamps.

"And I am certain that any creatures abroad upon the moor tonight will know better than to get upon the wrong side of you."

The Captain put his hand to the peak of his undress cap in formal salute. The words were clipped and urbane, his real feelings bitten back and kept in check.

"You may rest assured of that, Miss Hammond."

Then he wheeled the big white horse swiftly, clattering on ahead, the stiff set of his shoulders indicating his displeasure.

Carter could see the amusement dancing in the girl's eyes but he did not dare comment on this situation aloud; that would have been presumptuous and, from what little he knew of the female psyche, might well have persuaded her to take the Captain's side if he were seen openly to reap advantage of the situation.

Instead, he simply leaned toward her on the seat as she urged the pony on. His voice was so low that she had to strain to hear it.

"Thank you."

She looked at him artlessly.

"For what, Mr. Carter?"

"I think you know, Miss Hammond," he said casually, drawing away from her again.

"Perhaps," she said dreamily.

In the light of the carriage-lamps he could see that she was smiling; though whether at the smouldering figure of the Captain, pirouetting in front of the carriage, or at some secret thought of her own he could not make out.

In any event Carter soon forgot the grudging presence of the military man because he and the girl seemed suspended in a small, intimate world of their own in the dusky interior of the carriage; bounded only by the gyrating light of the lamps as it jolted on over the rough roadway.

Ever afterward Carter was entranced at the memory of the girl's live, eager face; her lazy smile; her tawny hair flying in the lamplight; the scene impregnated with the pungent smell of burning lamp-wick and hot metal mingled with the aroma of polished leather from the fittings.

The girl talked easily and fluently on a variety of topics; of literature and music and painting; and even of some of the more intricate points of architecture, of which she seemed to have a respectable knowledge. Carter was already engaged with this girl's physical attractions, but he realised she had a well-stocked mind and now, as they chatted easily, over the staccato beats of the pony's hooves, he forgot their misty surroundings, the damp uplands of the moors beyond their enclosed world; and the rawness of the November night that was rapidly closing in.

2

It was quite dark when they reached The Priory but the great Palladian porch was adazzle with light from lanterns in the arcade, as though Mr. Hemming's house was the venue of some county function and they were the first of the guests. The girl got down easily from the carriage and Slade, who had appeared from some obscure region, gave a knowing wink to Carter as they clattered toward the stable area.

Henderson had already saluted the pair curtly and gone off ill-temperedly in the same direction so that the two were briefly alone, except for Mrs. Arkwright who hovered somewhat uncomfortably in the half-open doorway. A thin rain had started again now, but the weather was temperate compared to what it had been earlier and promised a fairly reasonable drive back.

Carter was about to say goodbye when, to his surprise, the housekeeper said, "You will stay to high tea, Mr. Carter? Mr. Hemmings is insisting, and I think he would like a further word with you regarding your plans."

"By all means, Mrs. Arkwright. If it will not put Slade out."

The housekeeper smiled pointedly.

"I think not, Mr. Carter," she said softly. "He makes himself comfortable enough below stairs."

She ushered the couple indoors as though they had been wayward children and slammed the massive front door behind them. Carter was about to cross to the painting in the hall when Hemmings appeared from the study door, a sheaf of papers in his hand. He smiled benevolently on his ward and the young man, beckoning them toward the comfort of the oval chamber.

"You do not mind if I monopolise Mr. Carter for a short while, Miss?"

The girl laughed, amused at her guardian's banter, and crossed to the leaping flames of the fire. She had left her outer garments with Mrs. Arkwright in the hall, as had Carter, and he felt a quickening of the spirit at the lithe, animal good health of her body as she traversed the room with quick strides, her tawny hair falling about her face and making a flecked brilliance in the lamplight.

"Let us have tea in here this afternoon, Fiona," said the Magistrate. "What say you?"

"An excellent idea," the girl responded. "I will let Mrs. Arkwright know."

She excused herself briefly and left the room. The Magistrate rubbed his hands together and smiled at Carter.

"A slight subterfuge, Mr. Carter. I would like to show you something of my workshop after tea."

A shadow crossed his face.

"Fiona does not approve of some aspects of my enthusiasm. I fear she regards the cellars as a somewhat macabre area."

He smiled again, reminiscently this time.

"It stems from her more tender years. She found her way down there without permission. She always had an adventurous spirit."

He gave Carter an apologetic look.

"I am experimenting with life-size automata of my own design. It promises to be an exciting field."

He lowered his eyes toward the parquet as though watching the shimmering reflections of the firelight in its brilliant surface.

"But perhaps you would not care for such a visit."

Carter hastened to express his interest.

"I should greatly enjoy it, sir. But I must not keep you too late this evening."

"Nonsense."

The Magistrate laid his hand on the other's arm.

"Possibly you have better things to do in Thornton Bassett?"

Carter was aware of the dancing amusement in the older man's eyes.

"You are joking, sir!"

Both were now looking toward the door through which the slim figure of the girl had disappeared. Hemmings gave a great jovial laugh and crossed to the fireplace, poking at the logs with a long-handled brass instrument. Carter hesitated a moment and then went to the desk, gratified to see his plans and drawings spread out over its surface. It was evident that the Magistrate had been studying his ideas in great detail. Hemmings caught the movement from the corner of his eye.

"Brilliant in its simplicity, Mr. Carter," he said softly. "I cannot fault it."

Before the architect could reply, the faint clatter of the girl's footsteps could be heard from the hall outside.

"What has happened to Captain Henderson?" said Hemmings blandly.

Carter shrugged. He had no wish to speak out of turn and he would leave it to the girl to explain if the Captain did not put in an appearance for tea. He could not help it if Henderson's pique made him display his dislikes in such an open manner.

"I think he had things to do at the stables, sir. Concerning the comfort of his troop and their mounts."

Hemmings nodded, a frown on his face.

"Yes, yes. He has great responsibilities."

His eyes were fixed almost dreamily on the big double doors through which the girl would at any moment appear.

"He will be going out with the troop tonight, I believe, if the weather holds."

He shrugged helplessly.

"Though what he hopes to do I cannot imagine. Unless we can find some local person to talk I do not see how we can lay these rascals by the heels."

His eyes were very sharp and attentive beneath the lenses of his gold-rimmed glasses now.

"Which reminds me that I must find someone from Thornton Bassett to guide Henderson and his troop about the moor."

He chuckled, his mood lightening.

"It would not do for the good Captain and his men to get lost on their first night out."

Carter and his host raised their eyes as the door opened. Fiona Hammond stood there in the gloom, holding the tall wing aside so that Mrs. Arkwright and the maid could manoeuvre the trolley through the open space.

Hemmings clapped his hands together like a schoolboy, making an explosive sound that startled the echoes from the massed ranks of the gold-spined books that lined the room.

"Ah, tea!"

Twenty-Nine
The Catacombs

1

"We have wine here as well, Mr. Carter, so you will not find it a wasted journey! You must allow me to present you with some bottles to take back with you this evening."

Hemmings' voice echoed and re-echoed beneath the vaulted archways of the long, sloping tunnel through which he lighted them. Their footsteps made muted, hollow noises that seemed to persist long after the sounds should have stopped. The girl looked around her cautiously, keeping within the protective shadow made by the two men who flanked her.

She held the lamp high, her eyes seeking Carter's, her face appearing pale in the pallid light. It was musty here too, and Carter fancied he could smell corruption in the dampness and the greenish fungi which sprouted from the shining pillars of the great arched buttresses which supported the roof.

It was indeed an eerie place, and he could see the girl's distaste on her face; could equally well understand her reasons for disliking this long, vaulted tunnel which apparently led a vast distance beneath the ground.

Hemmings looked at his guest shrewdly.

"Eigh, Mr. Carter?" he queried.

The architect felt embarrassed.

"I am sorry, sir. It is extremely kind of you and I appreciate your generosity."

"Think nothing of it. We have one of the best cellars in the county here. Eh, Fiona?"

The girl looked at him quickly, something of the spirited vivacity returning to her face.

"If you are talking of wine, uncle, then I agree with you entirely," she said drily. "But I have reservations about the rest of these catacombs."

Hemmings laughed shortly, the sounds making a jarring vibration against the massive studded door that barred their path.

"I quite understand that," he said equably. "My major passion, the study of automata, is mainly a man's pursuit, of course. And I agree that these vaults would appear gloomy to an imaginative young lady such as yourself. It is good of you to accompany us."

The girl tossed the hair back from her forehead.

"I do not want you frightening Mr. Carter to death, uncle."

Carter smiled and his host ventured another chuckle.

"I think this young man has rather more spirit than that, Fiona," he said equably. "And I certainly have no intention of frightening him off. His architectural services are far too valuable for that."

Guardian and ward exchanged another of those secret glances that Carter found so tantalising, and he was aware, for a few brief moments, of nuances here which it might be better not to pursue.

It was with relief that he saw Hemmings produce a big iron key from his pocket, and the elaborate ritual of unlocking and unbolting the enormous and extremely thick door made a welcome diversion.

He wondered what had kept Henderson. The man had not reappeared at the house, and Mrs. Arkwright had no comment, though both Hemmings and the girl had made somewhat pointed references to his absence at tea. Carter had, in fact, felt some concern in case he were keeping Slade from more urgent duties at Pollard, Bassett, but had been reassured by his host on the point.

The coldness and gloom here was inclining his thoughts to more charnel imaginings as they penetrated deeper into this underground world, and Carter noticed that Hemmings was now pointedly lighting oil lamps set at intervals on heavy stone brackets in the ancient walls.

The shadows fled before them and made strange, unnerving patterns on the groynes and on the dusty passageway at their feet and Carter had a brief vision of those charred victims of The Black Death which Jeremy Hands had hinted at so graphically.

He thrust the horrifying images away, aware that the girl was addressing him.

"You see what I mean about my guardian's activities here, Mr. Carter."

The latter nodded.

"I do indeed, Miss Hammond."

He looked round the bleak corridor, which was inclining even more steeply downhill now, repressing a shiver.

"It is certainly no place for a lady, Mr. Hemmings."

The landowner nodded affably, holding his own lamp high, concentrating on leading his charges in safety through this strange underground world.

"I can understand that, Mr. Carter. Unfortunately, it is the only place really suitable for my activities. I could use part of the stables but there is no security there and I could not trust my treasures away from the house."

"I quite see that, sir. I was wondering whether one might not establish some more practical lighting system here. Gas, for instance."

Hemmings smiled, his face expressing surprise.

"We have not even got gas in the house, young man. We are too remote here."

"You might establish your own plant," Carter went on, carried away by his enthusiasm. "If you wish I could prepare a scheme, and the office could work out an estimate."

Another amused glance passed between ward and guardian.

"My dear young man, let us get this major architectural scheme under way first. You have no wish to force me into bankruptcy, I hope?"

Carter joined in the general laughter and, the atmosphere lightened, they quickly came to a series of shallow steps and the vast main cellar where cobwebbed bins and wine-racks stretched out through the arcaded gloom, attesting Hemmings' taste and wealth, for Carter soon saw this must be one of the most important and extensive wine collections in private hands in the country.

2

Hemmings had lit several lamps now and as Carter and the girl stood a little apart he went from bin to bin commending the great vintages and pointing out wines of particular merit. Carter was not an expert but he appreciated the finer points of his host's discourse and apparently said the right things, judging by the flush of pleasure on the Magistrate's face.

He paused finally, taking his watch from his waistcoat pocket.

"Time presses, Mr. Carter, particularly when one is engaged in the more pleasurable activities of this world."

He pointed to a large, arched door at the far end of the cellar, almost lost in the dim light of the lanterns.

"Now for the *piece de resistance*. Fiona's Chamber of Horrors, Mr. Carter! The Workshops of the Clockwork Men!"

And his laughter pealed across the spaces beneath the vaulted arches as he led the way briskly forward, the two somewhat discomfitted young people following on behind.

If Carter had expected something outre or bizarre as soon as his host had flung open the far door he was disappointed. For the wine-cellar led merely to another dark passage. But here, oil-lamps stood prepared upon small wooden brackets at chest level, and it was only after he had carefully lit each, leaving a glowing and faintly trembling aureole of yellow light behind them, that Hemmings advanced, all the while giving the occasional dry chuckle. His dancing eyes scrutinised the couple shrewdly over his shoulder.

Carter now held the lamp Hemmings had originally carried, holding it to the spill the Magistrate was using to light the succession of vessels, while Fiona held the other; the combined result of these operations seemingly an absolute blaze of light after the sombre gloom of the cellar they had just quitted.

A few moments later Carter saw the object of this caution, for the narrow passage they were descending ended in air at the left-hand side. A cool breeze blew on his face as he looked down into impenetrable darkness and then his host's hand was at his side, urging him away.

"This is the ancient mediæval foundation of The Priory, Mr. Carter. I do not know what went on here in ancient times but it is a sombre, not to say lethal place. I should have had a balustrade erected long ago, but for the expense and the fact that few venture here except myself and favoured guests."

He smiled wryly.

"As you see I am careful to keep lights burning here at all times, extinguishing them only as I re-emerge into the wine cellar."

"Very wise, sir," Carter observed.

Hemmings nodded, the golden lamplight sending back small sparkling reflections from his glasses. The girl was silent, her face pale in the light of the lamp. She kept in close to the wall at the right, her expression seeming to Carter strained and tense.

Hemmings was poised, his feet not eighteen inches from the edge of the dark space which seemed to have eaten the ancient stone steps away; his nostrils distended as though he were sniffing the air like some wild beast. And a strange, almost warm draught blew from some unknown depth, bearing with it a faint, elusive perfume that Carter could not place.

He licked his lips, despising himself for the faint tremor in his voice, as he asked, "Is it a long drop here, sir?"

Hemmings nodded, giving his guest a curious smile.

"About thirty feet at this point, Mr. Carter; though of course it gets progressively shallower as one reaches the end of this passage. It is very dangerous, my boy. The drop here is direct on to a stone pavement."

The girl shivered, and Carter moved back from the edge of the tunnel, conscious that her hand was seeking his own. The silence was broken by Hemmings, who turned briskly.

"There is no need to be frightened, Fiona. Come along. The passage is wide enough and one needs only to keep close to the wall."

He was right, of course, Carter reflected, but as the two followed the tall figure of Hemmings, Fiona's hand still tightly in his own, he was all the time aware of the hidden danger of that unknown step into darkness and silence on his left hand and he was relieved when his host finally lit the last of the lamps. They stood before what the girl assured him was the entrance to these mysterious workshops of which he had heard so much.

Hemmings smiled, holding the creaking door wide. A gentle draught blew through; definitely warm this time, and with it the distinctive, sweetish smell of heavy engine oil.

He motioned the two young people forward.

Thirty
The Metal Man

1

"Astonishing, sir!"

Carter could not resist the exclamation as his host flung the door still wider. The girl stood back from the entrance and the young man felt her delicate fingers tremble on the skin of his hand.

His amazement, seemingly torn from his lips, was due to the bizarre sight which met them. For the golden rays of the lantern glinted on the soulless metal face of a man who stood near the entrance of the doorway in the great cellar-workshop.

He was six feet in height, proportionately broad, and was dressed in an exact replica of military uniform. The light winked back from his buttons and accoutrements and flashed on the metal parts of the pistol at his black leather belt and on the naked cutlass which he held in his gloved hand.

For a split-second Carter had felt fear flood through him at the unexpectedness of this menacing figure. Then he relaxed, aware that the creature before him was nothing more than a greater elaboration of his host's ingenious toys.

Hemmings stood watching him, enjoying the young architect's reaction, and now he advanced the lantern nearer. Carter saw that the eyes were indeed empty sockets; that the face was silver metal formed as a mask to resemble human features; and that the figure was another of Hemmings' incredibly clever automata.

"I have been working toward this for a long time, Mr. Carter," his host said, evident pride in his voice. "What do you think of it?"

Carter smiled, relaxing, as he turned to the girl.

"I believe I have already made my feelings evident, sir. Is this a working model?"

Hemmings beckoned the couple into the workshop, the girl advancing reluctantly, and he then closed the door behind him. Carter stood in thought for a moment or two, looking at the lifesize soldier and again marvelling at the model-maker's ingenuity.

"A prototype only," said Hemmings, answering his question. "But Fiona and I have great hopes for it."

The girl forced a laugh.

"You must not include me, uncle."

She turned hesitant eyes on the architect.

"Though I must admit I did collaborate, Mr. Carter. And that I designed and made the preliminary costumes, based on drawings in old books on military history my uncle keeps in the library above."

Carter glanced from Hemmings to the girl, aware of the amusement in the eyes of the former.

"You have not really answered my question, sir."

The Magistrate shrugged, putting down the girl's oil lamp on a massive wooden bench behind him and going farther down the shadowy, vaulted chamber, lighting two other lanterns which rested on wall brackets.

By the dancing, tremulous light that made the shadows of beams and inanimate objects undulate and shift on the walls in a disturbing manner, Carter saw there were other shrouded shapes, as though the white, swathed figures of an amorphous army stood there.

"I would not claim to be entirely successful, Mr. Carter." Hemmings said shortly.

His eyes glanced at the young man sharply from beneath the glinting spectacles.

"The technical details are nowhere near so complex as the miniature figures. The clockwork is robust, easily constructed and straightforward in comparison. But there are other problems, mainly due to weight and perambulatory considerations."

Carter exchanged a swift glance with the girl.

"You do not mean to say this is a marching figure, sir?"

Hemmings chuckled at his guest's astonishment.

"I do indeed, Mr. Carter. And there may be other surprises as well, by the time my work is finished."

"You intend Miss Hammond to paint the features and the eyes?"

Hemmings gave a short laugh which seemed to set the lantern flames jumping and dancing again.

"Without discounting my nieces's excellent contributions to my museum, Mr. Carter, I did not exactly mean that. It is really too technical to go into now. As I have said, the machinery is quite straightforward."

A frown passed over his strong features.

"But I am having trouble with the counterweights in the legs. Balance is the main problem. I fear it is proving fiendishly difficult. I will show you what I mean."

2

He bent forward to the chest of the giant silver-faced figure and instinctively both the girl and Carter drew back. Hemmings opened the front of the tunic and set a lever in motion. There came a strange whirring noise and then a jerky animation was imparted to the figure.

There was something remote and cruel about this thing with the metal face already, but when motion was transmitted clumsily to its limbs and it made a first attempt at a shuffling pace forward, Carter had to bite his lips to prevent himself from crying out. The girl averted her gaze as the first whirring was followed by an ugly grinding noise.

But Hemmings was completely absorbed, a smile of satisfaction on his lips as the metal figure made two or three tentative paces forward; stiff-legged, like some scene from pantomime, the golden lamplight giving back yellow reflections from the passive silver face.

The cutlass hung forward from the limp fingers, and Carter saw too that the feet were circular plates, no doubt temporary, which moved hesitantly across the rough cellar floor as though the thing had life of its own.

"Remarkable, is it not," said Hemmings softly.

Carter could not find it within himself to speak before the girl forestalled him.

"Dreadful, rather, uncle!" she said with a swift, jerky inhalation of breath, as though she were moved to imitation of this sinister inanimate thing which was yet endowed with uncanny life as it made a circular, crab-like circuit of the workshop. All the time there were strange whirrs and clicks and metallic noises from within its chest as though it suffered from some awful malady.

Frightening as it now was Carter realised it would be terrifying once perfected, with the face painted and the eyes gleaming in the mask-like visage.

Hemmings walked protectively, close behind the automaton as it moved stiffly, one step at a time, seemingly on the point of tottering, his arms held out widely in order to catch it if it fell.

"Is there any way of stopping it, sir?" Carter said, more to break the tension than anything else; there seemed to be an enchanted spell on the thing which imparted an almost menacing atmosphere to this strange cellar-workshop.

Hemmings shook his head, shooting him a quick glance as the young man moved over to follow.

"I am working on it. It is difficult to operate the switch on the chest. I am thinking of fitting a second, perhaps on one foot, which might be tripped by a wire placed two or three inches from the floor. But that would have its own dangers as the figure would probably topple."

He turned back to Carter, smiling affably.

"Of course, this is cheating, really. I had previously wound and set the clockwork, preparatory to this little demonstration. I hope it has not disappointed you."

Carter shook his head, looking at the white face of the girl.

"Rather the opposite, sir," he said drily.

"I think we have seen enough, uncle," the girl said, throwing her guardian a faint smile which the young man realised she had summoned up with some effort.

"Of course, my dear," Hemmings said abstractedly. "But I fear the demonstration could not have lasted much longer in any event. Ah, there it goes!"

As he spoke the thing caught one of its metal plates on an uneven projection on the floor and gave an angry whirring noise. It tottered, the silver mask gleaming sombrely in the lamplight, and then fell, the metal cutlass making a sharp clanging reverberation against the flagstones.

But Hemmings had darted forward and caught it before the bodywork could hit the floor. Carter realised he must be immensely strong. He held the automaton gently, oblivious of the angry humming, and whirring noises that were coming from its interior. The strange feet, dimly glimpsed beneath the white military trousers with their scarlet piping, made ineffectual scraping noises on the stone of the cellar.

Hemmings reached forward, operating the switch. The ugly sounds died away. He got to his feet, dusting the knees of his trousers. Perspiration gleamed on his high forehead.

"That is one of the dangers, Mr. Carter. A poor example of my work in the full-size field!"

"On the contrary, sir, an extraordinary achievement."

Hemmings held up his hand but his eyes were smiling.

"You flatter me, Mr. Carter."

He glanced round the cellar again before bending and restoring the military figure to the upright posture. He fussed about it, adjusting the uniform and brushing the dust from the epaulettes. Then he glanced at the two young people standing near the door.

"This is an unsuitable place for such an elegant young lady, Mr. Carter. If you will escort Fiona part of the way, I will extinguish the lamps and join you in a few moments."

Carter was only too glad to obey his injunction and he operated the latch of the heavy oak door with some difficulty, ushering the girl back into the heavy silence of the tunnel they had quitted a short time before. She had recovered herself now and gave him a genuine smile.

The couple waited while Hemmings secured the door, bringing one of the lanterns out with him to supplement those carried by Carter and Fiona Hammond. The three walked back along the great sweep of tunnel, each conscious of the brooding atmosphere in here; each conscious, Carter felt, of the weight of unspoken thoughts.

As though he had some means of reading the young architect's mind his host broke in suddenly, his eyes kindly and concerned above the furrowed brow.

"I was talking to Mr. Curtis earlier today, Fiona."

"Is there any news of his daughter?"

Hemmings shook his head. He turned his glance on his guest, standing aside courteously to light the couple up the slope.

"We are talking of one of my tenant farmers, Mr. Carter. He is a very superior type of man, who is not given to exaggeration. His daughter is missing from home."

His lips were set in a grim, stern line now.

"She disappeared about three days ago."

"I am sorry to hear that, sir."

Hemmings gave a heavy sigh.

"It may be something altogether more commonplace than we imagine," he continued. "It is my private opinion that the girl has run off with some sweetheart. She will probably turn up in Plymouth or some other town in due course."

The girl bit her lip.

"Let us hope so, uncle."

Carter looked at his host shrewdly.

"What makes you incline to that theory, sir?"

Hemmings smiled briefly.

"While an admirable person, Curtis is a dark, inflexible man. Like many people about here he holds strict religious, not to say puritanical views. He is a widower and inclined to be far too restrictive with his daughter."

Carter exchanged glances with the girl, saw nothing but mild curiosity in her eyes.

"Nevertheless, I have a heavy responsibility as the senior representative of the law in these parts, Mr. Carter. Apart from the local Inspector of Police, of course."

He sighed again.

"I suppose I shall have to accompany Henderson and his dragoons tonight to comb the moor. The girl may have wandered off somewhere and injured herself."

"Will it not be too late now, in that case?" Carter asked.

Hemmings shrugged, his glasses flashing fire in the mellow gold of the lamplight.

"Possibly, Mr. Carter. But what am I to do? The moors are a vast place. Curtis reported the girl missing only today; and even if she is upon the moor, she may well have taken refuge in some remote cottage if my original surmise is correct."

Carter heard the Magistrate's last sentence with quickening interest, but he was careful to make his voice sound neutral.

"Might it not be dangerous, sir?"

"Possibly, Mr. Carter. But I am not unused to that. And I fancy I know the moors a good deal better than any town-bred dragoon officer, however much he may fancy his own abilities in that area."

Carter was at some pains to repress the smile he felt spring to his lips. He was being unfair to Henderson, he knew. He was sure the man was an able enough officer. It was stupid to allow petty jealousy over Hemmings' ward to influence his judgement on the man's abilities. But Henderson had only himself to blame.

"You speak of danger, Mr. Carter."

Hemmings had an expression of cynical amusement upon his face now. He rummaged in his waistcoat pocket and produced a grubby sheet of paper.

"That was left upon my own porch a few nights ago. The insolent rascals!"

Carter read the roughly formed letters, in block capitals, with amazement. The message said: MAGISTRATE HEMMINGS. KEEP OFF THE MOOR AT NIGHT. YOU GO THERE AT YOUR PERIL.

He handed it back, feeling a faint trembling of his finger-tips.

"The night-riders?"

The Magistrate thrust the sheet back in his pocket with a grim smile.

"Or someone who wishes me to think so. The judiciary will not be swayed or deflected in its course by such arrogant nonsense."

A silence fell upon the three, which was not broken until they had once more regained the civilised comfort of the house.

THIRTY-ONE
Lights on the Moor

1

"THANK YOU FOR your generosity, sir!"

Carter extended his hand to his host in the dim light of the hallway, his eyes on the wooden case whose straw-lined interior concealed the six bottles of choice wine Hemmings had brought up from the cellar for him.

The tall, long-haired Magistrate smiled affably.

"Think nothing of it, Mr. Carter. I can assure you it is an excellent investment! A small token of appreciation for all you intend to do and will do for The Priory extensions."

He made no move to take Carter's extended hand and the latter changed the gesture to indicate the gift on the side-table next to his leather case.

"You may be sure I will do my best, sir, after seeing your collection."

Hemmings caught the query on his face as Carter glanced about the hall.

"My ward will be down in a moment or two to see you to the door, Mr. Carter. I am sure you can get along well enough in my absence and that of Mr. Henderson."

There was a faint smile in his eyes but Carter did not take him up on the remarks. Again, he felt a fleeting embarrassment. But with Mrs. Arkwright's withdrawal into the interior of the vast house and Fiona Hammond's momentary disappearance there would be time enough to examine the painting providing the Magistrate also withdrew.

Though his remarks indicated his intention to do so he currently showed no inclination to leave the young man there on his own.

Courtesy, perhaps. Carter could read nothing in the mildness of the eyes beneath the thick glaze of the spectacles.

"We were talking a few moments ago of inventions, sir," he prompted. "Following my expressed admiration of your own genius in that direction. Yet you yourself do not appear to keep a motor-car."

The eyes were dark and forbidding now as the Magistrate turned them upon him.

"The motor-car, sir. You surprise me. At their present stage of development they would be quite useless in a place like Dartmoor."

Carter shrugged.

"I appreciate it is early days yet, sir, but I would venture to say they are not just a passing fancy. I have seen and travelled in the Panhard in my time in London. It is a most exhilarating mode of locomotion."

The Magistrate smiled gently.

"You are young, Mr. Carter. And you may well be right in your percipient comments. But I am a much older man than you."

He smiled again, a little wryly this time.

"As *au courant* as I am with modern technical developments, I fancy this mode of travel will never replace the horse. Good night to you, sir! Come again soon and, of course, whenever you are upon this part of the moor."

He shook hands warmly with his guest and then turned on his heel, his footsteps ringing out strong and firm over the parquet as he strode back to his study. The door closed crisply behind him and then the great hush of the house descended once again.

Carter glanced around the hall. Nothing moved in all that dim expanse of luxury. In three strides he was at the painting, examining it minutely, almost anxiously. It seemed curiously different to what he had remembered. The swirling oils and the heavily ridged encrustations made, he believed, with a special type of palette knife, looked far darker and more sinister that he had recalled. Perhaps the lighting was different.

Then he realised he was perhaps being subjective; the images in the large canvas distilled through a mind which was becoming clouded with the brooding horror of what was happening upon the moor. Or rather, what was not happening, for he knew nothing of it at first-hand.

Jeremy's wild tales of charred corpses found there, the stories of police and other investigations, the Chief Magistrate's hints and official diplomacy, the roughly pencilled note threatening Hemmings' life, the veiled warnings given him by the Rector, his landlady, and even his employer. All these things had combined to warp and distort his normally sane judgement.

Yet he could not shake off the sorrow and conviction on the faces and in the voices of Jeremy and the Rector in particular; and though it had not been repeated he still retained the vivid memory of the wild, anguished sobbing he had heard from his window on a summer-like evening which now seemed so long ago.

That had never been explained yet it might, of course, have simply been the outpourings of an overburdened heart, possibly one of the bereaved relatives of a young man found dead upon the moor, giving way to long suppressed grief.

Carter temporarily dismissed the heavy thoughts which were thronging his mind and scanned the canvas intently. Though, superficially, the scene depicted might have been taken to represent that of a local hunt there was a great deal more to it than that. Even a kind of crude, pagan symbolism.

The artist might well have been a minor practitioner of the eighteenth century yet he was not without skill and talent; that the work dated from the previous century was never in doubt. It was not merely a question of style; for here, in addition to the solitary ruin of Rats' Castle, was a substantial and obviously prosperous mansion to the left of the ancient original and apparently contiguous to the picturesque ruins.

As the girl had said there may have been a passable road across there in those days, though there was no trace of it in the picture; but more than a hundred years would surely have been needed, not only to obliterate all vestiges of the track but those of such a large and well-built house.

Unless there had been a fire or some other disaster to demolish the edifice. Carter resolved to investigate further the next opportunity he found to pay the area a visit. He might try the excuse of essaying his own water-colour study of the ruins once suitable weather made this possible.

All these ideas had passed through Carter's teeming mind in fractions of seconds as he scrutinised the canvas keenly. That the scene was not a hunt seemed fairly definite for the hounds were not those normally used to pursue the fox or stag. They were huge, gaunt and half-famished creatures with slavering jaws and little red eyes which the painter had picked out on his canvas in a disturbing manner.

The horsemen, too, wore dark clothing and an aura of mist seemed to cling about their cruel and feral features; it was as though the painter had clothed them in a baleful light. The technique was just the opposite to religious painting, in fact, but doubly effective; for it was always easier to depict evil than good, Carter mused.

He turned his attention quickly to the upper portion of the huge canvas, which was lost in shadow, his ears attuned to the slightest sound from the house beyond. He located the mound; it was almost a tor, which apparently stood a fair way from the ruins.

There was the figure, dark and misshapen, yet full of suppressed power. It leaned on a stout staff and it seemed like the brooding presence of the moor itself, presiding over the wintry scene, so that Carter felt a faint draught pass across him, like an inward shiver of his very soul.

He turned away from the picture quickly, aware of a slight movement to his left. He had just time to see a scarecrow image at the far side of the canvas, that of a terrified man running out on to the moor. He had his head turned at an agonised angle over his shoulder, and the fear of death was upon his ashen features. Carter knew then that what the hounds hunted was a human quarry.

There was a striking parallel in the pose of Captain Michael Henderson. The officer stood some way off, at the far side of the hall. His body was in shadow, faintly silhouetted against the heavy panelling. From where he had come Carter could not fathom, though he had certainly not been there a few seconds before. His eyes were fixed upon the young architect with an expression of implacable hatred.

Then he had caught the other's gaze upon him; he gave a slight start as though recollecting himself; made Carter a stiff half-bow and passed on so silently and quickly that the guest was not now sure whether Henderson had indeed stood there or whether he had been the victim of some hallucination.

He turned with relief at the sound of Fiona Hammond's light footstep upon the stair.

2

It was a cold, clammy evening but with occasional patches of clearness among the clouds, through which a few stars gleamed palely. The hooves of the two black horses rang out hollow on the cold surface of the moorland road as Slade drove the carriage back in the direction of Thornton Bassett; and below them the hollows were filled with mist, pale as milk, lapping at the shoulders of the moorland like a liquid tide.

Carter's mind was full of the girl's parting words and he held the image of her face before his eyes, blurring the bleakness of the scene as they rattled out of Tor Bridge, the village already dim and indistinct behind them.

Slade kept silence for the first half-mile or so, while they were still on the uplands, his face strong above the beard; his hard hat still jammed upon his head, even within the carriage. Carter could sense that he was content enough with his day.

"Nice people at The Priory," the young man ventured presently, his gloved hands resting on the leather case which contained his drawings and plans for Hemmings' ambitious museum rooms. His mind was still full of the strangeness of the catacombs and the metallic silver face of the life-size metal soldier which the Magistrate was developing there, the whole atmosphere so different to the civilised and refined ambiance of the great house above.

Slade roused himself, as though from a reverie.

"They are that, sir," he said reflectively. "Mrs. Arkwright is a very fine woman."

His shrewd eyes caught Carter's own quickly.

"But, of course, you'd be thinking of the young lady, sir."

The architect sensed the amusement behind the driver's innocuous statement.

"I had not forgotten Miss Hammond," he said non-committally, aware of the dancing lights in Slade's eyes that were not entirely born of the mellow beams of the side-lamps.

"Does Mr. Hemmings approve of your plans for the new extensions, sir?" Slade went on quickly, as though removing the conversation from a difficult area.

"I think so."

Slade gave his companion a thin smile.

"Mr. Pollard will be pleased, sir, and that's a fact. It's a credit to the firm."

Carter felt a faint flush of pleasure and he warmed to this strange, enigmatic and yet upright man who was something more than his somewhat humble station might denote. He had meant that Carter was a credit to the firm for which he, Slade, had so much respect and the architect took it as a hard-earned compliment.

The wind was buffeting a little up here now and Carter looked about him keenly, suddenly roused to consciousness of the dreariness and loneliness of their position. It was not really late in the evening but he could not help contrasting the present wintry conditions of cold and darkness with the summer-like golden days of October.

Only a few short weeks ago, yet they might have been years for the contrast they afforded. He hunched deeper into his thick coat, again reflecting on the events of the past hours. He could not erase from his mind the look on Henderson's face. He had caught the Captain in an unguarded moment when he did not know he was being observed.

There was cruelty as well as hatred in the glances he had given Carter. Yes, and something of guilt and surprise too. Though why that should have been so the young man could not surmise. He was sorry that such a person was beneath Fiona Hammond's roof.

Ordinary jealousy and dislike of a possible rival for the girl's affections Carter could understand. But there was something a great deal deeper here that he could not yet fathom. Though on reflection, his mind may have been over-impressed by the sombre images conjured up by the strange, anonymous oil painting that hung in Magistrate Hemmings' hall. And, a little farther back in time, the even more horrifying imaginings painted by the vivid conversations with his friend, Jeremy Hands.

He glanced quickly at Slade. The driver had slouched back into a more somnolent position in his seat, his keen eyes half-closed, which meant that he was not inclined for any further conversation. For all that he missed nothing that might be going forward on the moor about them and he was equally alert to the faintest break in the horses' confident stride.

It was he whose keen ears caught the muffled thunder on the road behind them long before Carter himself heard it. Slade looked at him grimly and pulled the carriage in to the side, making sure their lamps were bright and well-trimmed. In a surprisingly short time the roaring sound and the clash of metal had resolved itself into the somewhat terrifying collective apparition of Henderson's troop; the Captain himself as usual mounted upon his white charger; his troopers on coal-black horses, looking like spirits of the moor, the mounts seeming to glide above the thin mist that hung over the surface of the road.

Slade raised his whip in silent salute as the troop of dragoons swept past at the trot, the horses' hooves raising vivid sparks against the flinty surface underfoot. The Captain, who had a grim face as though the devil himself rode at his elbow, gave Carter a stiff bow as they passed and then pounded swiftly onwards, his back a straight, uncompromising column as the cavalcade faded from sight.

Slade put his tongue in his cheek and looked at Carter blandly as though he knew of the veiled enmity that existed between the two men; and urged the horses on. For a long time they could hear the dragoons' progress on the road ahead of them.

"I wish them well of it," he said at last as Carter continued silent.

"You do not think they will have much success against the moor-riders, then?"

Slade looked at him sharply from beneath the black brim of his hat.

"If they exist, sir," he said cautiously.

They were slowly descending the curving road, the whole expanse of the moor; silent, mysterious, the mist, milky-white in the hollows, spread before them. Strange points of light suddenly pricked the horizon. Carter felt a faint thrill of fear as he stared at them. He could not be certain but he felt that they originated in the general direction in which he took Rats' Castle to lie.

He glanced at Slade but it was obvious the man had seen nothing, for his eyes were fixed upon the road before them in the direction the troop had taken.

Carter was about to draw his attention to the phenomenon when something stopped him. Jeremy Hands' warnings came back and he had a vivid impression of his colleague's pale, earnest face, enjoining caution. He said nothing, compressing his lips, a sour taste of fear in his mouth.

When he again turned in his seat the lights, shifting and insubstantial before, had already vanished in the dark and dreary moorland blur.

Thirty-Two
The Hounds Gather

1

GAS LAMPS FLARED and made shimmering pools on the wet cobbles as the horses clattered into the shuttered streets of Thornton Bassett. Carter got down thankfully near the bridge, gathering up his case. Slade bid him goodnight and urged the horses on toward the tangled mass of alleys where Carter had walked with Hands. He understood the firm owned stables there though he had never yet seen them.

He was about to turn away to seek his lodging when a shadow detached itself from the darkness near the edge of the stream. Carter recognised with a startled shock the features of Jeremy himself. His face looked pale and set, and his eyes burned with strange fires.

The ruby ring on his hand flashed beneath a nearby street lamp as he raised it toward his hat in salutation.

"Jeremy! What are you doing here?"

"Waiting for you, John."

The voice was sad and resigned and Carter found it impossible to read his colleague's mood. Hands looked round the deserted streets almost furtively and drew Carter back into the shadow.

"I must speak to you urgently, John. There may not be time after."

"Well, let us go to our lodgings."

Hands shook his head.

"I have reasons for not going back now, John. The office is near. We could speak much more comfortably there."

Carter looked at his companion in silence for a moment.

"Very well. As you wish."

The two young men hurried over the bridge, the thin tendrils of mist raw and clammy at their throats. Lights glowed comfortingly from The Bassett Arms opposite and the high, thin notes of a piano sounded from one of the nearby houses. The church clock chimed as they let themselves in at the front door of the office.

To Carter's surprise it was still only nine o'clock. He had felt it to be so much later. But then a good deal had happened today.

"Did you see the dragoons?" he asked Hands, more to make conversation than anything else, as they mounted the stairs that led to Carter's office.

Hands nodded, his expression thoughtful in the dim light from the street that filtered through the big windows at the stairhead.

"I was drinking at the inn when the troop passed."

He gave a hard, cynical laugh.

"What do they think they are doing?"

"Searching the moor," Carter said. "I take it you do not feel they have much chance of success."

They were in the office now, which struck chill as the fire had died in the grate.

"I will leave that to you, John," said Jeremy as the architect lit his green-shaded desk lamp, the wild look in the former's eyes quite evident. "But with Henderson leading them I cannot feel much confidence in their mission tonight. Why are they out there, anyway?"

"Magistrate Hemmings has ordered them out," Carter told him. "A farmer's daughter has been reported missing. And the troop has other purposes on the moor."

That reminded him of something else and he sat down at his desk with a corrugated brow, motioning Jeremy into the leather visitor's chair.

"Mr. Hemmings told me he was accompanying the dragoons on their search to guide them. Perhaps he is meeting up with them later tonight."

Hands shrugged, his mind evidently elsewhere.

"Even so, I do not give much for their chances. Such a body of horsemen can be heard coming from miles away."

Carter gave his friend a shrewd look.

"But they must try, Jeremy. And there is the girl, too . . ."

Hands twisted his lips, the lamplight shining on his sandy hair.

"I see that," he admitted. "But such a body is a clumsy way of conducting a search over a wide and desolate area . They will be of nuisance value and nothing else."

"To Satan and his Hounds?" Carter put in quickly.

Hands drew his breath in with a little emphatic noise and sat back in the chair, his eyes on his friend's face.

"Perhaps," he admitted cautiously.

"But does not the reverse also apply to these horsemen upon the moor?" Carter returned.

Hands put the tips of his fingers together on Carter's desk and studied them reflectively. His voice was so low that the architect had to strain to catch his drift.

"They have entirely different functions, John. The soldiers are casting in circles, aimlessly perhaps. These others have a diametrically opposite purpose. One is to confine and terrify. The other is to congregate in a given spot."

Carter nodded, a slight shiver traversing his frame.

"You may be right, Jeremy. I saw lights upon the moor tonight. I do not think it was imagination. And they seemed to be coming from Rats' Castle.

2

"The devil you say!" Hands observed in deep and serious voice.

A long silence fell between the two young men. Carter was about to resume the conversation when he noticed something white shimmering on the office floor, just beyond the range of the lamplight. He excused himself hastily and got up, crossing to the door.

The envelope was addressed to him, inscribed in a flowing, elegant hand. He realised it had been thrust beneath his door during the day while he was at The Priory, probably by Miss Harkness. It had not been posted but had been delivered by hand to the office. He returned to the desk and put the envelope down face uppermost on the green leather surface.

"And Magistrate Hemmings has himself been threatened by these people," Carter went on. "He showed me the roughly scrawled warning which advised him to keep off the moor."

There were dark spots on Jeremy Hands' frank, open features. He nodded slowly, as though he had made up his mind.

"That does not surprise me, John. It should be an interesting evening upon the moor tonight."

Carter's eyes widened.

"You are not thinking of going out there?"

Hands nodded.

"I must. Too much is at stake."

He smiled quickly at the architect's expression.

"Do not fear, John."

He went on before Carter could voice any further objections.

"You must give some excuse to our landlady this evening. Say that I have been called away to the north on urgent family business."

"Without even having time to pack, Jeremy? And you will have to return by morning, surely?"

Hands bit his lip; then his face cleared.

"Say that you have had a message, John. That I am staying the night with the young lady's family. That her parents are providing for my overnight comfort. And that I am travelling north from there."

Carter nodded.

"Very well, Jeremy. Though it does not sound very convincing. Was that why you wanted to see me this evening? To tell me you would be away tonight?"

Hands turned his eyes down to the floor of the office, the pupils catching the faint flicker of the dying firelight.

"Partly, John. As you know I have been about the moor a good deal these past months. There is a pattern to these alarms. And to the murders also, if one studies them. They follow certain phases and regular periods of time."

Carter felt a sudden quickening of the breath. He looked at his friend sharply.

"What are you telling me, Jeremy?"

The young man shook his head.

"I do not really know, John. Except that I am on the brink of something important."

He broke off as though he had heard a faint sound and stared toward the door. Carter had noticed nothing untoward and waited for him to continue. Hands sat so for fully a minute, his face alert, his body bent in a contorted and fearful attitude that his host found unnerving.

Then Hands relaxed with a muffled apology. He turned back to the architect.

"The people hereabouts talk of the Hounds of Hell, John. Now even you, a newcomer, talk about them. Farmers and other people living in lonely spots on the moors have heard them howling on winter nights. On summer nights too, come to that. And I have heard them myself."

Carter was startled both by the other's information and his manner, but he strove to keep his face blank and untroubled.

"I believe you, Jeremy. There may be dogs of some kind out there. I examined the painting at The Priory today."

There was vivid interest in Hands' brown eyes above the stickpin in his cravat, which made a liquid blob of gold in the lamplight as he moved.

"And what did you find?"

"The hounds were not ordinary ones, Jeremy. They were lean and famished-looking. And they were not hunting deer or other animal prey. They were hunting a man!"

There was mingled fear and triumph in Hands' eyes. He leaned forward at the desk, his broad, spatulate fingers spread out on the leather surface. The ruby in the curious ring glowed with dull fire. He spoke in a low and urgent voice.

"Listen carefully, John. We will talk of this again tomorrow. But I have made certain discoveries which can only be corroborated by field-work upon the moor. I have been out and about a good deal, as I have already said. On my spare days and evenings in the summer I have travelled extensively both by rail and dog-cart around the fringes of the moor—hopefully, without attracting too much attention. Surveying and sketching was my excuse and I carried the tools of my trade with me."

He went on again after a moment.

"I did not know there was such a business in the conveyance of livestock. I found a good deal of wicker baskets, both full and empty upon the platforms of lonely railway stations. Some of them interested me greatly. They were never more than singles or in pairs."

Carter felt faint irritation rising within him at the other's mysterious manner but he strove to keep his voice normal.

"What about the baskets?"

Hands lowered his voice still further.

"They were always to be called for. So there were no addresses for their destinations."

He smiled thinly.

"That was a shrewd touch."

"But what are you implying, Jeremy?"

Hands leaned forward until his eyes were boring into Carter's.

"Dogs, John! Irish wolfhounds mostly. Great, half-starved brutes for the most part!"

Thirty-Three
At the Rectory

1

IT WAS NOT until long after Hands had gone that Carter remembered the letter. Nothing that he had been able to say would dissuade his friend. His conversation came back, reverberating like doom in Carter's numbed mind though it was almost half an hour since Hands had taken his departure.

It was gone ten before he recalled the envelope upon his desk. The last vibrating notes from the church clock were just dying away when he tore the letter open with slightly trembling fingers. It was from the Rector and its contents crept like a ray of hope into the blackness of his mind.

It was crisply worded and brief. It merely said: Dear Mr. Carter, I must speak with you on a matter of the utmost importance. Come to the Rectory tonight no matter how late the hour. No-one must know of your visit. Do not fail me. Yours, David Sennen.

As soon as he had finished reading, mindful of Hands' admonitions, he took both envelope and enclosure and burned them in a brass tray set upon a corner of his desk. When they were consumed to a fine ash, and only then, did he stir himself, as though awakening from a long sleep.

He quit the office precipitately, closing and locking the big front door quietly behind him. He turned to the right, making for the network of small alleys and squares that would take him to the Rectory by quiet and devious ways. He stopped in the shadow of the buildings, conscious of the crisp echo of footsteps over the stone setts nearby.

Peering cautiously from his place of concealment he saw the tall figure in dark clothing walking upright and confidently. It was Slade right enough, just returned from stabling the pony; the light from a gas lamp catching the strong, bearded face beneath the brim of his hard hat.

Carter stayed where he was. He felt half-ashamed at hiding in the shop doorway like a thief from such an honest, upstanding fellow but then recalled the admonition in the Rector's note. He had most likely delivered it himself, pushing it through the front letter box toward the office closing time, so that Miss Harkness would see it before she went home and take it to his private room.

Carter left his place of concealment, conscious that the faint beat of Slade's footsteps was dying away up the street. The fret of water from the swollen stream, washing round the stone piers of the nearest town bridge, was uppermost now, cloaking his own movements.

He went quickly through the nearest alley, walking in the middle of the road, keeping in the shadows between the street lamps. There was no-one about in any case, but if the Rector did not wish his nocturnal visit to be known to the general public of Thornton Bassett then he must have good reason.

His mind was continually revolving Jeremy's weird suppositions regarding the moor. That hounds had been heard there at night was supported by testimony from many local people, according to his colleague. But that dogs were despatched to lonely railway stations and then, by implication—for Jeremy would not expand further upon the matter—assembled into a pack in some fastness upon the moor, was too fantastic for belief.

Yet there was evidently some sort of basis in legend for hounds hunting humans upon the moor. The strange picture at The Priory would appear to bear that out. Jeremy had not implied, in so many words, that people were hunted to death upon the moors. That would not account for the charred and blackened corpses that had been found.

But that the hounds existed in reality to frighten and prevent people from venturing upon the moors at night was another supposition altogether; Carter could give that some credence, though his bewilderment and apprehension at the slow winding of the invisible net that seemed to be closing about him was growing.

The Rector was the man; he was the person who knew most about local legend and history, Mr. Pollard had said. Was he not the town's own historian? Perhaps his researches had revealed something important, and he was now going to open up his heart to Carter? That itself was not without its own dangers, as Jeremy had already hinted.

And, in view of Hands' anguished admonitions to keep his fears and suspicions to himself, should he now take the Rector into his confidence; tell him of Jeremy's lone and potentially dangerous expedition upon the moor tonight? For despite all Carter's questioning the young man had remained tight-lipped about his real reason for going out there at dead of night.

Carter would think him insane, he had said; and he had refused to be drawn further. Indeed, all along, Jeremy's hesitations, hintings and revelations—which were never quite what his listener had hoped for—had reached a maddeningly tantalising stage in Carter's mind.

He realised he was probably cruelly misjudging his friend; and had he been in his place and had actually seen the shrouded remains of those unfortunates who had perished in the night in a lonely and most horrific way, perhaps he too would have kept silence in the face of indiscreet questioning.

He was close to the Rectory now, where a dim light burned in a lower window and another in the shadowy porch. The fret of the stream was in his ears, its noise overlaying the sound of his footsteps, and he quickened his pace as though at the end of a long journey. He passed swiftly through the churchyard, the path clear in the light of the moon, crossing the drive to the Rectory. The Rector was opening the front door as soon as he heard him approach.

2

Sennen's face looked even more worn and fine-honed in the light of the oil lamp on the hall bracket than Carter remembered. But his eyes lit up with relief, and there were lines of resolution carved at the corners of his mouth as he greeted the architect with unfeigned pleasure.

"Thank God you got my note, Mr. Carter. This is deep business, and I have great need of your help and advice."

Carter raised his eyebrows, lingering at the porch entrance until his host almost dragged him inside. He re-locked, bolted, and chained the front door with elaborate precautions, Carter felt.

The dark-haired cleric put a finger to his lips to enjoin caution and led the way across the gloomy hall, unlit except for the one oil lamp; and opened a door on the right where a pale beam of gas-light gleamed cheerfully, enhanced by the large fire of coals burning in a great stone chimneypiece.

The room was a study, lined with thousands of books and with an encircling gallery up toward the massive beamed ceiling, but Carter had little time to take in its detail.

"I am at your disposal, Rector," he began. "I have only just received your note, I am afraid."

Again Sennen enjoined caution, closing the study door softly. He came back down the room to where Carter stood hesitating.

"My housekeeper is a light sleeper, Mr. Carter. I would not want her to witness our meeting here."

Carter's first inclination was to smile but one look at the Rector's sad features made him realise the seriousness of the man's purpose.

"But what is there to fear from your housekeeper, sir?"

Sennen led him over to a deep leather chair by the fire before replying.

"It is not my housekeeper, Mr. Carter. It is just that she is a nosy and garrulous old woman. If she knew we were conferring here at this time of night the information—together with her own wild speculations—would be all over the town by tomorrow morning."

Carter sank into the chair, grateful for the warmth of the fire.

"I see."

He watched uncomprehendingly as the Rector bustled about at a sideboard. He heard a clink of glasses, and then the cleric was back with a tray on which reposed a decanter and several bottles.

"I do not usually indulge at this time of night, Mr. Carter, but what I have to say is serious indeed and whisky is a great fortifier."

Carter gave the other a thin smile.

"I will not argue that, sir. Half and half if you please."

There was no sound except the faint fretting of the fire as the Rector bent to pour from the crystal decanter. He passed the gasogene to his guest before re-filling his own glass.

Carter noticed, as he filled his tumbler to the brim with the soda-water, that the big circular table at the Rector's elbow was scattered with layers of books; together with sheets of paper covered with notations.

He glanced idly at the gold-lettered spines as the Rector went across to take the chair opposite; and was astonished to see that so far from being the religious works of his imaginings they were learned treatises on such esoteric subjects as demonology, secret societies and witchcraft. The Rector gave him a somewhat strained smile and raised his glass in silent salute. The two men drank, absorbed in thoughts too deep for words.

Now that his ears were attuned to the atmosphere within the library Carter could faintly catch the roar of the stream that ran outside the Rectory; the room in which they sat was obviously at the nearest point to where the edge of the garden debouched on to the bank of the flood, now swollen to a sizeable river with the autumn rains.

A gilded clock on the mantel shelf chimed. Carter realised it was only half-past ten. In London the evening would be just beginning. Down here in the fastnesses of the moor was another world; ten-thirty was dead of night in a place like Thornton Bassett though the inns and bars would only just be turning out.

Carter wondered idly why Sennen's housekeeper would already be abed. Then he realised she would most likely be up in the very early hours to lay fires and prepare for the churchman's busy day.

Sennen himself seemed sunk in a brooding silence now that Carter had arrived, the urgency of his note apparently forgotten. He roused himself at Carter's gentle question.

"I am sorry, sir. I was just wondering how best to tackle this business."

Carter put encouragement into his voice.

"You have decided to confide in me, then?"

The Rector nodded.

"I must, Mr. Carter, or go mad. One or the other."

"Would it help you, Mr. Sennen, if I told you that I am already involved in these weird events upon the moor? Through my friend Mr. Hands. Or that I have myself tonight seen strange shifting lights near Rats' Castle, out there upon the moor?"

There was astonishment in the Rector's troubled eyes, immediately replaced by hope.

"Ah! You ease my mind considerably, Mr. Carter. Would you care to enlarge upon your remarks? I can assure you I will be equally frank in return."

Carter drew his chair a little further forward so that the two men were sitting squarely opposite, quite close to one another. Before he could begin Carter was startled to hear a low, shrill whistle, as though from a kettle but muted and far away. The note persisted for a few seconds more and then died. The Rector smiled faintly at his guest's expression.

"It is only the train leaving Princetown Station, Mr. Carter. You forget that sound sometimes carries a long way on the moor at night. One can often hear trains, even though from far off, when the wind is in the right direction."

Carter thought that it was merely one more strange phenomenon, apposite to this weird landscape but he kept the notion to himself.

"Of course, sir."

He was answering the Rector's earlier question and not his last remark, and the Rector seemed to sense this because he waited, his eyes fixed upon the architect's face, his smooth, well-kept hands clasped round the breadth of his whisky glass.

"Mr. Hands would not approve of my confiding in you, sir, but we must trust one another."

The sharp words were out the Rector's mouth almost as quickly as Carter sensed fear on his face.

"You have not told him you are coming here, Mr. Carter?"

The latter shook his head, he would have been inclined to laugh had not the matter under discussion been so serious. For here were two men, manifestly on the same side, each worried at the other's knowledge.

"You are both upon the right, Mr. Sennen, are you not?"

The Rector nodded gravely.

"Perhaps, sir," he said cautiously. "But if you had lived so long upon the moor with such secrets as I have had to live with you would give your confidences with some caution."

Carter shot him a frank glance.

"Yet you have no hesitation in confiding in me, sir."

The Rector shook his head, the gas-light catching and making a brindled mass of the grey sprinkled in his dark hair.

"You misunderstand me, Mr. Carter. In the first place you are a stranger. Therefore you can have no knowledge of, nor any part in, these terrible events which have plagued our parish. And secondly I have now had some little time to consider your character. What I see I like. Apparently Mr. Hands sees the same things in you which also impel me to confidence."

Carter nodded gravely.

"I am flattered, sir. I think the three of us should put our heads together at the earliest possible moment."

The Rector took a quick sip at his glass, his head cocked on one side as though he were listening for something.

"Perhaps, Mr. Carter, perhaps. We shall have to see. But I believe you were about to tell me something. You were speaking of lights in Rats' Castle."

"Not only that, sir. Jeremy Hands has some wild theory about these hounds which have been heard in lonely parts of the moor at night. He has been travelling by train of recent months, visiting obscure stations. He has discovered some interesting statistics."

The Rector's eyes were very bright as he put down his glass on the circular table at his elbow.

"Go on, Mr. Carter," he said gently.

"Mr. Hands discovered dogs, Mr. Sennen. In crates and boxes and baskets, waiting to be collected on lonely station platforms. He has some strange idea they were there for a purpose."

The Rector's face was ashen now.

"To assemble into a pack, perhaps," he said quickly. "What sort of dogs?"

"Savage Irish wolfhounds, for the most part," Carter said.

The Rector swallowed hard as he stared at the architect without speaking. Then he nodded his head several times as though he had made up his mind. He rose abruptly.

"Come with me, Mr. Carter, and be very quiet. As I have said, my housekeeper is a light sleeper."

He stared at the young man reflectively, his mind evidently a long way away.

"You will need your coat but we will collect that on the way through the hall. I think you will find this very interesting. And, afterward, I will offer you some explanations."

He led the way quietly out of the silent room and into the chill gloom of the hall.

Thirty-Four
On the Tower

1

THEIR FOOTSTEPS ECHOED on the treads of the square Norman tower as Sennen led the way, the beams of yellow light from his dark-lantern brushing strange patterns on the dusty walls.

"So Magistrate Hemmings is riding with Henderson's troop upon the moor tonight?"

"That is correct, sir."

The Rector turned a furrowed forehead to him as he negotiated a bend in the stairs.

"God send him success then!"

"But you personally doubt it, sir?"

Sennen gave a dry chuckle, his hand trembling slightly on the wooden rail which protected them from a dizzy drop into the darkness on their left.

"The past efforts of the judiciary in that direction have not given me great confidence, Mr. Carter."

"And yet one must do something."

They had stopped for a moment or two on a broad wooden platform and now the Rector faced his companion, his features grave as a marble statue in the rays of the lamp.

"Of course, Mr. Carter. But still this terror continues."

Carter nodded.

"Mr. Hemmings himself has been threatened. This afternoon he showed me a roughly worded note which had been left in his own front porch, warning him off the moor."

Sennen looked startled and he took a half-step forward, the hand holding the lantern again trembling slightly so that beams of light flickered up and down the massive stone walls at their back in a disturbing manner.

"I will reserve comment upon that until later, Mr. Carter," the cleric said in a low voice, his lips tightly compressed. "But you see the advantage of pooling one's knowledge and resources in the way I have suggested."

"I begin to, sir."

The couple again began their ascent, their shadows fleeing before them in monstrous rushing motions. There was a faint light from the sky through the discoloured glass windows let into the slotted embrasures in the tower's side, and once Carter glimpsed a wild moon riding high above jagged clouds.

They were at the top at last, and the pair again paused to catch their breath. Then Sennen handed the lamp to his companion and advanced toward the massive oak door, banded with broad iron strapping that was bolted through the woodwork. He lifted the latch with a harsh scraping noise that echoed in startling fashion about the tower. It was followed by a brief scuttering sound that sent Carter's nerves aflame until he realised that it was nothing more than roosting birds, disturbed by the light and the noise, on their perches among the great beams high above their heads.

Sennen took the lantern and turned the metal shutter until there was nothing but a dim glow directed toward the floor.

"We do not wish anyone to know we are up here," he said simply.

He opened the big creaking door, letting in a gush of chill night air. Carter saw the wild, streaming clouds, the small town below bathed in the light of the moon, and the yellow holes torn in the darkness by the gas-lamps.

The wind was fresh and bracing and he waited, crouching a little below the square battlements of the tower as Sennen put the lantern down on the flags at their feet.

"One of my hobbies, Mr. Carter," the Rector said softly. "And one I have put to good use in recent years. Though no-one knows I come here or what for. I hold the only set of keys, you see."

"So you have already been up here once tonight," said Carter.

His eyes were adjusted to the lower intensity of the moonlight now and he again caught the sorrow on the Rector's ravaged face.

"You are perceptive, Mr. Carter. You noticed that I did not unlock the door. Yes, you are right. There are few nights this time of year when I do not come up for an hour or so. And I do not wish the verger to know what I do here. So the door is kept locked."

"But what is it that you do here, sir?"

The Rector smiled faintly.

"The impatience of youth, Mr. Carter, as I have already observed. This way."

The two men moved forward to a point halfway along the battlement on this side of the square tower. They were at an acute angle to the town here and Carter could see the flood-swollen river like a silver ribbon as it ran foaming some hundred and twenty feet below them.

Above them rose the moor, dark, faint and mysterious with long scarves of mist hanging about it.

The Rector sighed.

"That is one of my major problems, Mr. Carter. As you have already seen, Dartmoor is a strange and mysterious place. We are some 1,400 feet above sea-level here, though one might not imagine it. The northern part of the moor rises to over 2,000 feet and the weather is among the most changeable in the world. It can be brilliant sunshine at one moment; and then, an hour later, the clouds have closed in, it is raining and thick mist has come down."

He shot a quick look at the architect as though he were a student and the speaker a lecturer addressing a class.

"This can obtain even in summer. And people can easily die of exposure out there. As well as of other things. You catch my drift?"

"Not entirely, sir."

The Rector moved forward to a shape shrouded in canvas that stood in an embrasure in the stonework.

"Of course not. Forgive me. I was referring to my telescope. I use it to scour the moor at many different times of the day and night. It has uncovered some very interesting things, I can tell you. People come and go at various times of day and night, of course. But sometimes in quite large bodies, which I find very interesting indeed."

Carter felt a faint thrill of apprehension run through him, though he could not have said why. The Rector had unsheathed the powerful instrument, whose dull brass eyepiece glinted faintly in the moonlight.

"You can see Rats' Castle from here, Mr. Sennen?"

The cleric nodded.

"On clear nights, Mr. Carter. The weather is the most frustrating thing about my vigils. I will tell you why I do it when we get back below."

He bent to the eyepiece and swivelled the heavy telescope on its stand, making a gentle arc across the landscape.

"There is a shoulder of hill between, which makes viewing difficult."

He sighed again.

"I only wish I could afford a more powerful instrument."

He kept to the eyepiece for a minute or so. Then he straightened up, shrugging.

"I am afraid I have brought you here on a futile errand, Mr. Carter. The mist is closing in."

Carter felt a stab of disappointment. He in turn applied himself to the telescope at the Rector's invitation. He did not know what to expect; certainly not the vague blur that presented itself. Then he realised his eyesight was naturally far keener than the Rector's and adjusted the focusing screw.

Sennen had already aligned the instrument in the direction of Rats' Castle but he could see nothing for the moment, except wreathing masses of white vapour. He remained in a stooping position for several minutes, now and again slightly altering the angle of vision.

Presently he made out a faint scar against the blackness which Sennen told him could only be the road. The Rector himself bent to the eyepiece to verify this. It was cold up here and the chill was beginning to penetrate to Carter's extremities, but still the two men lingered, as though held by some invisible resolve.

Once Carter thought he made out a gauzy incandescence far away, on the horizon, but it was swiftly blanked by the encroaching mist. Then vague shadows swirled across the lens. Carter rapidly re-adjusted the focus. He gave a faint exclamation which brought the Rector to his side.

"Horsemen, Mr. Sennen!"

The Rector grunted as he adjusted the focus to suit his own vision.

"You are right, Mr. Carter."

He gave way to the architect once more though there was now nothing but an amphorous mass which slowly disappeared into the mist. The two men remained for a long time on the battlements, straining with their naked eyesight to make out anything in the long black slope of the uplands before them, which was slowly being drowned by the deadening white blanket.

"Henderson and his troop, Mr. Sennen?"

The Rector looked at his companion grimly.

"Or Satan and His Hounds, Mr. Carter."

2

"There is a darkness here, Mr. Carter, which is something beyond even the horrors of those murders which local people attribute to The Black Death."

David Sennen's thick hair, brushed with grey, was momentarily lost in clouds of tobacco smoke as he leaned forward to the tray and poured his visitor a glass of wine.

It was eleven-thirty now and the last trembling notes of the church clock had just died away.

"This will keep out the night chill, Mr. Carter."

The guest raised his glass.

"To your health, Mr. Sennen."

The Rector put down his goblet on the silver tray at his elbow and looked at the young man sombrely. In the clotted silence of the library with its massed books and shadowy gallery it was cloistral and at peace but to Carter it seemed as though naked horror lapped just a short way outside of the walls; much as the mist was encroaching upon the moor above the town.

"You remember our conversation earlier. One thing that telescope has taught me is patterns. People leave the village at certain times at night. Late at night, sir. In ones and twos and threes, eventually to form groups on the roads above the town."

Carter felt another quick thrill of excitement pass through him.

"You think this is something which Jeremy has also discovered?"

"It is possible, Mr. Carter. It is quite possible. And he has stumbled upon something even of more vital importance with the information about those dogs of which you spoke."

Carter clasped the rim of the wine glass between the palms of his hands and slowly revolved it as he listened to his host. Sennen's eyes were very bright as he went to the nearest bookcase with quick, alert movements. He returned with several thick volumes which he placed upon the table.

"Patterns, Mr. Carter. Patterns of movement which I have been observing of late years. People, gathered in ones and twos to form a larger body. Dogs now, according to Mr. Hands, in ones and twos, on the platforms of lonely railway stations. Perhaps to be formed into a larger body in due course."

He shrugged heavily.

"I leave aside the blacker horrors of this business. Of why people should be murdered and found as charred corpses in this way. We have first to establish the circumstances; once we have done that then the solution to these mysteries will follow."

Carter shifted uneasily in his chair.

"I follow that, Mr. Sennen. But I fail to see exactly what it is you are driving at."

The Rector shook his head vigorously.

"Does it not strike you as strange that both the police and the troops have had no success whatever in their searches for the murderers of these wretched people?"

He leaned forward until his eyes, almost lost in their mass of wrinkles, were boring into Carter's own.

"Someone in the town; someone perhaps close to the military, knows what is going on. Knows every move the authorities make and is thus able to warn these people."

Carter felt uncomfortable. The ground was beginning to crumble away from his feet at an even faster rate now.

"Are you able to point a finger at anyone, sir?"

Sennen shook his head quickly.

"Not for the present, Mr. Carter. But it stands to reason, does it not. Whatever is going on on the moor could not continue otherwise."

Carter agreed.

"And these people who drift out of the town on certain nights. Could you put a name to them?"

Sennen glanced at the other sombrely.

"Two or three times only, Mr. Carter. On clear nights when I have had my telescope trained on the upland road. Unfortunately, the glass is too powerful to identify them as they leave the outskirts of Thornton Bassett as they are too close; and they cannot be made out with the naked eye. You saw the impossible angle up there. And a shoulder of hillside cuts them off as they mount the slope just outside the town."

He reached forward to one of the large volumes he had placed on the table earlier. Its title was in Latin, and he lifted it so quickly that the young man could not properly make it out. Sennen ruffled the pages anxiously.

"Have you been to Rats' Castle, Mr. Carter?" he said absently.

"I went there fairly recently with Miss Fiona Hammond," Carter said somewhat defensively. "It seemed an interesting spot."

"It is," the Rector rejoined. "I could tell you much about it but this is neither the time nor the place. I have written a monograph about the later building and the earlier structures which stood upon the site. Did you notice anything particular about it when you were there?"

Carter shook his head.

"Not that I can think of."

The Rector picked up his wine glass and took another cautious sip.

"There is no reason why you should have done, of course. I was referring to its orientation. The window orifices are all in line with the west, to catch the setting sun."

Carter smiled.

"Like the Druids in reverse."

The Rector put his stubby black pipe back into his mouth.

"Something like that," he agreed.

Carter suddenly saw what he was driving at.

"You mean there is some sort of sect or secret society involved? Here in Thornton Bassett?"

The Rector widened his eyes, staring up at the gallery which housed his thousands of books.

"Perhaps, Mr. Carter," he said dreamily. "It is not beyond the bounds of possibility."

"Lights perhaps burn there too conveniently, within easy view of the town."

Carter shifted in his chair.

"I do not quite follow, Mr. Sennen."

The Rector smiled faintly.

"It is a place full of history and an excellent decoy. What I mean is this. On several occasions bright lights have been seen at the Castle. Both police and military have hastened there as fast as horse or conveyance could carry them."

The smile lingered on his face.

"When the authorities arrived they found nothing. It took them a long time to make their way across the rough and tumbled ground from the road. But perhaps you have already found that so?"

Carter agreed.

"They made lots of noise, of course," the Rector continued. "That was inevitable. Half a mile off, all the lights were extinguished. They found nothing when they arrived at the ruins. Not even a candle-end. But ten miles away, on the other side of the moor, horrors had been perpetrated. On each of the three or four occasions I have specified."

"The lights were a decoy?"

"Exactly, Mr. Carter," the Rector said softly. "After that, the authorities no longer took any notice. The odds were too great. But some nights the lights remain burning."

He shrugged.

"Perhaps a challenge, or a mockery. Who knows?"

Carter stared at his host. Some things were becoming clear now.

"So one person might get close where a body would fail."

"It may well be," said Sennen sombrely. "But I would not advise it."

He broke off suddenly, his eyes wide again.

"But perhaps you think I have been too long upon the moor, Mr. Carter."

The architect shook his head.

"Not at all, sir. That there is something monstrous and evil here cannot be denied. But I am sure you have other things to tell me."

Sennen put down his glass upon the table, consulted his intricately chased silver watch.

"All in good time. I wanted to make sure tonight that we were allies."

"We are certainly that," said Carter warmly.

"And, above all, I wanted to make sure you were within the sanctity of this building tonight."

Again Carter felt the strange uneasiness creep over him.

"You do not think I am in any danger, sir?"

Sennen stared at him sharply.

"I do not know, Mr. Carter. But when you have been consulting such books as I have here, month in, month out; year in, year out; one realises that nothing is impossible. It is a very strange and shadowy world we inhabit, Mr. Carter, at the best of times; it is certain to me, after years of study of various arcane subjects, that we see only a fraction of what might be visible had we but greater powers of perception."

Carter felt out of his depth, and this must have shown on his face for Sennen went on hastily. "Do not misunderstand me, Mr. Carter. I have not gone off my head. Though there is darkness enough and horror enough to unhinge a less steadily-nerved man than yourself."

He put the watch back in his pocket and resumed his musings.

"Have you seen the sign of the goat that is carved high up on the west side of the church? It is one of our local curiosities. It is to be found in a niche and was only discovered by accident during some renovation work several years ago. I commend it to you."

He fixed his guest with brooding eyes again.

"It has a pagan connotation, has it not?"

"Surely, sir, mediæval carvers often embellished buildings, particularly churches, with such symbols. The powers of darkness as well as of light. They were supposed to be reminders to the backslider, were they not?"

The Rector was smiling now.

"Indeed, Mr. Carter. I agree entirely. But I did not mean that alone. To me it indicates that the parish has long held pagan beliefs beneath the veneer of Christianity that passes for organised religion hereabouts."

"Just as there is an oil painting at The Priory which depicts hounds hunting a man across the moors, with what is obviously Rats' Castle in the background," Carter observed.

The Rector looked at the architect with deep-set brooding eyes.

"I have heard of that picture, Mr. Carter, though I have never been invited to Mr. Hemmings' home."

He smiled wryly.

"Mr. Hemmings is not in my parish, you see. And congregations upon the moor are so sparse that poaching by incumbents is much frowned upon."

"What do you think of the content of that picture, sir?"

Sennen hesitated a moment, the gaslight gold and mellow upon his troubled face.

"It seems apposite to what we were discussing," he said gently. "I have done much research upon the subject. But it is, after all, too long and involved to go into tonight."

Carter remained silent and Sennen went on after a moment.

"Are you familiar with the paintings of Bosch, Mr. Carter? He was a Flemish artist of great genius, though little-known outside his native land."

Carter shook his head.

"I'm afraid not, sir."

"A pity. One glance at any of his paintings and you would have seen what I was intending to convey earlier."

Sennen made an expressive gesture with his hand at the pile of books on the table. Carter leaned forward to read the embossed lettering on the spines. He could see them clearly now. The titles included: *Magick, The Black Arts,* and *Malleus Maleficarum.* They were obviously rare and had equally obviously been well thumbed by the Rector.

A curious sort of library for a cleric, Carter thought, and Sennen had evidently read his glance for he gave a smile of great insight.

"It is a poor priest who does not get to grips with the opposition, Mr. Carter. Those old Bible writers knew what they were up against. To those able to read the message aright, some passages of the Holy Testaments are far more terrifying than even such authors of genius of our own day as Edgar Poe."

He got up abruptly and stretched himself, again consulting his watch.

"But I digress, Mr. Carter. I had a particular reason for wanting you here with me this evening. Put it down to a middle-aged man's imaginings, if you wish. Tonight is a particular occasion in the calendar of evil. I had noted some stirring about the town earlier. Which is why I was so disappointed at the descending of the mist."

Carter understood then the general thread which had been running through all of David Sennen's remarks and he felt a great warmth for this unusual and remarkable man who had chosen to bury his talents in such a small place as Thornton Bassett.

"You wished to preserve me from something harmful tonight, Mr. Sennen? If so, I am much indebted to you."

"Not at all."

Sennen became brisk again.

"I would like you to look at some of these books, however briefly, Mr. Carter, before you leave here tonight. And we must lay our plans for the future with some care. Your friend Jeremy must be made party to all our proceedings."

The mention of Hands' name recalled Carter abruptly to the realities of the present.

"Certainly, sir. In fact I think he has some inkling of what might be afoot tonight."

The Rector frowned, turning his strong features toward his guest in the mellow gas-light.

"I am sorry to hear it. I hope he has not done anything precipitate. If I remember correctly, he is a somewhat impulsive young man."

Carter felt alarm rising within him.

"You do not think he is in danger, sir."

Sennen's eyes met and held his own with burning intensity.

"What do you mean, Mr. Carter?"

The young architect rose.

"I mean that Jeremy has gone out upon the moor tonight to try to penetrate to the heart of this mystery."

There was a sudden crash which set Carter's nerves jumping. The Rector's glass had fallen from his convulsive fingers and lay smashed upon the study floor.

Sennen turned an ashen face upon his guest.

"Then God help him, Mr. Carter! God help him!"

Thirty-Five

Fiona Again

1

CARTER BENT LISTLESSLY to his drawing board and pencilled in a detail of the commission for Simon Hemmings. But his mind was not on the work, and he was glad when Slade rapped smartly on the door and brought him his afternoon tea. A week had gone by since his conversation with the Rector and their vigil with the telescope on the tower. A week in which nothing had been heard from Jeremy; a week in which it seemed as though the brooding fastness of the moor had swallowed him up.

True to his promise Carter had given Jeremy's excuse to Mrs. Tregorran when they had met at breakfast the following morning. She had seemed surprised, as well she might, but had merely accepted his explanation. But things had been different at Pollard, Bassett. The senior partner had wanted Jeremy for a particular commission and Carter had, of course, to repeat the same story he had given his landlady; it would have seemed very odd otherwise. One thing had led to another and now Carter found himself additionally enmeshed in small, trivial lies which supported his original story.

He did not like it; his nature was straightforward and he had almost told Mr. Pollard the truth. But a moment's reflection strengthened by the Rector's vehement urgings, had decided him against that course. It would have been too dangerous altogether.

Instead, he had suggested the sudden call from Hands' relatives in the North of England—the simulated reason given him verbally by Hands—to his colleagues at Pollard, Bassett; though the pretext had seemed more and more hollow to Carter as the days slipped by.

Sennen, in whom he had confided when Jeremy did not return, had been out and about the moor in a dog-cart; ostensibly on visits to his parishioners, but in reality to try and locate the missing man or at least some word of him. He had also visited the young lady to whom Hands was pledged and though worried at the situation, she had seen or heard nothing.

The weather had not helped. It was turning toward winter in earnest now and great gusts of freezing wind blew out of a leaden sky. Carter's sombre thoughts were also coloured by the absence of any real news from The Priory; it was true he had received two notes from Hemmings regarding the major building works which were soon to commence, comments or questions on detail, nothing more; and once, a verbal communication through Mr. Pollard, which had spoken well of Carter's professionalism.

But the note for which he longed, a mere word even, scribbled on a single sheet of paper, from Fiona Hammond, which would have lightened the darkness of his thoughts, was not forthcoming. Mrs. Tregorran had noted the change in him and had attempted to cheer him in her own subtle way.

She had said little about Jeremy's absence but had made no attempt to let his room; which at least gave him some small comfort. It was evident that she, at least, hoped for his speedy return. Since the night they had talked together, the Rector and Carter, as though subdued by Jeremy's mysterious disappearance, had maintained only the most tenuous of contacts, though the young architect knew he would be the first to hear should his friend find some tangible evidence of Jeremy's whereabouts.

Beyond that he had no wish to think and he pursued his professional tasks mechanically, his mind a mass of churning emotion beneath the blank façade. The small affairs of Thornton Bassett went on about him, almost disregarded. The morning gatherings for coffee in the Pollard, Bassett board-room; the bantering exchanges between the partners into which Carter entered with little real enthusiasm; his small round at Mrs. Tregorran's, where he was now accepted into a widening circle which encompassed the bank clerks, who had made room for him at their own table, despite his somewhat obvious desire to be left to his own devices.

The one real topic which had buzzed about the taprooms and public bars of the small town had concerned the dragoons' encounter with the moor-riders, the night they had ridden out to rendezvous with Magistrate Hemmings. Shots had been exchanged, that much was certain; as the Rector had surmised, the lights at Rats' Castle had been a ruse to draw off the military.

All traces of the illuminations had disappeared long before they got there, and it was a disgruntled troop which had blundered across a pack of riders and their hounds crossing a lonely moorland road at right-angles to their path, some miles distant.

The Magistrate had led the charge with commendable courage, Carter had learned; and the melee in the dark, with the hounds barking and snarling, horses plunging and falling on the slippery slopes, and the air full of angry shouts and the whining of bullets among the boulders, must have been a nightmare.

One trooper had been wounded and several cut and bruised by heavy falls among the rocks, but the entire cavalcade had disappeared into the enveloping mists within a minute and a half, as though they had never existed.

No-one had obtained a clear description of them; the horses were jet-black, as were the hounds, and the riders themselves wore dark clothing with black cloths across their features. The affair had penetrated far beyond Plymouth and Henderson and Hemmings were local heroes for several days after.

The Captain himself had been thrown early on and winded and wore his arm in a sling for a day or two, which gave him a somewhat exaggeratedly romantic aura among the ladies of Thornton Bassett, Carter felt. The cavalcade of dragoons had straggled back, muddy and exhausted, through the town the following morning, where Hemmings had made certain depositions at the court-house; and Inspector Pepper, a lugubrious police officer from Plymouth on secondment from that city, had been making a very busy show for a while.

But it was obvious that the riders, whoever they were, knew the moors in great detail. With extreme cunning they had led the soldiers on to boulder-strewn and then swampy ground; and though their progress could be heard for some quarter of an hour, until every last trace of their passage had been erased, as though with the mist, the brief glimpses the searchers had caught as the cavalcade crossed the road had been their last as well as their first.

Sennen had nodded with gloomy satisfaction as Carter had imparted the news. The two men had legitimate cause to meet as Carter was again inspecting the church to present a further schedule of improvements to the Rector. The two men stood before the altar, a single shaft of winter sun penetrating the stained glass far overhead and imparting a bloody tinge to Sennen's face as the two talked in low tones.

"It was well done, Mr. Carter," he said.

The latter looked at him, slightly startled.

"You must forgive my ignorance, Rector, but I do not see . . ."

Sennen stopped him with a wave of his hand.

"I have the advantage of long and serious study of these matters, Mr. Carter. I see farther than the average person, my senses sharpened by my delving into this darkness."

Carter looked at Sennen shrewdly. He wore a dark soutane this afternoon and he was a distinguished, even somewhat awe-inspiring figure in the blood-red glow which enveloped him from the armorial window.

"You have never married, Rector?" he asked, somewhat irrelevantly.

Sennen looked startled in his turn, shaking his head vehemently.

"Marriage is merely shared loneliness, Mr. Carter," he said wryly.

"Oh, come, sir!" the architect protested. "You must have performed so many wedding ceremonies . . ."

There was amusement dancing in the cleric's eyes now. He put an affectionate hand on the other's wrist.

"We will not go into that today. But I will perform your own nuptials with the greatest of pleasure when the time comes, Mr. Carter. And for a much reduced fee."

Carter joined in the other's laughter but again he felt inward confusion. It was true that this remarkable man seemed to see deep within one; it might even be that he knew, or guessed, what had happened to Jeremy Hands and was keeping the knowledge to himself for some unspecified reason.

"You were saying, Rector? About these riders? At least we know that both they and the hounds exist."

Sennen nodded.

"I never doubted it," he said gravely. "Think of this. As we have already seen, lights are placed within the ruins. These people know the military is out. After all, there is no secret about it. They are drawn to the place but find nothing there. Some hours later they are given a hare to chase."

Carter took a step forward.

"You mean . . .?"

"A feint, Mr. Carter," Sennen said evenly. "Something for the troopers to chase. For the real events taking place were back at Rats' Castle. I went up to the tower once more after you left. The mist had cleared a little and the lights were again there."

He looked sombrely at Carter, the deep light from the window still staining his face.

"I think your friend Jeremy Hands knew of this, Mr. Carter. That was why he was out there. He had found out something. Something important of which only he knew the workings."

Carter lifted his head from the drawing board, threw down his pencil irritably. It bounced to the floor, its tip breaking against the skirting. There was a sudden tap at the door which startled him more than he could have imagined.

"Come in!" he called, slightly louder than he had intended.

He started to his feet as the door gaped and Fiona Hammond stood framed in the opening.

2

"We have missed you at The Priory, Mr. Carter."

There was a flush of health on the girl's cheeks beneath the tawny gold hair but her eyes were reproachful as she stared at Carter for a long moment.

He felt awkward and at a disadvantage but he moved quickly, closing the door behind her and motioning her toward the desk.

"It was not my intention, I can assure you."

The flush on his own cheeks matched hers.

"Will you not come and sit near the fire. It is a cold and inclement day. I will ring for some more tea."

The girl looked round Carter's office with approval and allowed herself to be installed in the client's chair, near the architect's leather-topped desk. She was about to protest his invitation but Slade solved Carter's small predicament because he appeared at the door almost immediately, bearing a tray of the firm's best silver tea-things, together with slices of walnut and currant cake.

He beamed on the couple like some genial gnome, Carter thought.

"Mr. Pollard saw the young lady through the window, Mr. Carter," he offered by way of explanation. "He ordered me to make her comfortable."

The girl's cheeks were more highly flushed now; it may have been from the glow of the fire.

"That was extremely kind of Mr. Pollard," she ventured.

"Not at all, Miss," Slade beamed. "If I may be so bold, you and your Uncle entertain me most royally at The Priory whenever I go there. One must reciprocate."

Carter and the girl exchanged amused looks which were not lost on the tall man because he drooped one eyelid to Carter in a somnolent wink that could not be caught by the girl; put his forefinger up to his nose and withdrew quietly and unobtrusively through the door.

The girl was laughing as he disappeared.

"He is a most delightful man," she said softly. "And you are too kind."

"Not at all," Carter said hastily. "Let me pour for you."

He got up quickly and came round the desk, standing over her. She wore a thick riding habit today and carried a heavy plaid blanket over one arm. He guessed she had come down specially in the dog-cart and took the blanket from her gently, placing it on a chair in the corner. He was aware that the busy clatter of the office went on about them, albeit faintly along the corridors and up the stairs.

The humdrum background added to the piquancy of their meeting.

"Mr. Pollard has given you a splendid office," Fiona Hammond said, her eyes travelling about the walls, taking in the opulent fittings. Her gaze rested longer on the drawings he was preparing for her guardian, it seemed to him.

"He is a very kind man," Carter said. "And I am a junior partner," he added with obvious pride.

The girl's eyes were dancing now as she looked at him across the desk.

"You are indeed," she said softly.

The ordinary words seemed to him to be so charged with hidden meaning that the tea he was pouring into her fine china cup suddenly made an erratic arc in the air, before he had regained control. The girl bit her lip, though whether with vexation or to repress a sudden urge to laugh, he could not tell.

"Perhaps I had better do that," she said. "Would you like another?"

Carter swiftly brought his own cup over; it was made of ordinary thick china and he realised she had not missed the contrast. He went to sit back in his own chair, putting the desk between them after he had urged on her an assortment of fruit and walnut cake. Fiona Hammond bit fastidiously into the first slice with very white teeth.

"I hope I am not keeping you from your work?"

"Of course not," Carter hastened to assure her. "You may tell Mr. Hemmings that I have almost finished. If he would like to order the workmen for this day week I will be up to supervise."

The girl's expression changed abruptly and she bent her head.

"We shall all look forward to that, Mr. Carter."

"I hope your guardian is well," the architect went on. "We were all shocked with that terrible business upon the moor. He might have been killed or badly injured."

A cloud passed across Fiona Hammond's face as she raised it to him.

"Indeed. So might Captain Henderson."

Carter had unconsciously stiffened at the mention of the dragoon officer's name and he was almost immediately aware that the fact had not been lost on the girl. But she merely brushed a crumb from her fingers and wiped her hand with one of the firm's best linen napkins that Slade had brought for her.

"I have, of course, touched on the matter in my business correspondence to Mr. Hemmings," Carter went on quickly, as though to make amends. "But you might give him my warm good wishes."

"I will certainly do that, Mr. Carter."

"Has the Captain found anything that might lead to the arrest of these villains, Miss Hammond?"

The girl shook her head. She looked at him pensively, as though she wished to confide in him but felt perhaps that this was not the moment. The young man had a question trembling on the tip of his tongue but a further look at her expression decided him against. It was not the proper moment. But there would be occasions at The Priory.

"They tell me you have a minor mystery at the office here?" the girl went on.

Carter furrowed his forehead, leaning back in his chair, taking in the agreeable heat of the fire set between the two big circular windows.

"I am not quite sure . . ." he began.

The girl tossed a few strands of hair back from her face, the brown eyes watchful. He noticed that she still wore the small gold brooch at the breast of her jacket.

"Why, your friend, Mr. Jeremy Hands," she said. "I understand he left Pollard, Bassett without a word to anyone."

Carter felt himself colouring.

"Hardly that, Miss Hammond," he protested. "Jeremy has been over-working of late. He said he was called back to his home on an urgent family matter."

The girl continued to regard him coolly.

"But it is strange nevertheless, that he has chosen not to write to you or to Mr. Pollard, is it not?" she persisted.

Carter dropped his eyes.

"Unusual, perhaps. Unless he has had such bad news that the matter of writing has gone completely from his head. I expect we shall hear something soon."

The girl finished her tea in silence.

"You may be sure I shall write to give you news the moment I hear anything," Carter said after an interval.

He was astonished to see that Fiona Hammond's shoulders were shaking. He thought for a moment that she was crying but then, looking more closely, saw that she was laughing quietly.

"Dear Mr. Carter," she said apologetically. "I am not at all interested in Mr. Hands, only inasmuch as he is your friend. But I should perhaps enjoy receiving a letter from you on my own account."

Carter rose from his desk, again amazed at the frankness of this young girl. He put the confusion of his thoughts firmly into the background. He bent across the desk so that his face was only a foot or so from Fiona Hammond's own upraised features.

"You may be sure I would be delighted to correspond with you, Miss Hammond. It was just that I did not mean to appear presumptuous either to your or your guardian."

Carter thought the girl had never looked more beautiful at that moment, with her lips slightly parted, and he made haste to plunge on.

"Please tell your guardian . . ."

Fiona Hammond made a little explosion of breath.

"We are not talking about my guardian, Mr. Carter," she said firmly. "We are discussing ourselves. Mr. Hemmings is well able to take care of himself. What I should like is for you to . . ."

The couple were posed like that, the girl in mid-sentence, when there was another interruption and Slade's jovial features were again framed in the half-open doorway.

"Just thought I'd see how the two of you were getting along!" he said chirpily.

Carter resisted the sudden savage impulse to throw the teapot at his head and bit back the irritable words that sprang into his mind.

But the girl smiled sweetly at Carter as he slowly drew himself into an upright position.

"Everything is perfect, Mr. Slade!" she said calmly. "And I really must be going."

Despite Carter's protests she quickly gathered up her gloves and the blanket and went downstairs with long strides, Carter clattering at her side. He was not at all mollified by the second more pronounced wink Slade gave him as he went by.

In the square the girl briefly lingered, her gloved hand on Carter's own.

"You are altogether too reserved, Mr. Carter," she said at parting. "While it is true that Captain Henderson is in the house, it is equally true that you are in the town. It is entirely up to you to see that the position is reversed."

Carter was left with the brief impression of the dazzling smile as the remarkable girl clattered forward over the bridge spanning the foaming stream. For a long time he followed her progress in the encroaching dusk.

Thirty-Six
Questions from Pollard

1

"AND YOU ARE certain that Mr. Hands gave you no further indications of his future movements?"

Carter shook his head. The two sat alone in the board-room, the half-empty coffee cups at their sides. The other partners had dispersed about their business, but the senior had indicated that Carter should stay.

There was no irritation in Pollard's eyes, but considerable puzzlement as he stared at the newest addition to the firm.

"Do you not think his action is strange, even incredible if one may so put it?"

Carter felt helpless and at the other's mercy; he had dreaded this moment but it was something that had to be faced. He dared not tell this kindly and well-meant man Hands' secret fears. Apart from the danger to himself and Sennen that might follow, he owed it to Jeremy himself. He might well reappear at any moment with some quite plausible explanation for his week-long disappearance.

"He was very upset," he returned, inwardly regretting the small tissue of lies into which he was being led. "I gathered it was some serious family matter."

Pollard nodded, drumming with his thick, capable fingers on the polished surface of the board-room table.

"Thank you for your helpfulness, Mr. Carter," he said.

The latter glanced at the principal quickly.

"If I knew more I would tell you so, sir," he said somewhat stiffly.

Pollard shifted in his seat. He looked uncomfortable and a fleeting expression Carter found difficult to read passed across his face.

"I am certain of it, Mr. Carter. And I certainly did not wish to imply otherwise."

Pollard nodded affably. He wore one of his well-cut grey suits this morning, and the cold winter light coming through the board-room windows glinted on his gold pince-nez. The fragrant smoke from his fat cigar, clamped between the fingers of his right hand, went up straight as a ruled line toward the panelled ceiling.

Carter felt a sudden remorse deep down inside him at his attitude toward a kindly employer.

"Do you wish me to telegraph his home, sir?"

Pollard slowly shook his head, the friendly expression back on the frank features beneath the clumps of immensely thick grey hair.

"I think not, Mr. Carter. But if we have heard nothing from him within the next few days, I will write to his family and ask if they have any news of him."

He hesitated a moment and then went on, his eyes now clouded and far away.

"Have you spoken to Mrs. Tregorran of the matter?"

Carter nodded.

"She knows nothing, sir. And she is not, in any event, a very forthcoming lady."

Pollard smiled faintly.

"You have a point there, young man."

He made an obvious effort to change the conversation.

"I understand you are making good progress on the additions for The Priory. Hemmings speaks very well of you. I am delighted, as much for your own sake as for the firm's."

Carter warmed to the principal's generous words.

"I am glad that you are pleased, sir."

Pollard hesitated again and then went on, more cautiously.

"I hear that Miss Hammond was here to see you yesterday afternoon. An unusual girl, is she not?"

Carter kept his eyes down on his shoes. To his dismay he saw that they were muddied from an outdoor survey he had been carrying out earlier that morning.

"I think so, sir," he said in a low voice.

When he again glanced at the senior partner he fancied he saw a faint flush on the older man's features. He was not the only one then, who sometimes felt inner embarrassment when talking about quite innocuous things.

"I have no intention of prying into your private affairs, Mr. Carter."

The voice was bland and neutral but to his surprise Carter felt resentment growing inside him.

"Of course not, sir."

He raised his eyes. Pollard was actually beaming now.

"As I have said, it is no concern of mine."

He hesitated again and then ejected a last sentence in a rush.

"But if you were to set your sights in that direction I fancy you could not do better in this world."

Carter gazed at Pollard in astonishment. The principal's eyes were twinkling.

"Thank you, sir. I am inclined to agree with you one hundred per cent."

2

The two men sat on in silence for a while. Then a cloud seemed to pass across Pollard's face. The junior partner suddenly sensed its cause.

"You have heard nothing further from that quarter? From The Priory, I mean? Those riders and hounds upon the moor. I understand it was a disturbing and dangerous business in which both the Magistrate and Captain Henderson distinguished themselves."

There was no danger in such a query, surely; Carter remembered both Hands' and Sennen's admonitions to secrecy. But the affair on the moor was not only all over Thornton Bassett but widely discussed throughout the county and beyond.

Certainly Pollard saw nothing strange in his questions. He gave a heavy sigh.

"I do not know what to think, Mr. Carter. You realise my views upon such matters. Pollard, Bassett as a corporate entity does not meddle in politics, revolutions or any forms of sudden or violent death."

There was a faint smile curling the corners of the heavy lips now.

"Are you asking me as the principal of this firm or as an ordinary human being, Mr. Carter?"

Carter smiled in turn.

"As an ordinary human being, sir."

Pollard shrugged. He suddenly looked very much older, sitting there in the seat of honour at the board-room table, before the embers of the dying fire. In the far window, beyond his shoulder, Carter could see the bleak contours of the moor, now partly shrouded in mist.

"As an ordinary human being I deplore these dreadful mysteries, Mr. Carter. They disrupt life, disseminate tragedy, and interrupt business. But I feel for the people concerned and the relatives and families of those unfortunates who have come to an untimely end upon the moor."

He tapped his breast at this point with a quaint, old-fashioned gesture such as might be made by a stage-actor of an older generation, Carter thought.

"But Dartmoor has always been a strange and tragic place, Mr. Carter. From time immemorial. From those Bronze Age dwellings upon the moor and the pagan era of human sacrifice, to the cruel and rapacious age in which we now live."

His manner slackened and became less serious.

"But from a purely business point of view, Pollard, Bassett has no thoughts on the matter; takes no stand; strikes no postures. Though as an ordinary human being I am as bewildered as I daresay you yourself are."

The blank eyes were shuttered now, as if waiting to explode some theory and Carter became suddenly wary.

"You have no views upon the subject I suppose, Mr. Carter?"

The question was casually put but Carter was immediately aware of danger; the room was unconscionably hot and oppressive. He kept his eyes fixed on the toes of his shoes and gave a passable imitation of a shrug.

"I, Mr. Pollard? Why should I have any particular views? And who would be likely to take any notice?"

The tension suddenly lifted as Pollard opened his eyes and took a quick puff at his cigar.

"That may be so, Mr. Carter. But it is open to any of us to hold views on such subjects."

He eased back in his chair, keeping his eyes on Carter's face.

"Your friend Mr. Sennen, for example. He is an historian and a man immensely learned in the ancient lore of Dartmoor. What does he think of these matters?"

Once again Carter felt a constriction of the heart, and the room seemed to darken before his eyes. He reached for his coffee cup, drained it to gain a little time. He hoped he appeared as casual as he intended.

"He is not my friend in particular, Mr. Pollard. I thought he was your friend. It was you, if I remember rightly, who recommended him to me as the author of learned papers upon the history of the moor."

Pollard chuckled deep down in his throat.

"So I did, Mr. Carter, so I did," he observed.

"I have seen something of Mr. Sennen recently," Carter plunged on, aware that he was over-protesting now. "But that has merely to do with my duties regarding the renovation of the church."

"Of course, Mr. Carter, of course," said Pollard soothingly.

He regarded the tip of his smoking cigar through half-closed eyes.

"And now I must not keep you from your duties any longer. I am glad we have had this little chat. Most illuminating."

Somehow, Carter found himself outside the board-room door, without being conscious of how he had arrived there. Cold sweat beaded his brow. Why, he could not have said, but he felt as though he had escaped from some very great danger.

THIRTY-SEVEN
The Thing in the Stream

1

IT WAS SO COLD, there was a feeling of snow in the air. Carter had been working hard, and as it still needed an hour to supper-time he had stepped into The Bassett Arms for a while. He sat by himself in an alcove, his mind oppressed by his racing thoughts. It was a dark November night, and when he at last left the hotel it was to be confronted by a relentless mist which cloaked the square and made the few pedestrians seem like drowning men.

He turned across the bridge and had gone only a few yards in the direction of his lodgings when he became aware that someone was walking quietly behind him in the murk. Though Carter was young and not inclined to be over-impressionable he felt a disagreeable sensation at the base of his spine. He instinctively quickened his pace and turned toward the maze of alleys which led back to the other end of the town.

The steps behind him hesitated and then came on again. A moment later Carter had lost them. He stood in the shelter of an overhanging porchway, straining his ears. But there was nothing save the distant roaring of the stream in the silence of the night and the faint footfall of an occasional wayfarer over the cobbles.

His suddenly racing heart had steadied. He felt cold and out of sorts, the bright cheerfulness of the bar of The Bassett Arms instantly erased by the dampness and sombreness of his surroundings. For the first time since coming to Dartmoor he wondered whether he had been wise to quit the capital.

For a moment he longed for the cheerful bustle of London. But then he remembered what local people had said about winter on the moors; he had a fine future with Pollard, Bassett. The moor and its atmosphere was something he had to learn to live with. And he was forgetting Fiona Hammond.

For some reason too he recalled the anguished sobbing he had heard on a summer-like evening in October which now seemed so far away. December was only a few days off and a vaster gap than some eight weeks in time yawned between the John Carter, architect, who had descended from the train at Princetown; and the strained, almost frightened figure who crouched in a dark doorway, and who seemed a lifetime older.

He hesitated a moment longer and then moved on. He was not quite sure of his direction now, the mist was so thick. He tried to circle round, orientating himself by the noise of the stream but to his mild consternation it seemed all about him, the cloudy vapour was so all-embracing and muffling in its effect.

Carter again walked a little and then stopped; he searched around helplessly, his eyes blinded, his ears straining for the faintest sound that would give him the right direction. He was in the mouth of an alley that he could not recollect.

The strange thing about Thornton Bassett was the unexpected corners that one was constantly discovering. When he had first arrived, fresh from London, it had seemed the merest village, then it had appeared as a small town as its environs were discovered, now it seemed mysterious and baffling in the strange byeways and courtyards its tangled thoroughfares kept throwing up.

He moved to the nearest street lamp, trying to make out the plaque on the corner house, which would give him the name of the road. He could not discover it because of the mist and shadow.

He was still standing there, his mind a confused turmoil, the surroundings a blurred mass of vaporous mist, when a boot gritted on the setts, a shape grew at his elbow, and a firm hand held his wrist in a grip that made him wince.

2

"Quiet, please, Mr. Carter! I did not wish us to be seen in the square, so I waited until you had quit the inn. We have not much time to lose!"

Carter fought for breath, his heart pumping in a ridiculous fashion. The kindly face of Sennen faded and receded in an alarming manner before its image steadied and settled in his eyesight.

"My dear boy! I am extremely sorry. I did not mean to startle you in that manner."

Carter shook his head.

"It is nothing, Rector. It was just that your approach was so unexpected."

The cleric drew back into the shadow of the alley. Carter was still trembling and he fought to gather his ragged nerves.

"Forgive me. You may rest assured I would not have approached you in this furtive way if it had not been extremely important."

Carter forgot his fears.

"Something has happened?"

Sennen nodded gravely. His tortured, sorrowful face seemed almost part of the mist as it eddied and billowed about him.

"I have been out upon the moor. I have made a discovery of the most horrifying and tragic nature. You must prepare yourself for the worst."

Carter lowered his voice to the whisper the Rector was using.

"You want me to go with you? Now?"

"Of course, but only if you are willing."

"Naturally I am willing, Mr. Sennen. Anything to help you. May I know what you have discovered?"

Sennen drew him through the alley, and the two men walked on quietly for some moments.

"All in good time, Mr. Carter. You must just trust me. This is an ideal evening for the expedition I have in mind. There is no-one about and we are not likely to be followed in these conditions."

"But where are we going?" Carter persisted.

"To the Rectory in the first instance. Or rather my stable near the churchyard. I have already harnessed up the cart. We use it for funerals and other heavy work, and it will be ideal for its purpose tonight."

Carter forbore to ask any more questions, his troubled mind turning without any point or focus. He knew where they were now; they had come out of the mouth of a narrow road and were crossing the small square where he had walked with Jeremy that evening when they had watched the ponies come down from the moor. A few paces on and they would be close to the approach to the churchyard.

"Would it not be better if I sent a message to Mrs. Tregorran? She will wonder why I am not at supper."

David Sennen shook his head. His voice was uncharacteristically sharp as he replied.

"By no means, Mr. Carter! It would only draw attention to us. And I wish to avoid that at all costs tonight. It will take us an hour or so to reach our destination and the same time to return. You will be abed the right side of midnight. And I have brought some sandwiches for your refreshment and to make up for your missing supper."

"That is extremely thoughtful, sir."

"You had better take them now. And eat them on the way. It is certain that you will have little appetite after."

Carter took the packet the Rector thrust into his hands with a muttered word of thanks. Something of his companion's gloom seemed to have penetrated his own thoughts. He was silent as they threaded their way through the small lanes to the churchyard entrance.

The blanched marble faces of saints and angels seemed like demons of the night as they swung mysteriously from out the long swathes of mist as they crossed the cobbled pathway. The Rector led the way unerringly; it was obvious that he had passed across here a thousand times or more over the years, and however thick the mist he neither slackened his pace nor hesitated when turning a corner.

They were out at the far gate now and the Rector, with a muffled admonition to silence, ushered Carter across to a low stone building which adjoined the lane. The latter caught a faint glimpse of the Rectory, with gas-light shining from the windows and once more heard the sound of the stream which, he remembered, looped round and bordered the lane at this point.

The pony was in the stable, eager and willing to start, its ears cocked and its eyes bright as the cleric fished in the pocket of his thick caped overcoat to find some sugar lumps. Carter took in the shallow cart, the tarpaulins and spades in the back with a sinking heart. He was about to ask some question when the Rector stopped him.

"All in good time, Mr. Carter, all in good time," he repeated gently.

"Now if you will just get up on the seat I will lead Bessie to the lane and close the doors behind us."

In a few moments more the stable was drowned and lost, and Carter waited impatiently in this white, mysterious world; his limbs chilled by the dampness and cold; his mind as numb as his fingers as he wondered for the hundredth time how he had become enmeshed in these problems of darkness and death that seemed to beset the small town in which he had come to make his home such a short while ago.

Then Sennen, a dark, powerful figure, had clambered up alongside him and taken the reins. The pony and cart went lurching and grinding on into the mist; once out near the far bridge the Rector, looking sharply about him, urged the pony onward.

They were clearing the town now, rising slowly up the hill, the mist cloaking and muffling their movements until all traces of Thornton Bassett were left behind them.

3

The two men were walking on the steep slope, to rest the pony; the only sound the faint rattling of the cart in the raw, all-encompassing mist which swirled about them.

"Can you find the place?" Carter asked for the third time.

Sennen nodded, his face dark and haunted.

"I left a marker at the side of the road, that only I can read." he said.

He pursed his lips grimly.

"But the place is half a mile over rough ground. I hope we shall be able to manage."

Carter's throat was dry and his mind full of whirling impressions, but he was afraid to ask the vital questions that were hovering at the back of his consciousness.

"Is that why you brought the tarpaulin and the dark lanterns?"

"Yes," Sennen said simply.

He shuddered slightly.

"It is a bad place and dark. That is probably why the moor people did not bother. And there would have been few traces in the spring."

Carter marvelled at the man's courage and restraint. David Sennen was an even more remarkable person than the architect had imagined. And he had guessed to what the bald, bare statements referred. He only hoped he would have the strength to play his part.

The slope was levelling out a little now. Carter judged they were about two miles from Thornton Bassett, though it was difficult to be sure in the mist. The road was a continuation of the one up which he had escorted Miss Hammond on that sunny evening when she had stayed overnight with friends; the large iron gates they had passed about a mile and a half back were probably those of the new municipal graveyard of which he had heard.

Since then there had been no identifiable features and they were obviously on the fringes of the moor, for the road had looped and turned in a baffling manner, Carter truly understood the dangers involved. Two yards off the road and one would be irretrievably lost in the swirling whiteness.

One could die of exposure up here, even so close to such a town as Thornton Bassett, and lie undiscovered until spring.

"Does this road link up with Rats' Castle?" he asked, more by way of making conversation than anything else.

Sennen nodded.

"It leads to other villages, of course. But it loops to the west as it levels to avoid the higher slopes of the moor. If you study the maps, Mr. Carter, you will learn to read the ground. It is essential to memorise the lie of the land if one wishes to survive."

Normally Carter would have remarked on such a statement and questioned his companion eagerly; but it was a measure of the sombreness of the occasion and the mysterious errand on which they were bound that he merely absorbed the information without querying it.

The Rector was smoking his pipe now and the stubby bowl with its glowing dottle made little stippled red marks on his face through the tendrils of mist. Carter consulted his watch for the third time. Incredibly, they had been travelling for less than an hour. They should be near their destination soon.

As though he had taken notice of Carter's unspoken thought Sennen slackened his pace and looked keenly about him; then Carter caught the milestone through the mist. Sennen stopped the pony and tied the reins round the base of the stone, making sure the animal could not wander off.

He put the blanket over it and went round to the back of the cart. He returned with a folded tarpaulin which he handed to his companion.

"I think this will do. Take it and one of the spades and for God's sake follow my lead in all things. These creatures may still be out here."

His words struck a chill to Carter's soul but he made no comment. Sennen had also produced a lantern. By contriving to put the tarpaulin under his left arm Carter was able to manage the spade and the unlit lantern under his right. Sennen had reappeared now, after securing the tail-flap of the cart. He carried a spade and a second lantern, together with a coil of rope.

"I am sorry to leave the lion's share to you, Mr. Carter, but you are a much younger man, and I need to keep my wits about me if I am to retrace my footsteps without mistake."

"That is perfectly all right, Mr. Sennen."

The architect followed the thickset clergyman as he led the way, keeping to the right-hand side of the road. The Rector had his lips pursed and was mumbling to himself as though in prayer. Carter knew that he was counting so he did not interrupt. They had gone about two hundred yards in this fashion when Sennen stopped and looked keenly about him.

The young man then saw the fragment of white glistening in the sparse grass at the edge of the road. It was one of the small splinters that Sennen used as a pipe-spill, and he spotted it at the same moment with a grunt of satisfaction.

"Over here, Mr. Carter. We shall be going downhill pretty steeply so keep your wits about you."

The two men crept slowly downward into the growing darkness. It was a bad place and Carter remembered his Biblical teachings and the Valley of the Shadow. They were threading between boulders now, and the air struck even more chill and raw than on the open moor.

Sennen was negotiating the slopes with extraordinary agility and skill and Carter realised something of the stamina of the middle-aged man bred of long years tramping these bleak and lonely moors. Aided by Sennen's whispered admonitions, he did his best to slither in the cleric's wake, the white mass of mist like a bottomless sea in which they were being slowly drowned.

At length he could hear the sound of water rushing over boulders and Sennen motioned him back with a cautionary word.

"Stay here," he said.

Carter sank on to a boulder, spreading out the canvas at his side. He rested on the handle of the spade after putting his unlit lantern by the edge of the rock. He saw the flare of a match ahead and the faintest glow through the fog. The lantern disappeared, and then followed a long and profound silence.

Carter had expected to see the light returning but was instead startled to observe a dark shadow as Sennen materialised from the mist. He realised that a city-bred person such as himself was hopelessly unsuited for such work on the moors. The Rector sat himself down on a corner of the boulder and looked at him with haunted eyes.

"Now, Mr. Carter, I must warn you to prepare for a shock. It is not a pleasant sight and I only hope your nerves are up to it. But I cannot do what I have to do without the help of someone young and strong like yourself. And it is also a question of identity."

Carter laid his hand on the other's arm.

"You can rely on me, Mr. Sennen. Is it a body we are to bring back?"

The question was a mere formality as he had gathered that from the first. The Rector nodded assent and grunted something in a low voice which the other was unable to catch. Carter stood up, gathering his things together.

"I am prepared, Mr. Sennen. And thank you for your great consideration."

The Rector stood up also, stopping to light Carter's own lantern. He trimmed the wick until the flame was low and then led the way forward without another word. The farther down they went the darker it became.

They were in a great fold between two flanks of hillside; it was almost a ravine, and cold draughts of dank air blew out of it. The noise of rushing water was louder now, and Carter could see the faint light of the Rector's own lantern ahead of them. The boulders were wet, and they had to use extreme care. By the dancing beams of light through the mist Carter could see the black race thundering by at their left-hand side, the water whipped to white frenzy as it scoured the edges of rocks and boulders.

There was a maniacal laughter in the horrendous sound which seemed to have all the brooding horror of the moor in it; and given the sombre history to which he had listened over the past weeks, Carter felt he could not have come here alone. It said a good deal for the Rector's courage and tenacity that he had been out and about by himself, probing the mystery at the heart of the bizarre happenings which had baffled both police and military alike.

Carter's thoughts were abruptly interrupted by the Rector stopping and holding the lantern high. He made the sign of the cross in the air and bowed his head. Then he turned sorrowful eyes to Carter, sweeping the lantern in a wide arc.

"There!"

Despite his mental preparation the young man felt a thrill of horror run through him and he had to reach out for the boulder at his elbow for support. The wavering beams of the lanterns shone on the great mass of racing water. Shone on something else too, which had been thrown free and caught between two rocks. It was like a blasphemous parody of a man who appeared to be clad in some sort of shining oilskins.

Sennen's face was set as hard and sharp as marble.

"Give me the tarpaulin, Mr. Carter," he said between clenched teeth. "Do not go closer unless you have a mind to."

He was too late, for the architect, his curiosity aroused, had taken two steps nearer. Then, a groan escaping his lips; his face ashy-white, he dropped the lantern. Fortunately, Sennen was able to prevent it tumbling into the stream and caught it by the wire handle.

Carter leaned against the other, sickness and anger fighting within him. For the waterproofs he had imagined were no such thing; what he had taken for them was a blackened, charred mass which the drifting spray had coated with moisture, gleaming in the light.

The thing was hunched and shrivelled as though with blasting heat and there were no fragments of clothing or ornamentation to identify it. The hair and eyes were gone, but the skull and teeth had resisted the searing incandescence and gave back a mocking smile in the light of the lanterns.

The blackened bones of the hands were held out in supplication, and Carter turned away numbly, retching uncontrollably. He came to himself with the Rector's hand on his shoulder, water splashing into his face.

"Forgive me, Mr. Carter. The shock was too great."

Carter shook his head, anger again invading him. Energy returned, and he trimmed the wick of his lantern to give a brighter light. Gently the two men bent to lever the shrivelled remains on to the tarpaulin with the edges of their spades.

It was then that Carter noticed on one of the thing's hands, as it rolled sluggishly over, the melted remains of the curious gold and ruby ring that he had last seen on his friend Jeremy's finger.

Thirty-Eight
The Broken Lock

1

CARTER COUGHED AS more of the raw spirit trickled down his throat. Sennen's face was concerned in the dim light of the lantern as he held the rim of the silver brandy flask to the young man's lips.

Carter looked round wildly, but there was nothing save the waving tendrils of mist, the pony's patiently nodding head as it settled to its work between the shafts, and the sound of gentle slithering in the rear of the cart as the tarpaulin mass that contained the mortal remains of Jeremy Hands shifted with the changing gradients.

Carter was invaded by an aching sense of bitterness, failure and helplessness.

"We must get the police and soldiery in!" he raged. "Before dawn the moor must be scoured."

Sennen shook his head, taking the flask from him and drinking briefly before returning it to his pocket. His left hand resumed the reins while his right dimmed the lantern. The fog was still thick, but he would not want the light of the cart to be seen as it neared Thornton Bassett.

"That is just what we must not do, Mr. Carter," he said softly, as though he were speaking to a child. "It would be no good. And you are forgetting that your friend's body had probably been there for the better part of a week."

Carter gazed at his companion with burning eyes. He hardly knew what he had been doing for the past hour, though the sense of the clergyman's remarks was beginning to penetrate. He had a vague recollection of them manhandling the remains in its roped canvas covering across the moor, like an an obscene parcel, and loading it on to the cart. Then he seemed to have fainted or become unconscious for a short period. He was only really taking in his surroundings now. He tried to concentrate his understanding as Sennen went on.

"Your poor friend was probably killed a short while after he left you to embark on his foolhardy expedition. We may be in deadly danger ourselves. We will tell no-one of this discovery."

Carter stared at him incredulously.

"You will not inform the police? Or hold a Christian service for as good a man as ever walked in shoe-leather?"

Sennen shook his head, a kindly expression on his worn face. Carter felt a sudden stab of pity. Tonight could not have been easy for Sennen either, even though he claimed no intimacy with the dead man. He must have iron self-control.

"Do not misunderstand me, Mr. Carter. We do no good to Mr. Hands' memory by running about like chicken with their heads cut off. There are sharp brains, cunning rascals, and cruel enemies abroad upon the moor. We do not, above all, wish to play into their hands."

"What do you suggest then?"

Sennen smiled faintly. He put his hand affectionately on the other's shoulder.

"Leave things to me. We will talk more of our future plans when your anger has grown colder. Your head will be clearer then. In the meantime we will unload the cart at the rear of the church; hopefully, unobserved. There will be few people stirring by the time we get back to Thornton Bassett."

"But what about Jeremy?"

Carter could not resist the question.

"You are certain it is Jeremy?" the Rector said gently.

Carter nodded.

"There is no doubt about it. I would recognise that curious ring anywhere."

He swallowed heavily.

"And did you not see? By some freak of fire there was still one lock of reddish hair clinging to the scalp."

The Rector whitened visibly but said nothing for a moment. Then his grip on the other's shoulder tightened.

"What do you think now that you have seen The Black Death for yourself?"

Carter turned a grim countenance, matching the other's own.

"That I shall not rest until I have avenged him."

Sennen nodded approvingly, encouraging the pony on a downward slope.

"That is the spirit, my boy," he said. "We must plan for that."

"You have not answered my question, sir," Carter continued, watching Sennen extinguish the lantern. They were travelling by the faint light from the sky now, the pony keeping in to the edge of the road.

"Do not worry, Mr. Carter. Everything will be done properly. We will take him to the catacombs. There, I will inter him decently and with a simple form of service, until such time as I can arrange an open and proper burial."

Carter looked about him wildly, as though he would rend the veils of mist about them to reveal the monstrous beings responsible for such a cruel death; only the latest in a long series, he realised.

"But what about Jeremy's parents? His fiancee?" he continued.

The Rector gave him a twisted smile.

"You are still not thinking clearly, Mr. Carter. If we tell one, we must tell all. The creatures who murdered Mr. Hands in such a barbaric fashion obviously did not expect his remains to be found for some considerable time. They probably tipped him into the stream, hoping the corpse would disintegrate and be dispersed over a wide area of the moor. It may have never been found in recognisable form if I had not intervened."

"You knew where to look?" said Carter.

Sennen, his black hair powdered with grey, was a faint silhouette against the mist now.

"Not really. But I have learned patience in my years here. I quartered the moor. I felt sure I would discover evidence in due course. You forget that what we have in the cart behind us is also police evidence. The coroner will wish to examine the remains. So there is simply no question of burial at this stage."

To Carter's distress he found his eyes filled with tears. Then he reached over impulsively and wrung the Rector's hand.

"You are quite right, sir. I have been foolish. But I was quite overcome out there."

"There is no need to explain or apologise, Mr. Carter," the Rector said gently. "We have both been under considerable strain tonight."

He looked at his companion shrewdly.

"Under the circumstances, after we have concluded our business in the vault—of which I retain the only key, incidentally—you had better have supper with me at the Rectory. That will give you a chance to calm down."

He gave the other another long look.

"And you had best wash and clean and tidy your clothing before returning to your lodgings. Mrs. Tregorran is a sharp-eyed lady, and she may still be up."

He put great emphasis upon the words.

"All must appear normal there."

Carter was himself now, all anger burned out of him.

"Of course, sir," he said readily. "Everything shall be as you desire."

"We must discuss our plans within the next few days," the Rector went on, braking slightly as they started to go downill again. Carter realised they were on the outskirts of Thornton Bassett.

"You have some ideas about these crimes?"

"Perhaps, Mr. Carter," Sennen said slowly. "I have no wish to go into it tonight. I think we have both had enough for one day."

Carter gave the other a brief smile.

"You are certainly right there, sir. What would you suggest?"

"I think it best if I approach you in a business way. We have to discuss further restoration work at the church, have we not? Let it be there, open to the eyes of the town. When we have need of maps and more detailed schemes then we can always meet at dead of night with no-one the wiser."

He got down from the cart to assist the pony, and Carter followed. The two men walked quietly on the rough grass at the roadside. Far below the chime of the church clock came up sharp and clear.

"But above all, Mr. Carter, I do not think I need further emphasise the necessity for absolute caution in this terrible enterprise. One false step and we are both lost men."

Carter nodded, vainly trying to expunge from his brain the image of the seared horror that lay shrouded in the cart at his back.

2

It was late when Carter reached his lodgings; so late that the last street lamps had long been extinguished. He was vaguely aware of the rushing of the stream when he crossed the bridge, but beyond that things were a vast, numbing blank. Perhaps it was better so. The ghastly fate of Jeremy Hands had driven everything else from his spinning brain.

He even had difficulty in remembering the events of the past hour; of the melancholy procession to the vault, where he and Sennen had with great difficulty conveyed the shrouded canvas. Of its bestowal, of the furtive stabling of the pony, of the locking of the doors and their repairing to the Rector's study, he retained no recollection.

That they must have done these things was obvious, for Carter had a vague remembrance of the low conversation with Sennen, backgrounded by thousands of leather-bound books; of the bottles and food on the table before them; and of the Rector's solemn warning; of his urgent exhortation to discretion.

He must have drunk too much. Perhaps that had been part of Sennen's purpose too. Whatever his motives Carter was grateful to him for many things, of course, but mostly that, for the fiery spirit had numbed his brain and inclined him toward sleep. They would think more on these matters in due time. That much had Carter retained in his addled mind of the Rector's conversation.

Sennen had availed himself more than once of his brimming glass. That was understandable too; he also had gone through a great deal that night. Far more than Carter himself, and he was a much older man. Not only had he descended into that horrendous gorge to make his appalling discovery but he had summoned the resolve to return and recruit Carter for the recovery and temporary interment of his friend's remains.

Carter's mind went blank again at this point. He recovered to find himself leaning against the wall of a house only some hundred yards from Mrs. Tregorran's dwelling. The roaring of the stream was still in his ears, and though it reminded him of many things he would rather forget, at least the clamminess of the fog and the feel of light rain upon his face restored him somewhat to his senses.

He looked about him clearly for the first time. It had long gone midnight, and nothing broke the stillness but the rush of the torrent. There would be no-one abroad at this hour in Thornton Bassett other than those with evil designs; even they would be hard put to it to pierce the blanket of mist. Though he could not be sure, Carter felt he had not been followed from the Rectory.

He should have come the back way, of course; but in his present state of mind he must have gone boldly through the main squares of the town. It did not really matter now. Young men do stay up late and drink, and no normal person would think twice of his presence in the town centre at that hour. No person who did not already have his suspicions about Carter and his activities upon the moor.

As he felt this the brooding horror again seemed to settle upon Carter's soul. From what he had gathered through the Rector, there was no reason to feel he was suspected by these night-riders who struck so cruelly and so ruthlessly at persons who sought to discover their secret. Carter felt perspiration start out upon his forehead.

Absolute secrecy was the only thing that would preserve them, Sennen had said. Jeremy had told him the same; but what could he and a middle-aged cleric do to lift the curtain on this terror and sudden death that blighted the small town and the dark moorland that lay around it? If Jeremy were to be believed, even police agents on the track of these mysteries had met the same fate as innocents upon the moor at night.

Yet there burned within Carter a fierce core of hatred against the persons—or things—that had murdered Jeremy. That, allied to a stubborn determination endemic in his character, impelled him now. And he had other interests that were working toward the same ends. The warmth of the girl's presence and her support. Warmth and support expressed only a short time ago.

And surely Magistrate Hemmings and Henderson and his troop would ultimately prevail, despite their failures of recent weeks? Carter was himself again; an icy cold was permeating his limbs and he had to get within shelter before he collapsed. He was due at his office in the morning, and everything must appear normal there. Both he and Sennen would be marked men unless they presented their customary visages to the world.

Again he realised what inner resources of strength and resolve Sennen must have brought to his solitary task. Both men had to go through with the business and rid the moor of an unutterable foulness that used night and murder and death to terrorise and have its way as ruthlessly and efficiently as any Eastern European secret society.

Carter moved on, being careful not to make any noise on the cobbles. He reached the garden gate and closed it gently behind him, fearful lest its hinges squeak and betray his presence. The church clock struck while he was doing that, and under cover of its long-drawn vibration he covered the remaining yards to the front door.

He moved the key gently in the lock and secured the door behind him without making any undue noise. The house was quiet and still; the warmth from the dying fires still filled the air and took the chill from his limbs. He replaced his key in his pocket and started up the stairs. He knew where the squeaky treads were by now, and negotiated them all without mishap.

The lamp still burned outside the bathroom door; its pallid luminescence speaking of normality and the humdrum routine of small town life. The stairhead grew before him as his eyes became adjusted to the lower intensity. Carter stopped in the corridor leading to his room, again overcome by a fit of shivering.

Jeremy's chamber lay to his right, the place to which he would now never return. How his disappearance was to be explained; or how his tragic reappearance for that matter, did not concern Carter now. He would leave everything to the Rector. But something that concerned Jeremy; something he had once told Carter a long time ago—perhaps during one of their talks at The Bassett Arms—hammered at the back of Carter's muddled mind.

It returned to him at the same moment his darting eyes became aware of a dark shadow at the edge of Hands' room door. The young man's heartbeat suddenly became irregular; the shivering arose again, and he leaned against the flowered wallpaper while he fought it down.

The door was not only unlocked but open; there was nothing unusual about that, of course. Pauline or the other girl would need to go there to clean and change the linen from time to time. But the mundane fact combined with the fragment of conversation which had just sprung unbidden into Carter's mind now had a dread significance for him.

He hesitated but a moment. A second later he was at the door, pushed it wide, making sure it did not creak. There was enough light spilling from the end of the passage for him to make out the broad detail of the room; with its shrouded bed as though the still form of his dead friend lay there.

The thought was so shocking that for a moment Carter actually felt it to be so. He stood for a second, his teeth locked tightly together, before forcing himself on. Jeremy had spoken of evidence taken from the corpse of the murdered police agent on the moor and which he had locked in a cupboard in his room.

There was the cupboard; it was the only one in the chamber which would fit the bill. It was a large mahogany affair, elaborately carved, which stood to the right of the fireplace. Jeremy had had the only key, he had told Carter. The young man stood in front if it, ice cold, his face drained of blood.

That door, too, gaped open; he could see the marks made by a knife or chisel around the woodwork at the edge of the lock. The bottom shelf inside had been ransacked, for books and papers had been thrown about in careless disorder.

Carter knew fear then. He spun on his heel as though the Hounds of Satan were indeed behind him and went swiftly out of the room and across the corridor to his own door, biting his lip and trying not to make too much noise. Blinded by sweat, he got his key in the lock and put the wooden panel between him and the silent corridor where the light burned, lonely and menacing now, rather than reassuring.

His brain was too disturbed to digest this new information. It brought terror home to him with the realisation that these people could strike with impunity even in the supposed security of his own lodgings. He had to warn Sennen in the morning. He would think again on the matter then.

He was crying now, like a strong man broken by forces impossible to resist. He stuffed his handkerchief into his mouth and fell upon the bed. Presently he drifted into a troubled sleep.

Part Three
WINTER

THIRTY-NINE
Work in Progress

1

THE CABLES RAN through the sheaves with a screaming noise that tore at Carter's nerves. He stood on the terrace in the searing air, his shoulders hunched into his thick overcoat, his feet in the stout boots spread far apart. The foreman, a squat, bearded man with piercing eyes, saluted Carter deferentially as he came up.

"I hope you are satisfied with the standard of the work, sir. We have had some trouble getting materials up from Plymouth. And the weather does not help . . ."

Carter smiled faintly.

"Your men are doing admirably," he said. "Everything one could have expected. And you may tell them so from me."

The foreman nodded, his eyes searching Carter's face.

"I will tell them sir," he said slowly. "They will be glad to know."

Carter glanced at the massive façade that was rising into the air, in an astonishingly short time, it seemed. He was pleased with the way his designs for Hemmings' new galleries were working out in practice; in fact he would have been intensely happy had it not been for the oppressive thoughts which kept dark shadows on his face, shadows which were only temporarily lightened by the presence of Fiona Hammond.

He walked back down the terrace a little way, ostensibly to check the progress of the work from another angle but in reality to master his thoughts. Two weeks had gone by since that terrible night when he and Sennen had returned from the moor.

Life had flowed on normally about them. Carter had said nothing to anyone about the disappearance of his friend; he did not think it wise. Other than retailing Jeremy's own prepared story, of course.

He had returned blank, noncommittal answers to Mrs. Tregorran's questions and to those of the two girls who served.

Gradually, public interest in Jeremy Hands' absence from his familiar haunts had died away. As the weeks had passed and the winter advanced into December, he might never have existed, Carter thought bitterly. Even Mr. Pollard and his colleagues at Pollard, Bassett had ceased their questions, and Hands' place in the drawing-office had been quietly filled by a new apprentice.

Pollard had, Carter had since ascertained, written to Hands' parents in the north but either he had the wrong address or they were away, for he never received any reply.

At Sennen's suggestion Carter had taken to frequenting The Bassett Arms public bar in the early evenings on his way home. The Rector was a shrewd man, and as he had so wisely said, a public bar was a great place for gossip. Perhaps someone, some time, might let a morsel of information drop which could lead to the culprits responsible for Hands' death. But though Carter had applied himself with enthusiasm, albeit with some caution, to this task, he had never heard so much as a hint which might have led the two men in the right direction.

Indeed, as week followed week, he had become greatly discouraged, and it was only Sennen's patience and strong direction from the shadowy background of the Rectory that had kept his hopes alive. Apart from the major commission at The Priory, Carter had been much about the district with Slade and the other partners as the early December days hardened into frost, with howling winds that came down from the north and made a bleak fastness of the moor.

Here again, Carter had kept alert at all times but he had never heard anything; either from workmen engaged in the firm's commissions; from Slade; from the partners; or from clients who needed new farm buildings or renovations to their houses, that might lead him in the direction of vital information.

One hope only sustained him. Of Sennen's hinting of something important planned on the moor. He would not give Carter more precise information than that, but during the last week he had immured himself in the Rectory library with his ancient books and sheets of notepaper, which he covered with inches of pencilled notations. It was drawing toward the season of Christmas yet the young man could not regard it this year as being anything but a terrible mockery.

Carter was thus left to his own resources and when Hemmings' commission began in the first week of the month he had thrown himself into it with notable energy, glad to be back in the luxurious atmosphere of The Priory, where a glance from Fiona Hammond's eyes would warm him on the most cheerless day, where the enthusiasm of Hemmings and his housekeeper would sustain him, and where even the sullen presence of Captain Michael Henderson could not chill his spirits.

Now, as he anxiously compared his inked notes with the foreman's scribbled heiroglyphs, he became aware that the owner of The Priory was regarding him from a position some hundred feet farther down the terrace. He had obviously just emerged from one of the museum rooms giving on to the paving, and in fact the door still gaped ajar.

The Magistrate smiled as he caught Carter's glance and came down toward him with typical energy, the cold winter light glancing on the gold-rimmed spectacles. Today he wore pale grey clothing, which the architect understood he affected on the bench, and his thick grey overcoat of herringbone tweed made him a somewhat dashing figure. In addition he wore highly polished brown top-boots which were splashed with mud, indicating that he had already been abroad on the moor.

Carter cast a quick look at the sullen sky which was pressing in on the rounded slopes of moorland at his rear, shading off into the misty distances of the tors, while he waited for his client to come up.

"Hard at it, eh, Mr. Carter!"

Carter smiled.

"It is these men who are doing all the real work, sir!"

Magistrate Hemmings pumped his hand enthusiastically, looking at him sharply from beneath the brim of his soft country hat.

"I hope you are satisfied with them, Mr. Carter?"

The young man shrugged.

"It is hardly for me to say, sir. I have never met better workmen, if that is what you mean. But are you satisfied, with both my efforts and theirs? That is more to the point."

Hemmings' smile widened.

"Ever self-critical, Mr. Carter! You will go far, sir. I am amazed, in fact, at what has been achieved in less than three weeks. The extensions will be a credit both to you and Pollard, Bassett."

"I am glad to hear you say so, sir."

The two men walked farther down the terrace to inspect the work at closer quarters. Indeed, Carter himself had seldom seen better set-up workmen, bold, muscular and self-confident craftsmen, even down to the bricklayers and labourers, who had an almost arrogant self-regard in their fierce glances and steady eyes.

They had no need to quicken their pace as Carter and his client approached. They were already working as hard as the architect had ever seen artisans work. Perhaps it was because Hemmings was the Chief Magistrate hereabouts? Perhaps. Carter pondered the question to himself a while longer.

He dilated on the finer points of construction though it was obvious Hemmings was *au fait* with the most abstruse technical terms; and the Magistrate's eyes glistened and his smile broadened as the architect's discourse continued. It was a somewhat puzzling reaction until Carter realised it was not so much the building that absorbed his client, but that the collector's instinct was aroused. Hemmings was mentally envisaging how his extraordinary clockwork toys would look when displayed in his new galleries.

Not that Carter would have employed such a term to his face. The man was a genius in his own way; and Carter realised the skill and precision which went into Hemmings' enthusiasms, even if he could not fully appreciate them. Which brought him back to the subject of Fiona Hammond. He had recalled the superb needlecraft in such costumes as those for the monkey orchestra and he put a stammering question to his client.

Hemmings' smile broadened.

"Ah, yes, Mr. Carter. My niece. You will see Miss Hammond at lunch. You will stay to lunch, of course? I understand there are some critical roof trusses to be raised this afternoon."

"It is very good of you, sir," Carter retorted.

"Not at all."

Hemmings smiled again.

"And I believe that she really has her own plans for these new extensions."

2

Carter felt a slight puzzlement
"I do not follow you, sir."
The Magistrate chuckled.

"If I am not careful, Mr. Carter, these new galleries will become nothing more than the Dartmoor Museum of Needlework!"

Carter joined in the other's laughter.

"I see."

The two men were in the lee of the extensions, sheltered from the wind, and the young man was able to point out more of the ideas he had been able to develop and refine from his original concepts. The Magistrate was silent for a long time when he finished, turning his gaze from the energetic scene before them to the brooding fastnesses of the moor.

"It is remarkable to me that you were able to obtain the services of such a firm, sir," Carter said in the end, more to break the impasse than anything else. "I must confess I have never heard of them."

Hemmings abruptly switched his gaze back to his companion.

"I am not surprised," he said mildly. "It is part of a small combination I have myself formed with a number of fellow-directors. I am Chairman of the company, which operates mainly in Cornwall and the far west of England."

"I see, sir. That accounts for their zeal, no doubt."

The Magistrate smiled faintly, the low winter light glinting off his glasses until he reminded the architect of some old drawing of Pickwick from his childhood.

"Perhaps, Mr. Carter," Hemmings said softly. "It would certainly account for some of it. All the same I wish I had had these fellows with me rather than Henderson's troopers the night we met the moor-riders."

Carter was glad of the diversion. He had not wanted to broach the subject direct and here was a golden opportunity.

"As I have already indicated, I was sorry to hear about that. And we have not yet had an appropriate moment to discuss it. You and the Captain might have been killed."

Hemmings made a solemn clicking noise through his teeth. His eyes were cold and irritated behind the glasses. He shook his head savagely.

"It was a wonderful opportunity thrown away, Mr. Carter. If we had been a little later along the road and had surprised them before they had got fairly across . . .And if the mist had not come down when it did . . ."

He shrugged.

"But there it is. I fancy we wounded more than one of the rascals in the first volley we gave them. I have had inquiries made up and down the moor but I have not yet heard of any injured person seeking medical advice."

He shrugged again, more expressively this time.

"But when I do . . ."

He gazed smoulderingly into the far distances of the moor.

"And you, Mr. Carter? Have you no theories regarding these terrifying beings?"

Carter was emboldened by this but retained his cautious attitude, with the recollection of the Rector's haunted eyes.

"I, Mr. Hemmings? I am a stranger here. I know nothing of these matters."

He smiled at the Magistrate's obvious puzzlement.

"And Mr. Pollard is extremely anxious that a member of his firm should not be drawn into speculation about such melodramatic and colourful goings-on."

Hemmings gazed at him paternally, putting a hand familiarly on the cuff of his overcoat.

"That is an old man's philosophy, Mr. Carter. But who is to say that Mr. Pollard is not wiser than either of us. Dabble not with the fiends of the moor, eh? He may be right. But just wait until you have been a few years upon Dartmoor. You will be just as bold in your speculations as any four-ale bar gossiper, I'll be bound."

Carter was inclined to agree.

"You may be right, sir," he said cautiously.

Then he was reminded of something else.

"Now that we are talking of the subject, did you hear anything of that farmer's missing daughter?"

A cloud crossed the Magistrate's face.

"I do not quite follow you, sir."

Carter was puzzled but he kept the emotion from his voice.

"I thought it was part of your purpose, sir, the night you rode out."

He glanced over Hemmings' shoulder at the blackish-brown vista of moorland, now being enveloped in a soft, milky whiteness. It was a winter landscape he was beginning to hate.

"Do you not remember you said something about a local farmer, whose daughter was missing upon the moor? You were hoping to gain information about her whereabouts."

The Magistrate's face cleared.

"I am sorry, Mr. Carter, I have much to distract me these days, what with my official work upon the bench, as well as these problems on the moor. The matter has reached as far as Whitehall, you will be surprised to know."

Carter raised his eyebrows.

"Indeed, sir."

"You may well say so."

Hemmings was looking down at the flagstones of the terrace now, his brow knotted and heavy with thought. He sighed, uncharacteristically. Then he shook his head.

"We found nothing, sir. Neither could we gain any information. But it is early days yet. The farmer himself thought she may have run off. Perhaps she will in due course be found and returned to her home."

"As you say, sir," Carter returned.

The two men resumed their slow pacing, seemingly oblivious of the busy clatter of the men employed before them. There was again satisfaction in the Magistrate's eyes as he glanced keenly over the panorama of toiling workers.

"It may well be your *magnum opus*, sir! And now, let us join my niece for lunch."

Forty
Accident or Design?

1

"GOOD AFTERNOON, SIR!"

Captain Michael Henderson's sullen face was contorted into an insincere semblance of a greeting as he stepped from the shrubbery, a half-smoked cigar clamped between his strong teeth. He looked beyond Carter, giving a half-bow to Hemmings, who had just emerged into the full light behind the architect.

Carter was not sure to whom the pleasantry had been addressed so he contented himself with a stiff bow in turn. From the corner of his eye he could see the faint amusement on the Magistrate's face, instantly erased by the mellow greeting.

Before Carter could venture anything in reply he was startled to see a grey blur in the long walk behind the Captain. The tall form of Fiona Hammond slowly drifted into focus. Her eyes looked cool and amused as they found Carter's own.

"You and Uncle seemed so busy, Mr. Carter, I accepted the Captain's kind invitation to a short walk before lunch."

Carter bit back the unkind thoughts about Henderson.

"My loss, Miss Hammond."

He ignored the expression on Henderson's face, concentrating instead on the Captain's fancy boots. Obviously hand-made, and non-regulation, they featured a faint red stripe running vertically from the soles to the straps by which he pulled them on. His grey walking-out uniform was plain and unostentatious, the only things breaking its monotony being the polished brown leather belt which held his revolver and two faded ribbons on his breast which Carter could not make out.

He was not in any way a specialist in military history and so would not know which campaigns they represented. Unless they were for good conduct; he suppressed an inward spasm of amusement at the thought.

The girl fell in between the two young men, her guardian walking discreetly behind. Carter could feel Hemmings' cynical amusement almost boring into his back.

"And what have you been talking about, Uncle?" the girl asked across her shoulder, her dancing eyes passing from Carter at her left to Henderson on her right.

"Little that would interest you, my dear. Mr. Carter's commission, of course. It is coming along splendidly!"

"I am glad to hear it. Nothing else?"

Carter cast a surreptitious glance at Henderson's face. It was dark and shuttered; its expression impossible to make out. Probably like his own.

"Only some talk about that girl lost upon the moor. As I have told the Captain here, I should imagine that she will turn up safe and sound somewhere in due course."

Fiona Hammond bit her lip. She cast a quick glance at Carter. For a moment there was something like fright in her eyes. Carter was startled but he covered the moment well, keeping his face blank, looking down now at his footing on the flagstones of the terrace.

"You may be right, Uncle," the girl said in a low voice. "Let us hope so."

Henderson had a somewhat sneering look on his coarse, handsome features.

"Come now, Miss Hammond," he was saying. "Do you not think this talk of ghosts and demons upon the moor is somewhat exaggerated?"

The girl shrugged, her eyes still on Carter.

"Perhaps. Perhaps not," she said softly. "You must admit there have been terrors enough. And these poor people burnt to death. What fiendish hand could have been behind such horrors? And for what reason?"

The three men were struck silent for a moment at the girl's vehemence. Then the Magistrate observed mildly: "We agreed not to talk further of that, Fiona. The matter is *sub judice*. Surely the police and the authorities in London, who have matters in hand, know best."

"I am sure you are right, sir," put in Carter in a neutral voice. His eyes looked a warning at the girl. No-one had seen the quick glance that passed between them. She took the hint.

"No doubt, Uncle," she said. "But it is hard indeed for those poor people upon the moor who are terrified out of their wits these dark winter nights."

Hemmings' voice was level and equable.

"There is a deal in what you say, Fiona. But you are not being courteous to the Captain here. He is our guest, after all, and no-one could have done more. He and his troop have been riding early and late. It is no easy task, I can assure you."

He smiled ruefully.

"As I have cause to realise if the one night I rode with them is anything to go by."

The girl bit her lip.

"Of course not, Uncle," she muttered. "I meant no discourtesy to the Captain. I pray he will be successful. Perhaps we had better leave the subject. It is too disagreeable for such a lunch as Mrs. Arkwright has prepared for us."

The four had paused at the corner of the house, the bleakness of the moor to their right. Something of its oppressive, brooding mystery seemed to have permeated the company.

Carter suddenly remembered he had left his surveying instruments upon the site of the building works. He made a quick excuse, saying he would rejoin the party, and went back down the terrace.

2

The clatter from the workmen seemed to have redoubled. They were certainly doing their best to meet the planned programme that Carter had worked out. He had promised Hemmings that they would try to get the roof of the extensions covered before the worst of the weather set in in January, and it looked as though they would achieve this in good time, providing the snow held off.

Granite blocks were being hoisted aloft now, to complete the exterior walls, and the roof beams should be in position within a few days. Carter paused a moment to watch the men scaling ladders and mixing mortar in the heavy wooden trugs they were using. His presence was not really necessary; he knew that. These men were directly employed by Hemmings and tolerated his supervision as the architect.

Carter well understood this; he was used to it, but it had taken him some while in the profession to become accustomed to the contempt and resentment some artisans had for a man in his position. It was partly compounded of fear; a fear of superior knowledge and education, and another fear that his calculations might be awry and that beams and joists would not support the loads he had calculated, which could lead to accidents causing injury and death.

There had been many such incidents in the great railway works that were now going forward the length and breadth of England, and Carter understood something of the men's attitude, though he both loathed and deprecated it. The condition of the labourer was harsh and demeaning, he knew. Their wages were poor compared to many people in cities. But that was not his fault, and he had always tried to treat them well and encouraged them in turn to give of their best.

These men were expert but they had a dark sullenness about them unique in Carter's experience; the foreman in particular had a bearing like that of some great industrialist or financier who was lowering himself through working under the direction of someone like Carter. The architect had meant to speak to Hemmings about it, but he did not want to cause trouble on the site, and the work was going extremely well.

He found his velvet-lined case of instruments lying on the low stone wall of the terrace and snapped it shut, gathering up the sheaf of drawings held in place by a couple of the large stones found hereabout. Again he felt his eye caught by the bleak expanse of the moor.

The sky was black and overcast and the scudding clouds seemed to scrape the higher land. Far to the east the blue, jagged edges of the tors were almost lost in mist while nearer at hand the eye was caught by the winding steel ribbon of the stream which led from an escarpment near Rats' Castle to a point somewhere on Hemmings' estate.

The wind blew cold and penetratingly, and Carter realised it must be extremely uncomfortable aloft where the workmen were toiling on the walls. He would ask Hemmings to provide them with some rum before they set to again on the afternoon's work. They had earned it, and so far as he could see none of them wore gloves or particularly thick clothing.

His thoughts were interrupted by the sound of the cables running through the sheaves and he saw that the man operating the shear-legs was again swinging some of the granite blocks into position on the wooden cradle. He watched idly for a moment or two, his professional instincts engaged. A black-bearded man stood at the edge of the scaffolding, his fierce eyes on Carter.

The latter waited until the blocks had been manhandled on to the platform and then again turned his eyes toward the moor. His mind was too much occupied with his fears and concerns in that direction. His work was suffering too. Once or twice he had made trifling errors in his calculations, and Pollard had had to draw his attention to them.

It was obvious Pollard had some inkling of his troubles; but he probably attributed it to the inexplicable disappearance of his friend, Jeremy Hands. Carter wondered what he would really think had he known the true situation which obtained in Thornton Bassett.

A lot depended on the Rector's word in this; and yet Carter had himself seen and experienced enough horrors in this business to last the normal man a lifetime.

He gave a brief exclamation. His mind was wandering again. He had let go the sheaf of papers, and one set of documents, propelled by the stiff breeze, had bowled across the terrace. They were caught now against a wooden wheelbarrow in the shelter of the wall. He hastened across to retrieve them, his mind still absorbed by unquiet thoughts.

He saw the girl then, a tall, slim figure, her tawny hair the only bright spot against the dark winter landscape. She was turning the corner of the house, coming back with long, athletic strides; obviously in order to accompany him to the mansion in private; perhaps to converse on something she did not wish her companions to hear.

Warmth flooded through Carter, as he watched her approach from the far distance. He knew he was becoming too interested in this intriguing young lady; that he should keep his thoughts not only on the difficulties which surrounded him but on the strict pursuance of his profession.

Yet there was something about Fiona Hammond which defied all logic; she was a girl he would have trusted and followed to the end of the earth. He longed to confide in her but held back; not only because of the problems that would involve but because of the danger to her own person which might follow.

He watched her for a moment longer, then bent to retrieve the documents at the base of the wall. The breeze was blowing a little more strongly now and the edges of the plans eluded him. He was still in a stooped position when he heard the girl cry out. At the same instant he heard the cables run screaming through the sheaves.

He looked up as the shadow swept across the paving. The two vast granite blocks hung suspended against the sky. The girl screamed again as he went in a desperate, scrabbling dive across the terrace. He landed against French windows with an impact that almost sent the breath from his body.

The blocks drove into the terrace with such force that the paving was split and shattered for yards around. Dust filled the air and small fragments of stone rained about, half-blinding him. The rattle of the tackle through the pulleys went on.

Carter looked up, saw the dark beard and impassive face flicker and disappear among the scaffolding. He shouted, more in impotent rage than anything else. The foreman was swinging down the ladder, and cries filled the air.

Beyond the girl's hurrying figure he could see Hemmings and Henderson breaking into a run. Fiona was above him now stooping to lift him tenderly.

"Are you all right? I was so frightened!"

Her cheek brushed his momentarily as he got to his feet. He found difficulty in standing for a moment.

"Please do not worry. I am unhurt."

He smiled at her shakily.

"And thank you for the timely warning."

The foreman had reached the ground, putting a finger to his corduroy cap.

"Apologies, sir. I don't know how that happened. You had a lucky escape."

Carter shot him a shrewd glance.

"I am well aware of that," he said drily.

The girl put her arm round his waist and led him to sit on the low stone wall. The foreman busied himself in picking up his instruments and the plans. Two men were down from the scaffolding now, looking with amazement at the vast blocks, half-buried in the paving. Carter noticed they both had thick black beards.

He smiled bitterly. He was unlikely to identify the man who had been so careless. If it had been carelessness . . . He let the dark question remain at the back of his mind. Two other bearded men stared silently from the top of the wall.

Hemmings was up now, his face purple with rage. The foreman stood with head bowed, waiting until the storm had passed. Henderson kept at a distance, watching Carter and the girl.

"Are you fit to walk, John?" she said at last.

Carter nodded. It was the first time she had used his christian name.

"It is nothing, Fiona. An accident merely. Please let us go in."

At the corner of the house he turned. Hemmings was still berating the workmen. Carter could clearly catch his drift from here. The girl's troubled eyes searched his face as they went slowly in to lunch.

Forty-One
Golden Dreams

1

"Do you think it was an accident, sir?"

Slade's bearded face was sardonic beneath his hard hat. Carter was at a loss for a moment. He had come down to the stable block at The Priory after lunch to see whether the carriage was ready and had found Pollard, Bassett's most enigmatic servant polishing brass in a cosy tack-room by a single oil lamp.

"It is a difficult question, Mr. Slade."

Slade winked grimly, giving a final polish to the pony's harness.

"Just when you were beneath, sir. Those blocks could have fallen at any time. Why just when you were beneath?"

Carter stroked his chin contemplatively. The two men were alone for the moment though there were signs of activity about the huge stable wings; the jingling of harness as the dragoons of Henderson's troop tended their own gear; the stamping of hooves; and the sharp metallic clang of a farrier's hammer.

"You have a point," he conceded.

Slade got up abruptly.

"Give me ten minutes, sir, and I will have the equipage at the front door."

"Thank you. I would appreciate it. I have a few things to do in Thornton Bassett tonight."

"Very well, Mr. Carter."

Slade had his face bowed toward the floor now but Carter could see the doubt in his eyes.

"Five men out of that building crew with beards, sir? Coincidence or design? Think about it, sir."

Carter caught at the suggestion.

"You seem to know a good deal about the business, Mr. Slade."

The tall man straightened until he was looking Carter in the eye. There was nothing but honesty and steadfastness in the glance.

"I keep myself to myself, Mr. Carter. But I also keep my eyes open. There is a good deal going on upon the moor, sir, as you have no doubt discovered for yourself."

Carter remained non-committal.

"What are you trying to tell me?"

"That if you wish for any help, at any time, you know where to find me. At Mrs. Malpleasant's, in the town. Anyone will tell you."

Carter realised there was a good deal more to Slade even than he had hitherto supposed, but this was not the time to pursue the matter.

"I appreciate your confidence, Mr. Slade," he said. "And you may be sure I will avail myself of your offer should the opportunity present itself."

Slade nodded, satisfaction shining in his eyes.

"I thought you would see it that way, Mr. Carter. Mr. Hands thought the same, did he not."

Carter drew his breath in with a thin hissing sound. Then he remembered the Rector's reiterated injunctions to caution.

"You use the past tense, Mr. Slade. Could it be that you know more than you have told me?"

There was a strange expression in the man's eyes now. Carter could not read it despite his efforts.

"I might say the same about you, sir."

The other laid an immensely strong hand upon his sleeve.

"I am merely trying to indicate, Mr. Carter, in my own way, that we are on the same side. A young man like you needs all the friends he can get upon the moor during these December nights."

Carter nodded slowly. Despite the strange manner, he was sure of his man now.

"I am certain we are upon the same side, Mr. Slade. And I will call upon you if and when there is need."

Slade slowly withdrew his hand, his strong yellow teeth glinting in his beard. He patted the flank of the brown pony, which whinnied softly with pleasure.

"There will be need, Mr. Carter," he said significantly. "It is December. You may be sure of that."

2

The girl accompanied Carter to the porch. He again glanced at the strange painting in the hallway, but he was absorbed by other problems now. Though Fiona Hammond had not spoken openly of the matter, it was obvious she was deeply disturbed by what had happened earlier on the terrace. The apologies made by Hemmings were again sounding in his ears. Carter had made light enough of the incident, though he was inwardly greatly shaken.

He had told his host that those sort of occurrences were, unfortunately, fairly common on building sites and that it was the purest coincidence he had happened to be there when the blocks fell. Hemmings was eventually satisfied though he was still breathing fire against the workmen when the time came for Carter to take his departure.

The architect had examined both the blocks and the tackle used when building operations had resumed after lunch, but he could not assign any logical reason for the accident. No-one had owned to being in charge of the tackle at the time of the fall, of course; that was standard practice and, as Slade had hinted, with no less than five men on site wearing beards, it was impossible for him to identify the man he had seen.

It was almost dusk now and though the men would be working on for a while there was no real reason for him to remain. He had to report to Mr. Pollard before the office closed and, truth to tell, the girl had sensed this and had herself suggested his early return.

Hemmings had retreated to his study, still full of apologies and Henderson, who seemed equally concerned, had now gone back down to the stables. The girl wore a white gown this afternoon and she looked striking, almost ethereal, her bodice and her cloud of tawny gold hair seeming to float out of the dark background of the panelled hall.

"Don't let this business spoil the day," Carter said. "Despite that, I have enjoyed it immensely."

The girl put one small pink hand on his fingers as they held the document case. They seemed very close at that moment, not only physically but mentally. A faint click broke the silence; for a second or so Carter thought that Henderson had returned. He remembered the officer's inexplicable appearance within the hall on an earlier visit. The incident had slipped his mind until now.

But it was only the dark-haired housekeeper, Mrs. Arkwright, hovering there nervously at the dusky foot of the great staircase at the far side of the hall.

"I am sorry, sir, to interrupt your conversation with the young lady."

She came forward apologetically. Carter smiled at her reassuringly.

"It is quite all right, Mrs. Arkwright. What is it?"

"Only that you have forgotten these plans, Mr. Carter."

She held up the thin sheaf of documents as she spoke. Carter remembered then that he had put the drawings to one side when they had returned to the house for lunch, still too shaken to clearly recollect what had happened.

He laughed and the girl joined with him.

"Thank you. It is not only this. I must have left my instrument case either in the study or the dining room. I would be grateful to you if you could find out."

"Certainly, sir."

The dark-haired woman went out quickly, as though glad to be free from an embarrassing situation.

"Mrs. Arkwright is an extremely tactful woman," Fiona Hammond said, still smiling.

"Extremely," Carter agreed.

Then the girl was in his arms, her mouth and tongue warm upon his cheek. He held her very close, again conscious of the subtle perfume of her hair. He saw the tableau they made reflected darkly in a carved mirror the other side of the hall. For a second they looked like some study by Watteau. Then she had pushed him gently away as Mrs. Arkwright came back.

Carter took the leather case from the dark woman, his heart racing. The housekeeper looked gently from one to the other as though she had guessed the situation.

Long after Fiona Hammond had closed the great door behind him, Carter carried within him the burning image of her imprisoned within his arms, as though she were about to yield to him some vast store of golden dreams.

Forty-Two
A Deadly Gift

1

POLLARD'S FACE WAS GRIM and he no longer looked like a friendly uncle as he paced the board-room, occasionally stopping to glance at his junior partner as though to assure himself that the latter was still alive.

"Fortunate indeed, Mr. Carter," he boomed for the third time. "I am sorry that this should have happened."

Carter shrugged. He felt himself again now, and Pollard had added another glass of cognac to the restoratives pressed upon him by Hemmings at The Priory.

"It was no-one's fault, sir. These things occur in the profession, unfortunately. And at least it was not our own contractor employed."

Pollard stopped as though the idea had just struck him.

"Thank God for that, Mr. Carter. Yes, that would have been a serious business."

He drew a chair to the board-room table and poured himself a generous tot of liqueur brandy with a slightly trembling hand. Carter knew then of the affection the senior partner had for him and he again warmed to his generous nature.

Pollard's eyes brightened a little as he sipped at his glass.

"Your health, Mr. Carter!" he said ironically.

He glanced at the ornate clock over the mantel.

"I am sorry to return to the world of trivia after such serious matters as we have discussed; but I would just like to consider the progress of the work with you, if you can spare the time."

"Certainly, sir. Despite their apparent carelessness in the matter of lifting tackle, these men are making really remarkable strides."

"Glad to hear it!" Pollard snapped.

Then he looked at the junior partner closely.

"Perhaps it is because they are going too fast that they are becoming careless, eh?"

Carter shrugged again.

"It may be so, sir."

He chuckled.

"If you could have heard Mr. Hemmings this afternoon! After his tirade, I do not think anything like this will happen again."

"I should hope not," said Pollard severely.

Carter raised his own glass. He felt quite normal now.

"Mr. Hemmings was full of apologies. I expect he will be down in person to apologise to you tomorrow."

Pollard nodded, swivelling his chair; his eyes looked empty and were focused upon the dying heart of the fire in the grate opposite the board-room table.

"I must say, Mr. Carter, that you have taken to this hard and difficult life upon the moor in a way which is even more encouraging than I had dared to hope. I should not like anything to happen to you personally, or to your connection with this firm for the world. Do I make myself clear?"

Carter smiled faintly.

"Perfectly, sir."

"And you have heard nothing from Mr. Hands since his strange quittal of my employment?"

The question, innocuous as it was, struck another of those faint warning bells within Carter. He recalled the similar conversation with Pollard a while back. His employer had a slightly sinister way of looking at him at times, though it may have been Carter's overheated imagination which was to blame.

"Of course not, sir. You surely remember my promise to let you know immediately there was any word of him."

Pollard bit his lip as though he had been indiscreet and a strange look passed across his shadowed face. He again turned to face the junior partner.

"So you did, Mr. Carter, so you did. Forgive me. I am not myself this evening. What with these awful tragedies at Thornton Bassett, and then this odd business of Mr. Hands. And today, an extremely serious accident which might have had tragic consequences."

He cracked his knuckles with a noise that struck Carter's taut nerves as a startling intrusion into the silence.

"It might be an idea if I drew up a memorandum for Miss Harkness, setting out a table of rules for building firms employed by us. Further to the usual safety regulations, of course."

His eyes were serious beneath the tousled grey hair.

"Imagine, Mr. Carter. Even a crippling could involve this firm in horrific sums for damages in a civil court. We must cover ourselves properly, sir."

His employer's alarm at such a fairly mundane level would have been a source of amusement to Carter at any other time, but his own visage was just as sombre as Pollard's as he stared back at the other man. The senior partner held the younger in a magnetic stare.

"You have no theories about young Hands, Mr. Carter? I should appreciate your complete confidence."

He cracked his knuckles again.

"Such conduct is completely alien to his charcter. There is a vast gap between our ages, of course. And he might well have confided something in you, however trivial, which could lead to the solution of this mystery."

Carter shook his head, his conscience gnawing at him as he lied to this good man.

"I cannot think of anything, sir. There was no hint in his manner or conversation the last time I saw him."

Pollard let out another heavy sigh.

"And the young lady? I understand she and Hands were close to an understanding?"

"That is correct, sir."

Carter had a job to keep his voice steady. The shock of Jeremy's horrible death and the charnel scene in the ravine had unnerved him more than he cared to admit. That, coupled with today's accident, had put a severe strain upon his system which even Fiona's soothing image had not entirely erased.

This was to leave aside the further mystery. Namely, who had entered Jeremy's room and destroyed a piece of evidence which was locked in a cupboard and whose existence should have been known only to Carter and Jeremy himself.

The young architect had told David Sennen, of course, and the Rector had treated the news extremely seriously. Anyone could have gone there; the house was as open as any hotel, even in winter.

Carter imagined it would have been someone well respected, perhaps even a friend of the landlady, of the two clerks staying there, or even of the two serving girls.

He—or she—could easily have slipped upstairs on some errand and opened the door with one of the keys which hung on a board in the hall; it would have been indiscreet, even dangerous in view of police involvement in events on the moor, but then, as Sennen had said, the people with whom they were dealing would stop at nothing.

Carter and Sennen had been extremely cautious this last week or two; they had had minimal contact and the Rector had again told the architect he would have news of an important kind for him a little later in the month. Despite Carter's questioning, he would not reveal anything further, and Carter had had to contain his impatience as best he might.

Now he brought his thoughts abruptly back to the present. Pollard was talking in a general way of the firm's current commissions and of Hemmings' important contract in particular. He was reiterating his strictures regarding safety precautions on site and brought the discussion to a close with a flourish, repeating his vague invitation that Carter should visit himself and his wife for dinner one evening.

2

As he walked back to his own office, glancing at the dusky square through the stairhead windows, Carter wondered how closely Slade might be involved with these shadowy events which appeared to be gathering substance and body with the steady advancement of winter.

It was unthinkable that Slade should not be open and above board; it was well-known that Pollard, Bassett was his whole life, and Carter had not taken long to sum up his character as being courageous, steadfast and open. Yet even now Carter would not mention their conversation in the stable to Sennen.

There was something so hateful and horrible in the whole atmosphere down here on the moor that even innocent conversations with people like Pollard tended to be tinged with all sorts of wild suspicions.

Carter longed to sound out the other two partners on the subject, yet he dare not. Both Innsley and Bassett had made indelible impressions on his sensitive nature, and he had found their advice and support invaluable on his various commissions about the moor. Yet it was as impossible to question them openly about his fears and suspicions as it was to engage Slade in direct conversation on these matters.

Carter paused at this point in his musings. Here was the subject of his thoughts himself. He was just in time to see the enigmatic figure of the carrier pass the newel post at the bend of the stair, on his way to the drawing office floor.

Carter was certain it was he, though it was impossible to be absolutely sure; it was very dark in that corner, even with the lighting of the gas lamps in the square outside, and he was left with an unpleasant impression of the illumination glinting on the man's eyeballs as he passed from view.

The architect stood irresolute and then moved on into his office. It had just turned five and it was a fairly quiet time of day. The offices below would soon be closing, and the hour between five and six was usually devoted to clearing one's drawing board; and, for the lesser members of the staff, the checking and preparation of correspondence and plans for post and other such mundane tasks.

Carter paused, his hand on the brass knob of his office door. There was something slightly different in the room from the way he had left it when he had gone to the board-room. Then he noticed what it was. The client's leather chair in front of his desk had been pushed slightly to one side. Carter walked up to it, his senses strained and alert.

He saw that someone had left a parcel on his desk. It was wrapped in thick brown paper and tied with string which had been sealed with wax. It was very heavy, as he found when he picked it up. It was addressed to him care of the office in a thickly inked hand, in block capitals.

Carter went round the desk, staring at the package. He hesitated again, crossed to the door and opened it. Nothing moved in the mellow lamplight of the corridor. Footsteps sounded from the floor above, and there was the usual busy hubbub coming from the drawing office below. He went back in and locked the door carefully behind him.

He tore open the brown paper carefully, refolding it, together with the string, which he cut with the scissors on his desk. There was nothing in the packet but two plain cardboard boxes. He opened the larger, and found to his amazement a blued steel pistol, which looked extremely lethal. There was nothing else in the box, and when Carter checked he found all the pistol's chambers were loaded.

He knew how to use such a weapon. He had once belonged to a club in London which specialised in teaching its members target shooting with both pistol and rifle. Carter was familiar with the make but he was extremely puzzled as he opened the second box.

As might have been expected, this contained a plentiful supply of ammunition. There was a single sheet of paper in the box, bearing the same inked block capitals as the address. The message was not signed but there was no doubt in Carter's mind as to the sender now.

The message said merely: I HOPE YOU KNOW HOW TO USE THIS. I URGE YOU MOST SINCERELY, IF YOU VALUE YOUR LIFE, TO CARRY IT WITH YOU AT ALL TIMES.

Carter was smiling as he locked his office for the night. The string and paper reposed in his overcoat pocket; he would burn them at the earliest opportunity. His locked briefcase was heavy indeed as he turned his steps toward his lodgings.

FORTY-THREE
Friendly Stranger

1

CARTER BROKE HIS most recent habit this evening. Despite the entreaties of his new-found friends, the bank clerks, he politely refused to join them, giving as his excuse pressure of work and the necessity to master his notes. Instead, he resumed the old table he had formerly occupied with Jeremy and sat in silence, his office documents scattered around him, as he waited for Pauline to bring his first course.

Mrs. Tregorran sat at her side-table by the fire but after a welcoming smile she was much up and down, supervising things in the kitchen and attending to three other tables which had been laid for supper on the other side of the room. Carter gathered that the seven or eight people gathered there were an overflow from The Bassett Arms.

He remembered there were two municipal dinners of various sorts taking place at that palatial establishment this evening and that as a result dining accommodations there would be strained. No doubt Mrs. Tregorran was grateful for the custom, and he wondered if there were to be any more people seeking accommodation for the night.

He had locked the brown paper and string from Sennen's packet in the desk in his room, but after the shock which the rifling of Jeremy's cupboard had given him, he had felt it imprudent to leave the pistol and ammunition there. That in itself would be a minor problem for the future, but he took the Rector's point.

Instead, he had secreted the pistol in the right-hand pocket of his overcoat, the ammunition in the left; in both cases jamming the articles down with his gloves. He had told his landlady he would be going back to the office after supper and had carefully folded the coat and put it down on the chair next to him.

Now he carefully studied these new diners over the upper edge of the sketch-plan he was ostensibly perusing, but could not see anyone he knew nor the slightest cause for suspicion. Nevertheless, there was deadly danger in Thornton Bassett, and he must not slacken his alertness for one second if he were to be of any use to Sennen.

The truth was, Carter thought bitterly, he simply did not know where to begin. He dare not confide in the girl, or even Hemmings and Henderson, who presented the powerful forces of the law and the military respectively. Such confidences had not prevented at least one police officer, to say nothing of curious laymen, from suffering violent deaths of the most horrific kind. Leaving aside people like Jeremy, who had observed every precaution in his secret observations of the comings and goings upon the moor.

For the hundredth time Carter pondered the problems, not the least of them the savage necessity which drove mysterious persons to kill ruthlessly and without warning in preservation of their secrets. And in such a vile and unique manner. For what secrets could justify such elaborate and complicated movements at night, in which the military were lured from one end of the moor to the other? Or for gatherings at all in such bleak and remote spots on the moor in dead of winter as well as in summer?

Carter had finished the soup now and was waiting for his main course when a shadow fell across the table.

"Is everything to your liking, Mr. Carter?"

It was Mrs. Tregorran's invariable question but she made the uttering of it and the cheerful expression on her face seem fresh-minted each time it was enunciated.

"Very well indeed, Mrs. Tregorran."

The landlady hesitated, her vivid blue eyes in the smooth face looking beyond him to the newcomers at the far tables. For the first time Carter realised that she could be only in her late thirties. It was strange he had not noticed the fact before. Perhaps because like all landladies she had an official part to play, and a young man like himself normally did not look beneath the façade.

But Jeremy and now Sennen were teaching him to probe past the surface, and he felt extraordinarily alert tonight; perhaps it was the presence of these hearty strangers. He should not forget that danger could come just as easily from that quarter. Had Sennen not said that many people in Thornton Bassett were involved in whatever was going on on the moors; and that someone close to justice gave warning when the movements of the military or the police might threaten them?

2

The landlady showed no inclination to move from her position by the table, nor to engage him in further conversation, so Carter's thoughts spun endlessly on, unchecked. He recalled then the lugubrious-looking police officer, Inspector Pepper, who had come to see him 'as a matter of routine' when Pollard had reported Hands' disappearance.

Might he have broken open the cupboard in Hands' room? But then surely he would have made official report of the matter and given the landlady some sort of document to cover the damage. She had not said anything of it, of course; but then would she in any event? No doubt the police would have asked her to keep silence. And why had not Jeremy's family come forward, unless they were abroad?

There were other anomalies, too. The door of the room had certainly been opened with the key; there was no sign of damage there. But as Carter had already realised, anyone could have borrowed one of the keys from the hall below. He had ascertained that a number of them fitted more than one door. It was often so in small country hotels and boarding houses, the management saving money by using keys and locks of a common pattern.

He raised his head from the table as the girl Pauline came back. She smiled hesitantly, and he felt she might have spoken to him had not Mrs. Tregorran been there. The landlady had found her voice now. Her face was serious and her conversation low.

"You have still heard nothing from Mr. Hands, Mr. Carter?"

The latter shook his head.

Mrs. Tregorran bit her lip.

"It is a very curious business," she said, speaking more to herself than her lodger.

"I am in something of a moral dilemma."

"Oh?"

Carter raised his eyebrows.

"You will forgive me?"

She sat down opposite him, next to the chair containing his overcoat, putting her menu-card on top of it.

"I was wondering whether I ought to let Mr. Hands' room."

She shrugged.

"I am sure you will not take this the wrong way, Mr. Carter, but times are hard and it is difficult for a person such as myself to augment income in a small place like Thornton Bassett in winter."

"I quite understand, Mrs. Tregorran," Carter said.

He bit his lip in turn. He really must watch his conversation. He was about to observe that he was sure Jeremy would not have minded, but the emphatic past tense would have alerted the landlady to the fact that he knew his friend would never be returning.

"What do you think Mr. Carter?"

Mrs. Tregorran's vivid blue eyes were fixed disarmingly on his own.

"I, Mrs. Tregorran? It hardly comes within my purview."

"But Mr. Hands is your friend. I would not wish him to come come back unexpectedly and find his room taken."

"That would be awkward," Carter agreed.

"Mr. Hands has paid up until the end of December," the dark-haired woman went on brightly. "He always insisted on paying quarterly in advance."

"Well then, I do not see the problem," Carter retorted. "If you have heard nothing by then, I am sure no-one would blame you for letting the room from January 1st."

Mrs. Tregorran nodded, looking relieved. Carter saw a slight opening and took it.

"You have not searched his belongings?"

By the dismay on the lady's face he realised he had said the wrong thing.

"Mr. Carter! That is certainly not my place."

"The police officer was here," Carter observed. "You were present in the room, I understand."

There was a faint smile on Mrs. Tregorran's face.

"That was a different matter, Mr. Carter," she said quickly.

"Instituted by Mr. Pollard, I believe. Missing persons. There have been many such instances, for example during winter when people have been snow-bound or lost upon the moor."

"Please do not misunderstand me," Carter said. "I was not suggesting anything irregular. Only that a thorough search of Mr. Hands' belongings might bring to light a letter or other evidence that support the original information he gave me regarding his sudden summons home."

The landlady shook her head.

"There was nothing, Mr. Carter. Or at least nothing that Inspector Pepper cared to impart to me. Mr. Hands' things are, of course, in his cases and in his wardrobe and there they will remain until I receive instructions from Mr. Pollard or someone else in authority."

"I will take it up with Mr. Pollard if you so wish," Carter replied.

Mrs. Tregorran inclined her head, her blue eyes again fixed on the far table.

"I would be obliged, Mr. Carter. And if you do hear from Mr. Hands . . ."

"You will be the first to learn," he assured her.

He finished the repast quickly, his mind endlessly revolving the possibilities. He was sure there would be nothing in Jeremy's belongings. Truth to tell, he had thought of making a search himself, but that would have been too risky under the circumstances.

Even in the middle of the night Mrs. Tregorran or one of her staff might have discovered him. The last thing he wanted was for the police to suspect him of anything underhand.

Besides, as Mrs. Tregorran had hinted, if an official detective had searched the place there would surely be nothing for an amateur like himself to find. Carter reached the end of the meal and got up, his mind still in a turmoil. He was halfway to the door when he remembered his overcoat.

He came back, almost cannoning into a florid-faced, middle-aged man who had been dining with the party of strangers. He smelt the acrid tang of whisky. To his dismay the man made a clumsy gesture of apology and picked up the overcoat. He helped Carter on with it, the architect pulling away, conscious of the reek of whisky close to his cheek.

"My apologies, sir," the florid man said.

He had a foolish smile on his face but there was something in his eyes which Carter didn't like. The man patted the overcoat pocket, jovially.

"What on earth have you got in here?" he asked, embracing the room in his question.

"Ironmongery?"

He laughed loudly as Carter went quickly out and down the hallway. He could feel a hot flush on his cheeks in the freezing night air and he did not slacken his pace until he had gained the darkness of the porch at the Pollard, Bassett offices.

He ascended rapidly to his office. He must not make too much of the incident. Perhaps the man had meant well. But it had been an ugly moment. That was the trouble with subterfuge; one saw or suspected dozens of things which might be mere trivia or coincidence. He longed to talk with Sennen.

But the Rector had said he would send for him when it was necessary. Carter sat down at his desk, turning up the lamp. He wondered whether Sennen had heard anything of the incident at The Priory today. Surely it would have travelled via Slade long before now. Perhaps that was why Sennen had sent him the revolver.

Slade had certainly brought it. Carter stared at his drawing-board, which held a half-completed sketch of details of the museum rooms for Hemmings.

He got up, throwing all doubts and fears from him. Five minutes later he was seated before the white paper, completely absorbed in his professional duties.

FORTY-FOUR
Anti-Christ

1

"THERE IS SOMETHING big afoot," Sennen said.

His eyes looked enormous as he stared at Carter from his great chair by the Rectory study fire and selected a spill for his stubby black pipe.

"I should have something more tangible for you in a day or two," he went on.

He indicated the scattered papers on his desk.

"I am working on the details now."

"But how can you be so certain?" Carter asked.

"Patterns, Mr. Carter, patterns," the Rector went on gently. "If you have the time I shall endeavour to explain a little more fully."

Carter fought back his rising impatience. The Rector had listened stolidly to his long catalogue of fears and suspicions and had shrewdly extracted the grain from the chaff.

"You have that pistol by you," he said sharply.

Carter nodded. He tapped the faint bulge in his breast pocket.

"Is this your own weapon?"

"I had a pastorate in Africa once," the Rector said. "I quickly learned to shoot accurately and to react in moments of danger. I can assure you I would like a guinea for every time I have used that weapon in a tight corner."

Carter stared at the dark-haired cleric with a slight sense of shock. More and more layers were emerging as the top surfaces peeled away. Sennen really was the most extraordinary clergyman he had ever met.

Now the deep-set eyes in the ravaged face were fixed with riveting intensity upon the architect. The Rector got up quickly and came back with controlled energy to the desk. It was after ten now and Carter had arrived half an hour before, following an urgent summons delivered verbally to him by Slade, who had approached him unobtrusively in the public bar of The Bassett Arms.

Though it was obvious that Pollard's curious employee was heavily engaged in the Rector's enterprises Carter had not liked to broach the subject himself. Sennen would tell him in due time.

He waited while the Rector put his pipe down and went across for the decanter tray and glasses. He gave the other a quick smile.

"We must compensate for your broken sojourn at our local hotel," he said.

Carter waited until the drinks had been poured.

"So you think that accident at The Priory was no accident?"

Sennen's eyes were sombre above the rim of his glass.

"Undoubtedly not, Mr. Carter. It could have been an accident; there was the cleverness of it. If the girl had not come back . . ."

He broke off suddenly, once again bent over, as on the occasion of Carter's previous visit; as though listening for the faint tread of the suspicious housekeeper. Carter himself was becoming increasingly infected with the poisonous atmosphere of the town, which seemed to be gathering inexorably like the mist crouching on the moor.

"That was what prompted you to send me the pistol yesterday?"

The Rector shook his head.

"I should have sent it in any case," he said crisply. "If I had known young Hands' purpose I could have saved his life."

Carter's eyes held the other's for a long second.

"You have him . . .?" he began.

Sennen nodded slowly.

"He is safe enough," he said gently. "And in sanctified ground."

He resumed his discourse.

"But our first thoughts are for the living. You burnt the wrappings of that packet, of course?"

"Up on the moor, this morning," Carter went on.

The Rector picked up his pipe again.

"That is good. I cannot emphasise strongly enough the absolute necessity for you to obey my instructions to the letter if we are to deal with these abominations."

Carter went on staring at his companion, his glass untasted.

"You sound as if you think something supernatural is involved."

The Rector nodded.

"We are dealing with anti-Christ!" he said.

2

There was a long silence in the study and during that time the echoes of Sennen's last sentence seemed to reverberate and re-echo from every corner of the gallery and back from the serried ranks of leather-bound books. Carter was the first to break the silence.

"You do not mean that literally, sir?"

Sennen looked at him grimly.

"I most certainly do, my dear young man. Which is why I am entreating you to regard the matter as seriously as I myself."

"But the pistol . . ." Carter began.

The Rector gave him a quick smile.

"I see your problem. The Devil has never suffered from a shortage of corporeal servants. The people we are up against are flesh and blood all right. Though I do not yet know their identities. But they certainly work for an unholy Master."

That reminded Carter of something he had not yet told Sennen.

"There was a man, last night," he began. "A big, florid man who had had too much to drink. I had the pistol and ammunition in my overcoat pockets and kept the coat on a chair at my table as I ate my supper."

Sennen folded his hands on the desk and regarded his guest steadily through his curling pipe-smoke.

"Go on."

"The man tried to help on me with my coat," Carter said. "He made a joke to the whole room about the weight of my pockets. Something about ironmongery."

Sennen slowly shook his head. Little sparks of humour had replaced the concern at the back of his eyes.

"You were indiscreet, Mr. Carter, but I do not think any great harm has been done. The people we are up against do not operate in that manner. And they would not draw such things to the attention of all and sundry."

Carter felt relief flood through him.

"And in any event," Sennen went on, "it would not be too difficult to trace the man. Surely his identity would be known to Mrs. Tregorran. You may leave it to me to make discreet inquiries."

"As you wish, Mr. Sennen."

"We have more important matters to discuss, Mr. Carter."

The Rector got up and walked over restlessly to poke the fire. The flames flickered higher, making a tired mask of his strong, sorrowful face. Carter stared at the shadowed study with its gallery of books, its marching ranks of leather spines in the big oak shelves on the ground floor, and its scattered apparatus of scholarship.

He gave a shiver as he thought of the wintry moor outside, looming over Thornton Bassett like some malign presence; of the miles of black scrub, granite and boulders; of the tors, seemingly representative of some pagan presence; and of the sentient mass of the fog, white and ghastly as it rolled inexorably forward, smothering and drowning everything in its path, cloaking evil deeds. At that moment Sennen seemed to him to be the one representative of Christian sanity against the powers of darkness.

The Rector came back to his place at the desk and quietly sipped at his glass.

"What do you know of Black Magic and the unholy arts?" he asked gently.

"Nothing, sir," said Carter frankly.

Sennen smiled.

"That is well-said, Mr. Carter. It will save a deal of time if we leave out my years of study of such things; of my investigations here and in places like Africa; of my suspicions regarding the moor and of Thornton Bassett; and my strong belief that for some reason not well understood by me at present this area is a focus for evil presences and unnatural practices."

There was a breathless silence in the study now which Carter did nothing to disturb.

"In mediæval times, Mr. Carter," Sennen continued, "there were sporadic outbursts of sadism and flagellation throughout Europe. Their origin was obscure, partly sexual, entirely hysterical. Whole communities were involved."

His deep-set eyes held Carter's own.

"When I say that the activities of these flagellants often preceded outbreaks of The Plague, you may gather something of my drift."

"I am trying, sir."

Sennen raised his eyebrows.

"I think not, Mr. Carter," he said gently. "The plague was better known as The Black Death."

Carter felt a dryness in his throat and had difficulty in speaking.

"You think someone may have reanimated these practices?" he enunciated at last.

Sennen nodded, his eyes bright.

"For peculiarly modern purposes of perversion. And with a horribly up-to-date version of The Black Death. I will not—and cannot—go into these abominations at great length at the present time. We have so little information on the matter."

"You think something else may be happening soon, sir?"

The Rector's voice was so faint Carter had difficulty in catching it.

"Very soon, Mr. Carter. In two days' time, in fact. Which is why I have asked you here. We must lay our plans with some care."

Forty-Five
The Feast of Asses

1

"HAVE YOU EVER heard of the Feast of Asses?"

The fire was growing low again, and the Rector got up to replenish it. Carter shook his head. He felt an intellectual pygmy by the side of this man who was so learned in such arcane and esoteric subjects.

Sennen resumed his place at the desk.

"You need not look so nonplussed, Mr. Carter. Very few people have. It was a particularly blasphemous ceremony which took place in the Middle Ages, among depraved devotees of witchcraft and black magic. An ass was usually present and a Black Mass was performed, often in a sacred place such as an actual church. The perverted services and festivities sometimes went on for days. A Pope of Fools was chosen, and great sexual depravity was the rule."

"You are thinking of a particular location?"

Sennen nodded gravely.

"Of course, Mr. Carter. Rats' Castle was formerly a sacred place of worship, if I read my local history aright."

He leaned forward across the desk, his eyes boring into his guest's.

"I have often spoken to you of patterns during the past days, Mr. Carter. One sort of pattern was that of movements; of people coming and going across the moor. Another was a calendar pattern. Of a cycle of events in the Black Calendar of the year. Of particular days or seasons in which the Black Arts were performed."

"You spoke of something happening, Mr. Sennen. Can you be certain as to the actual day?"

Sennen nodded again.

"I can on this occasion, Mr. Carter. I have selected the day after tomorrow as being of particular significance. I think Rats' Castle will be the venue. I have my reasons for this; principally because there was a great display made of lights in the ruins on the last occasion when the military were out."

Sennen picked up his stubby black pipe and turned it over nervously in his restlessly moving hands.

"You may recall the lights were extinguished when the searchers were about half a mile off. The troops were on a wild-goose chase, while the actual meeting was taking place at a sheltered spot among the tors some ten miles to the west. My telescope confirmed that."

"You think that on the night you have selected there will be some visible demonstration to the west this time?"

Sennen put his pipe back in his mouth and rubbed his strong hands together with crackling satisfaction.

"I do, Mr. Carter. Because it follows the pattern established. I have been careful to keep off the moor in person, to allay suspicion. But I have followed much with my telescope from the tower. I needed a resolute young man on the ground. I have found that man."

He held his head on one side as though listening for some manifestation that was not audible to Carter. The latter was held in a strong thrall of something like horror now. If what Sennen said was true there were abominable things abroad upon the moor, even more vile and unspeakable than had hitherto been hinted. He knew the role the Rector had chosen for him and he would not flinch from it, despite the dangers.

"You think whatever is happening out there the day after tomorrow will happen at the old ruins, after the military have been drawn off to the west?"

"I do, Mr. Carter. Most sincerely."

"But would it not, in those circumstances, simply be best to go to the police and lay a trap for these people?"

Sennen's face expressed incredulity now.

"Come, Mr. Carter! I thought I had already made my purpose clear. As well advertise one's intentions in the local newspaper! Besides, it is of no use catching the rank and file. We want to destroy the ring-leaders, to bring these murders home to the true culprits; to do that, we must be as secret as they themselves."

"I cannot argue with that, sir."

"Good."

Sennen was looking at him inquiringly.

"The main question now, Mr. Carter, is whether your nerves will be equal to the strain I am proposing to lay upon them. I am, after all, asking you to undergo fearful risks."

Carter had no hesitation now. He briskly tapped the bulk of the revolver beneath the thick material of his jacket.

"Thanks to you, I have some form of life insurance, sir. I am your man."

2

"Can you put your affairs in order and be here at about seven o'clock on the night I have selected?"

Carter nodded. Another hour had passed but all his senses were alert and strained as the Rector had put his proposals. They were bold and well thought-out but there were appalling risks, as Sennen himself had been at pains to observe.

"I will be here, Mr. Sennen, unless I hear to the contrary. You do not wish me to come to the Rectory itself?"

Sennen shook his head.

"That would never do. Meet me at the tower door. Knock three times, and I will let you in. We will go direct to the telescope. Unless the mist be too thick I shall soon see if there are any visible signs of activity to the west. We must then base our plan of operations on direct observation."

He knocked out his pipe in a stoneware ashtray on the desk.

"I will drive you up the eastward road at an appropriate time. I have a sick call to make at a cottage that way, which will give me a plausible excuse for being there. I will then return to the Rectory with all speed to take my place upon the tower. But as you appreciate everything depends on you."

"What about the hounds?" Carter asked.

Sennen's face was grave and concerned.

"That is the most dangerous factor, Mr. Carter. I have not underestimated it. I have strong reasons for supposing them to be kept on leash unless some definite demonstration be needed. After all, they could not afford to have them running loose while they are engaged up there."

He made an ugly clicking noise with his tongue against his teeth.

"I can only hope and pray that you will not need to use your pistol under those circumstances. And urge you once again not to expose your person to unnecessary danger. After all, what we principally want is names and descriptions of persons taking part. I think I can trust you for that."

"You can indeed, sir," said Carter fervently.

He turned back to Sennen's books.

"It is comparatively early yet, sir. Can you not tell me more of these sects and practices of which you have already hinted?"

Sennen shook his head vehemently.

"The whole thing already sounds too fantastic for words, Mr. Carter. If I were to enumerate the details you might not want to go out there at all. If I were not certain of your nerve; if I were not equally certain of your tempered desire to avenge Jeremy Hands, I would not ask. But these horrors in the parish have to be stamped out. At last, after years of secret struggle, I have the instrument to hand. That instrument is you, Mr. Carter."

He replaced the cork in the whisky bottle with a harsh abrupt movement as though he were stamping out something unspeakably evil with the palm of his hand.

"If you have the desire and the courage to carry it through; I would not ask you to do something I would not do myself, except that I no longer have the physical resilience and strength for such a task, and that there must be someone to eventually lay the full story before the authorities in the event of failure."

"You think there is much danger, then?"

The haunted face was turned to him.

"There is much danger, Mr. Carter. I cannot over-emphasise it. But equally much of it can be minimised if we are fully prepared and properly rehearsed in what we are to do."

He glanced over toward the dying fire.

"Slade is a good man," he said irrelevantly. "He will be acting as a reserve."

Though he forebore to question the Rector further Carter felt strength and comfort in his words.

"We must be flexible above all, Mr. Carter. That is why I have given you an outline of the salient points tonight. If you come early on Friday then we shall be able to complete our plans in the knowledge of the latest information and in full cognisance of the weather conditions on that evening."

"I would like to see Miss Hammond again before I go out, sir."

There was alarm on the Rector's face.

"You are surely not intending to confide in the young lady, Mr. Carter? It would be extremely rash."

Carter turned toward his host helplessly.

"But if there is great danger . . . You see, something has happened . . ."

There was great gentleness on the Rector's face now.

"You are both very fond of one another, are you not? Close to an understanding, perhaps?"

Carter nodded.

"Nothing has been said in so many words. But one knows in such situations."

Sennen shrugged.

"One can imagine. Even so, I would advise against any such confidences, however hard it may be for you. You will attend at The Priory daily, will you not, to supervise Mr. Hemmings' new commission. Let your glimpses of this young lady suffice, Mr. Carter, until this dark business is over. You may put Miss Hammond in danger if you persist in such folly. I will act as your liaison with the young lady when I think it is safe."

Carter bit his lip. He had not thought of these things. Sennen was right, of course.

"I will do as you say, sir."

Ten minutes later Sennen let him out at the side porch into a pitch-black night, a rasping wind gusting round the building. The darkness of his surroundings was as nothing compared with the texture of his thoughts.

Forty-Six
Good News

1

"YOU ARE QUIET, JOHN."

Fiona Hammond looked up from her sewing at the other side of the elegant morning room into which Carter had been shown a few minutes earlier. It was dusk now and operations on Hemmings' new galleries had been completed for the day, though a few workmen remained, still chipping off loose mortar by the light of oil-lanterns.

Carter was well-pleased with progress, but tired by his tramping about the moor during the earlier part of the day and by his activities at The Priory since lunch-time.

Slade had driven him as usual, but Carter had not broached the matter which had been several times on the tip of his tongue. Slade was in some respects a strange and taciturn individual and he would not appreciate Carter's breach of protocol, except perhaps with the Rector's express permission. Carter again wondered how many other secrets the man kept from him. Perhaps he also maintained a watching brief for Pollard, a paternal interest to see that his junior partner came to no harm through an excess of youthful indiscretion.

Carter smiled wryly to himself. He and Miss Hammond were waiting for Mrs. Arkwright to bring the tea, and then he would seek out Slade in the stable for the homeward journey. He understood Hemmings was currently from home on judicial business and he had seen nothing of Henderson; neither had he enquired.

When the girl spoke he had been staring at the pattern of the paper on the opposite wall; it was an intricately whorled design of great complexity and reminded him all too vividly of the tangled skein in which his own affairs rested.

"It is so pleasant here, Fiona. Soothing and restful after the bustle of the office and the windy bluster of the moor."

The girl smiled, her eyes sympathetic beneath the tawny gold hair.

"I hope you are not still shaken from that dreadful accident. Uncle has been into the matter most thoroughly, and both he and I are convinced that, though criminally careless, there was no malice intended."

She frowned.

"Uncle will not leave it there. The man responsible must be made to own up."

She went on almost fiercely.

"Uncle is most explicit about things like that. He was always telling me from my earlier years that responsibilities had to be faced up to."

Carter smiled.

"He was quite right," he said gently. "And I am sure you have always faced up to yours."

The girl bent her eyes to her sewing again. Today she wore a plain dress with a faint floral motif that set off her youthful figure, and there was an intensity and brightness about her in the glow of the lamps within the dusky room that caught at his heart. For a moment he had almost blurted out a confidence and then the Rector's reproachful face rose before him to crush out the instinct.

"Uncle has a meeting with the board of the company next week," the girl went on. "He will convey to his fellow directors the gravity with which he views the incident."

"I wish he would not," Carter said softly. "Let us leave the subject, shall we? It was unpleasant but it is behind us."

The girl looked up quickly, her eyes searching his face.

"You seem to make light of it, John," she said, a slight note of reproach in her voice. "Uncle was concerned only with your safety and welfare."

"I am certain of that, Fiona," said Carter hastily. "I am only too conscious of his generosity of spirit."

The girl smiled again then, at ease once more. Carter lapsed into silence, his ears catching the faint squeak of the trolley outside as Mrs. Arkwright approached with the tea-things.

Truth to tell he was enjoying this brief twilight hour much as a soldier on leave would, when between two battles. He could not keep his mind off tomorrow night and the dangers it might bring. Most of all he was regretting that he could not convey to this charming girl something of his inmost feelings and his concern for her.

Carter was no more a coward than the next man, but he was not looking forward to setting off across the moor alone at dead of night on such a weird and reckless adventure. But he had given his word to the Rector and he would not back out now.

There was a mumbling of voices in the corridor and the double-doors were suddenly thrust open. There was bitter disappointment in Carter's heart as he stared into the unsympathetic face of Captain Michael Henderson.

2

"Tea! Good!"

The Captain rubbed his hands together briskly and glanced with scarcely veiled hostility at Carter, his gaze softening as it lighted on the girl. Mrs. Arkwright kept her face averted as she followed with the trolley. Carter knew he was being childish but the mood was wrecked, and he sensed that the dragoon officer was revelling in the situation.

The man was going round now, turning up the lamps as though he were in his own home, chasing the romantic shadows from the corners, reflecting back harsh light brilliantly from the mirrors.

"Good evening, Captain," said Carter politely.

It would not do to let his dislike show too evidently. The girl shot him an approving glance. At least he had done the right thing. Mrs. Arkwright went about the room briskly, preparing tea, apparently oblivious of the atmosphere.

Henderson glanced at Carter quickly, a little taken aback at the other's jovial greeting, and gave him a grudging bow. The girl had put down her sewing now and had come to the fireside to preside at the large silver teapot. The Captain stood on the hearthrug, bowing his legs slightly and holding out his hands to the blaze so that Carter imagined he had just come from the coldness of the stables.

He was glad he had locked the revolver and ammunition in his document case. True to Sennen's injunction, he never travelled anywhere without it now, but it would never have done to have carried it in the house. The architect was wearing a fairly thin suit today, and the trained eye of the soldier would soon have noted the tell-tale bulge of the weapon.

The case was on a chair quite close to where he was sitting and as he went to fetch his cup from Fiona Hammond he casually removed the article and put it down against the leg of his chair, as though to make room for the Captain. But Henderson had no intention of sitting so close to his rival. He remained on his feet, near the girl, watching her tea preparations with approval.

He wore the undress uniform that Carter had previously noted, together with the curious military boots that repeated the faint red stripe of the uniform trousers.

Then he sat down on a small stool at the girl's feet and engaged her in low, bantering conversation that deliberately excluded Carter. Despite his rising irritation the latter merely sipped his tea and ate the biscuits the girl had given him on a delicate china plate, and kept his expression neutral.

But Fiona Hammond had not missed the atmosphere in the room and did her best to enliven things, drawing both young men into the conversation, with an occasional appeal to Mrs. Arkwright, so that a stranger would have noticed nothing amiss. Carter realised now that he would have no chance to talk with the girl privately.

Henderson was obviously settled for an hour or two, and it would be difficult, not to say indelicate, to draw the girl out to another room for a private conversation.

So Carter took his leave a few minutes later, with profuse thanks, keeping his manner normal and commonplace. The girl was puzzled and a little upset—Carter could see it in her eyes—but she murmured some polite banality as she took his hand in front of Henderson and Mrs. Arkwright, who had remained on the pretext of replenishing the fire.

Carter walked back down the hall, anger burning inside him. He was arrested by the sudden footsteps of Mrs. Arkwright as he was shrugging on his overcoat. She brought him the case he had forgotten in his sudden departure and a note from the girl, which she produced from a pocket of her severely cut costume.

She leaned forward to Carter with a faint smile.

"Circumstances are seldom what they seem, Mr. Carter," she said mysteriously.

Carter smiled too, all his anger dissolved. He put the note in his pocket.

"Thank you, Mrs. Arkwright. I quite understand."

He went out into the glimmer of the porch-light, hearing the clatter of hooves as Slade brought the closed carriage round. He got up with the driver, aware of Mrs. Arkwright's face as a vague oval blur at the door as she closed it.

It was a cold, dark night with just the faintest trace of mist, and the inclemency of the weather seemed to have penetrated into the interior of the carriage. Carter made a faint clicking noise of irritation as he felt the case at his feet; due to his carelessness he had nearly left it behind. All was well; the revolver and ammunition were safe inside. He could feel their outlines with his finger-tips. But Mrs. Arkwright might have suspected something by the weight. That could not be helped now.

Slade's sharp eyes sought his beneath the brim of the hard hat.

"Something wrong, sir?"

"Nothing really," Carter said. "Just the Captain's attitude."

"Oh, that!"

Slade spat expertly through the open top of the side window, then closed it tight.

"Soldiers! I shouldn't worry about them! They come and go, sir."

He winked broadly at the horse's ears, avoiding such familiarity to Carter.

"But civilians abide."

He gave Carter a kind glance.

"But if you want to read your letter, sir, don't mind me."

Carter flushed slightly as he stared sharply at the other. Then he smiled, drawing out the sheet of notepaper covered with small writing in the girl's own hand. He smoothed it and leaned forward to read it by the light of the side lamp.

Slade glanced at him from time to time with deep satisfaction.

"I hope it's sort of good news, sir," he said at last, smiling faintly at Carter's expression.

The architect came to himself with a start. His cheeks were a little redder than the state of the weather warranted.

"Sort of very good news, thank you, Slade," he said.

FORTY-SEVEN
Flame in the Darkness

1

THE BREATH SMOKED out of Carter's nostrils as thick as plumes of steam in the bitter air as the patient pony drew the Rector's trap higher up the moorland road. The moon was obscured by heavy cloud, and Carter was aware of the moor merely as a series of dark, brooding humps that ascended in a series of waves to the even darker sky.

The two men got down as the road became steeper and the pony slackened its pace, glad of the easier load. Sennen had been silent ever since they had left the tower and his constant vigil with the telescope.

"You are certain this is the night, sir?"

Sennen shook his head.

"One can never be certain of anything in this life, Mr. Carter, except uncertainty. But people have been leaving the village on foot ever since dusk."

"I saw nothing of them, sir, even with the telescope."

The Rector shook his head impatiently.

"That is because you do not know what to look for. You have all the details of our arrangements in your mind?"

"Certainly, sir. A good deal may depend upon it."

Sennen gave him a bleak smile.

"You may be sure of that, Mr. Carter, if of nothing else."

He leaned forward to the other, fixing him with those sombre eyes.

"If you are in grave danger, fire the maroon. I have made certain arrangements for that eventuality."

Carter felt reassurance at his words, but he forbore to question the Rector further. The desperate adventure to which they were pledged seemed absolute madness, on quiet reflection. He had slept brokenly the previous night, his waking dreams tinged with the nightmare of Jeremy Hands' charred remains.

An even darker suspicion was colouring his thoughts even now; an unworthy supposition that made him search the Rector's dusky face with even greater attention than usual. Supposing—and it was an awful thing—the Rector was in some way connected with these terrible occurrences upon the moor; and that he had involved Carter's assistance under the guise of a friend? That Carter himself might be lured to unsuspecting death out there in the dangerous darkness? It was a thought not to be borne and the Rector's own face seemed clouded with doubt, as if his quick and scholarly mind had grasped something of the young man's difficulties.

He stopped the pony for a moment and faced Carter squarely. The moon, coming out briefly from the clouds, turned the lonely road to a ribbon of silver and made of Sennen's sorrowful face a steel engraving.

"You do trust me, Mr. Carter?"

Carter gazed for one second more and then all his doubts were dissolved away. He clasped the other's hand impulsively.

"With my life, sir!"

Sennen nodded, his face clearing.

"It is good that we two are involved in this great business. If we are successful there will be such a purging and cleansing upon the moor as has not been seen since mediæval times. Be strong, Mr. Carter. If we both keep our heads, right will prevail, never fear."

"I will do my best, sir."

"I never doubted it. I am only sorry that such a burden should be laid upon such young shoulders. You have the pistol there? And you know how to work the flare apparatus? It is fired automatically once you have cocked the handle."

He smiled thinly, starting the pony again.

"It is a nautical device which I obtained from a ship's chandler many years ago. It could come in very useful this evening."

"I think I understand everything, Mr. Sennen."

The two men walked on in silence for another half mile. There was no sound at all now except for the clatter of the pony's hooves and the creak of the trap-harness. The Rector looked anxiously at the dark sky.

"If only the mist holds off . . ." he said. "I will do my best to get back to the tower within the hour. And if I see the flare I will get your rescue party moving without delay."

The trap was travelling without lamps, a necessary precaution, and Sennen studied his watch by the dim light of the moon, his eyes wrinkled with concentration.

"It is only eight o'clock now. I should be back at the tower by half-past nine at the latest, which will give me time to stable the pony."

He gave Carter another of his faint smiles.

"I do not expect anything much to happen before midnight. You think you can find your way, following my instructions?"

"I hope so, sir. After all, I have almost four hours."

Sennen frowned.

"We cannot rely upon that. And you must be well concealed before these people assemble."

Sennen stopped the trap again, pointing to a small lane which led off among the frowning rocks.

"The cottages I seek are here. We must part now."

"Very well, sir. And if the mist comes?"

Sennen's eyes were troubled once more.

"We must take that chance. And if so, it may act in your favour as well as against."

"That is true, sir. Until we meet again."

Sennen grasped the young man's hand with great fervour.

"God keep you well, Mr. Carter."

He remained staring after the athletic figure of the architect; the moon had gone in now, and Carter's receding form was soon swallowed in the encroaching dusk.

2

It took another twenty minutes of steady walking before Carter found the milestone of which Sennen had spoken. He looked quickly up and down the faint scratch of road which bisected the moor. There was nothing visible. In fact he could not see more than a hundred yards in either direction, the night was so dark now. And, apart from the scream of a nocturnal bird, the moor itself, bleak, freezing and remote, seemed like a blanket in which every movement which bespoke life would drown and suffocate. Far off to the east and again to the west, where Carter knew the vast spaces of Dartmoor rolled beneath the sky, it was so gloomy that he had no way of knowing which was hillside and which was cloud. The night was freezing cold but Carter's stiff walk had warmed him pleasantly.

He put down the case he carried and checked everything anxiously. Sennen had insisted on him carrying an anonymous canvas bag, such as workmen used; which would not identify him if he had to leave it on the moor in a hurry.

Within it reposed the cumbersome flare pistol, with its printed instructions; pencils, and a sketch-pad; there was also a dark-lantern and matches in a waterproof wallet. Sennen had warned him of the wet places on the moor and had asked him to pay particular regard to the stream. He could see its course in his mind's eye and knew that it lay somewhere not two miles off from the ridge on which he was standing.

The bulk of the revolver made a comforting pressure against his chest, and the box of cartridges reposed in his right-hand overcoat pocket. For the rest, he had a small flask of brandy and a packet of sandwiches which Sennen himself had made up in the Rectory kitchen after his housekeeper had retired to her own quarters. Apart from that he carried nothing with him except a handkerchief.

All his personal effects, his pocket-book, and documents which could identify him had been left at the Rectory. It was only commonsense but it had sinister connotations to Carter as he stepped off the road, and he conquered his fears and misgivings with some difficulty.

He wished now he had insisted on retaining his watch; but it bore his initials which had made Sennen veto its retention. The Rector had told him he could easily tell the hour and the quarters by the chiming of the church clock which carried clearly up here, and Carter agreed that, once again, his mentor was right.

If he had his watch with him he would have been worried in case it smashed against the rocks; and he would inevitably be consulting it every few minutes. As if to mock his thoughts he caught the silver notes, sharp and clear, drifting up from the far distances of Thornton Bassett. He identified the chime. It was half-past eight, and he had only made his way some hundred yards, with great caution, down the scree-strewn slope, now bonded heavily with frost.

Carter slightly increased his pace, but taking great care even in the stout boots he was wearing; Sennen had also warned him of the dangers of turning his ankle on the rough ground. That could be fatal under the present conditions. If his presence were discovered by illdoers near Rats' Castle it might well be the end of him, handicapped by a sprained or broken ankle.

He was slowly descending, and his eyes made out the nearest detail, the slopes, the granite boulders scattered here and there and, once, a small hut-like structure made of flat stones which looked to be pre-historic in its construction.

Carter was progressing with incredible slowness but at least his exertions were keeping the cold at bay; despite his gloves his fingers were becoming slightly numb with the damp, freezing atmosphere here, and he changed the canvas bag from his right to his left hand.

The moon came out briefly while he was doing this and though its beams did not penetrate far into the ravine-like fold between the hillsides down which he was painfully making his way, it did at least help to locate his position. He was satisfied that he was roughly on the route he had worked out with Sennen and he noted carefully the sparse details of a possible passage between the boulders of the opposite hill.

He rested for a moment or two in the shadow of a vast rock at the foot of the slope and then went slowly on up the opposite mass, stopping every few yards to catch his breath. He looked back once but could see nothing but an impenetrable black wall with a slightly lighter segment which could only be the sky. He had got about two hundred yards up the opposing face when the clock struck again. This time it was nine o'clock. Carter must have missed the quarter hour when he was down in the ravine.

He felt rather blown, but he knew he must keep on if he were to reach his appointed place in time. His muscles were hard and strong; he had youth on his side, and his mode of life had kept him reasonably fit and active. For the next half-hour he put out every effort, winding round boulders, being careful how he trod the scree, and using every endeavour to conserve his energy.

Even so he was drenched with perspiration, his heart thudding uncomfortably when he again started going downhill into another long ravine which was filled with darkness. There was mist here too, and he looked anxiously up to the facing slope, concerned in case fog should descend and blot out his objective both from himself and from Sennen who should by now be preparing to get into position on the tower.

He had not heard the clock for some time; he had either been too absorbed or perhaps the direction of the wind had changed. It was cold on these upper slopes, the gusting breeze chilling the perspiration on his face, and he made haste to get down to a lower level. He could hear the stream now; it was in full spate and its sound carried a long way. He felt relief, knowing he was, perhaps not exactly, but somewhere near where he should be.

In another ten minutes he had come across the foaming white water, already overlaid with a thin ribbon of mist; he cast about him for some while, looking for a place to cross, chill beadlets coating his features where the moisture rebounded from the rocks.

He found a sort of stone bridge in the end, where flat blocks met crazily, and slithered uneasily across. Once up the opposing slope the going was a little easier; there was a beaten path that looped between great boulders. For moment Carter thought he might have discovered the same route he had covered so long ago with the girl. Then a moment's reflection convinced him that the supposition was unlikely. He and Fiona Hammond had approached their destination from the road far to the west. Even so the thought of the girl cheered him in his present situation.

He changed the bag back to his right hand again and went on, more cautiously this time, being careful where he put his feet and making sure he made as little noise as possible. Sound carried on these upper slopes, and a fragment of stone, loosed from its bonding of frost, could bounce and rattle its way from top to bottom with alarming noises in the still of the night.

At last, after dint of much hard climbing, Carter reached a plateau of rough grassland, emerging from a defile of dark boulders. He knelt down and surveyed the ground cautiously. He could see nothing suspicious; the moon was again obscured by heavy cloud, and the light mist persisted. There was only a stunted tree or two in the middle distance, and then the slope went upward to a scarp of massive rocks.

Somewhere up there must lie his destination. As Carter hesitated he again heard the brittle chime from far away in Thornton Bassett; the wind must be blowing directly from the town. His straining ears made out the half-hour again. Surely not half-past ten already.

Then a moment's reflection satisfied him that it must be so. He had been making uphill for a long time; the way must have been longer than he had imagined. He went across the turf at a crouching run, taking as little time as possible to cross the open space. Only when he had gained the shelter of the rocks at the escarpment did he draw breath easily. He rested then for ten minutes, eating one of the sandwiches in the packet and taking a sip of the cognac Sennen had thoughtfully provided.

His mind again revolved Sennen's weird suppositions. What if all the Rector's elaborate theories turned out to be chimeras, born of the man's solitude and his inward-turning, scholarly life? Yet nothing could be so fantastic as the reality of hounds and men riding in the night, of murders of innocent people, of victims being burned to death in some inexplicable manner, their charred corpses left as a warning to intruders such as himself.

Carter felt his resolution falter and he fought back the black thoughts that came crowding in. He reached for the pistol, took it from his breast-pocket. He put it in his right-hand overcoat pocket where he could get at it in emergency, transferred the ammunition to his left.

Then he picked up the canvas pouch and started on the last stage of his journey. He soon saw that he had made one serious miscalculation. He had landed beneath an almost precipitous ridge, where boulders were tumbled outward at bizarre angles.

It was an impossible place to climb, but if he went to the right there was an easy ascent over what looked almost like meadowland. But who knew what he might run into there? If sentinels were posted—or, even worse, if there were dogs—he would be discovered immediately, and the consequences could be serious indeed.

Carter persisted; he stayed over in the shadow and went down to the left. Presently his stubbornness was rewarded; he found a large fracture in the rock and within the granite walls so exposed, a small defile which led upwards in a zig-zag fashion. By dint of much work and squeezing, Carter felt his way. He emerged into the remains of thick gorse and furze, much blasted by cold of winter, but still presenting some cover.

From here he worked up to the rim of a great fringe of boulders. He was using the utmost caution now, and his heart leaped when he saw the faint outline of vast pillars and slabs of masonry against the dark sky. Rats' Castle! There was no doubt about it. If Carter had been an experienced navigator using chart and compass he could not have managed it better.

Sometimes, by sheer accident, amateurs triumphed where a more experienced man might have failed in the confused, baffling ground which he had covered that night. It was the merest good fortune, of course, and Carter determined to make the most of it. He could not afford any error now.

He wriggled over quietly, found a spot which commanded a good view of the ruins; concealed himself in a shallow depression among the encircling rocks and fortified himself with another sip of cognac.

He had not been there more than half an hour before bright flames leapt from the shattered walls before him.

FORTY-EIGHT
The Goat, the Skull, and the Ass

1

CARTER PUT HIS hands over his head and pressed himself down into the shelter of the boulders as the area suddenly became as light as day. The flickering flames grew and with them a crackling noise which was deafening, though Carter was about a hundred yards off.

He lifted his head briefly to see the dark silhouettes moving about, lighting the vast fires of logs in the iron braziers. He stared in amazement, wondering how this enormously heavy equipment could be conveyed in secret to this remote place. Torches were alight among the pillars of flame now. By the remotest chance Carter had placed himself in a position where he could see right down through one of the empty window embrasures, giving him a view of the tiled amphitheatre spread out below in the shell of the old monastery. Carter realised he was on one of the mounds scattered about the moor adjacent to the ruins.

Canvas sidescreens had been erected to cut the wind at floor level, and Carter saw that the structure thus created would be warm and sheltered. It would need to be, for he swiftly saw, as the flames shifted and strengthened, throwing their ruddy illumination over the flags and the massive pillars, that there was a large congregation of people assembled within, most of them in an advanced state of nudity.

There was a wooden altar hung with draperies set up at the far end, where one of the surviving walls still stood intact; and Carter made out the blasphemous insignia on the banners: the goat, the ass, the trident, all the images of Satan. There were many young girls among the gathering, which must have numbered almost a hundred, and white-robed officials moved among them, roughly divesting them of their clothing and urging them to drink from the stoneware bowls that were being passed around.

Carter, despite his revulsion and present anxiety, had not lost all sense of his mission here and he glanced anxiously about the bleak vista of moorland outside the Castle walls. There was no-one and nothing in sight, and he could see clearly by the light of the flames.

If there were any sentries or guards they were certainly not on this side. Then Carter remembered that the nearest point of the road was farther round to the east; they would be watching there if anywhere.

He searched in the knapsack for his sketch-pad and pencil; when he had it safely by him he raked the crowd quickly for features familiar to him. There was a low moaning sound, like chanting, coming from the gathering now, and its members commenced to shuffle to and fro across the flagstones, along the wide aisle toward the altar, then drawing respectfully back and taking their places in the rear again.

Carter could not make out the sentences; they may have been some debased form of Latin because he occasionally caught a few root words, thrown up among the jumble of voices. Most of the people present were fairly young; there were some mature women; some older men and very young girls.

The architect's cheeks were ashen now, and he trembled slightly as he started to write; for a few familiar faces were starting to compose themselves from out the blur. Carter's eyes were young and sharp, and the fires in the great braziers, tended by men in black robes who wore white masks upon their faces, shone clear across the flagged interior of the ruins.

Here was a man Carter had seen in the public bar of The Bassett Arms not three nights since, another a moorland farmer to whom he could put a name if he had a little more time. Then the sensuous nude bodies of young women with flowing dark hair were swirling across his field of vision.

The young architect's cheeks burned with shock as he saw, incredulously, the girl Pauline who served him at table, then the younger girl who assisted her. And here was Mrs. Tregorran herself, her magnificent body fully exposed, her lips opened in a soulless laugh as she shook her hair out and held up her arms toward the altar with the rest of them.

Perspiration ran down into Carter's eyes as he went on with his writing. He had no doubt about Sennen's sincerity now or the thoroughness of his researches. His calendar of evil was entirely accurate. Carter looked vainly for a figurehead in what had become like something from an ancient woodcut, his mind automatically evaluating the features of the people who passed before his incredulous gaze.

He could see no-one in charge for the moment. The people seemed caught in some ancient spell, not frenzy, not violence, but a sort of somnambulatory trance that impelled them on to a climax that would not come to fruition for some time. Their slow, voluptuous movements were planned to husband their resources for something later in these ancient ceremonies.

That it was something dangerous and unspeakably evil Carter did not doubt. His brain was overheated now, perhaps by the peril of his position up here, partly by the spirit he had drunk; but his eyes went on observing sharply, and where he could not put a name to a face, he roughly sketched a likeness with his pencil in the flickering illumination from the silhouetted ruins in front of him.

When he again looked up the ceremonies had changed; many of the congregation were lying on the slabs of the Castle floor. Amid much chanting the females were being penetrated by the males. Carter noted, in the sudden light of a brazier which had been kindled at the far side of the altar, the great carved wooden phallus, the representation of the female organ, and a figure wearing a wooden donkey mask.

Now there was further chanting as of a choir and the white-robed officials were passing among the naked supplicants, supervising the changing of partners. An hour must have passed in this way, in which the men and women, warm and lewd within the shelter of the ancient walls passed slowly from a quiet, hallucinatory state to one of sexual frenzy.

The worshippers finished at last with a great shout, and as it died out Carter caught, as though from vast distances in another world, the tinkling chime of the Thornton Bassett clock as it struck midnight. It might have existed on a planet remote from this one, Carter thought. He looked at the faint fringe of mist which was lapping the moor and turned his eyes to Rats' Castle once again.

A drastic transformation in the obscene ceremonies was taking place. New figures had appeared at the altar, as though from the depths of the earth itself. Carter shuddered as he noted the crimson robe with the skull motif, topped with the goat's head. The glazed eyes of the effigy seemed to fix the congregation with a hypnotic glance for a hush slowly fell among the writhing worshippers.

The other figure wore a black robe which was embroidered with cabalistic insignia worked with gold thread. He had chosen the carved image of a human skull as the headdress which concealed his features and he took his place on a platform at the rear of the altar, in a position slightly lower than that of the goat-priest.

Both men wore heavy boots, but apart from that Carter knew they were naked beneath their robes. The stillness was broken only by the crackling of the flames, constantly replenished by the black-robed novices, as the goat-figure lifted his arms toward the sky.

"The night of sacrifice begins!" he intoned. "Let the subject be prepared!"

Sick at heart Carter saw a great shadow sweep across the altar and something vast hung there in the darkness between the leaping flames in the braziers and the remains of the vaulted ceiling.

2

"What is the Law?" the goat-priest chanted.

"Do as Thou Wilt Shall be the Whole of the Law!" the congregation shouted.

They were on their knees now, the glow of the fires in the braziers imprinting the shadows of the bars across their naked backs in a pattern of red and black as though they had been branded.

Carter had his eyes on the two figures at the altar. Try as he would he could not penetrate the secrets of the heavy goat-mask or that of the skull. He felt fierce disappointment. These two were the prime movers in the terror which gripped the moor; organisers of this hellish cult which held sway in the dark places of the heart.

Carter knew he was within an instant of penetrating to the source of this mystery; yet he could only do so at the cost of his own life, and that would not be useful for the purpose of Sennen's carefully laid plans, even if Carter himself had the courage to make the effort.

He racked his brains for some answer, while his eyes still searched the congregation for further identities, his pencil occasionally sketching an easily captured likeness. Carter knew now that nothing could ever be the same for him in Thornton Bassett, not until every one of this depraved congregation had been exposed.

They worked by night; they terrified the area; and they were ruled and controlled by a very clever mind. Carter had listened carefully to every intonation and nuance of the goat-creature's voice but he could not place it, could not even guess its age. Apart from the obvious fact that its owner would be careful to disguise it, the interior of the mask made an echoing resonance of the syllables that further distorted them.

Carter guessed then that the identities of the two prime movers in this blasphemous sect would be unknown to their followers; they would work through intermediaries. It would be difficult, but it could be done. For what purpose other than sexual gratification and other depraved tastes the cult existed, he could not guess.

He only knew that Sennen had been right about everything. And that unless he behaved very foolishly tonight he would survive to confer with the Rector on what might best be done. Carter knew that he could himself be in very grave danger. He did not even know if he could go back to his lodgings.

It was obvious Mrs. Tregorran knew everything about Jeremy's death; yet with relaxed features and the heart of a fiend she had smiled blandly upon her lodgers and looked after their physical welfare while corrupting her employees and maintaining her place in these dark secret rites.

No wonder, Carter thought, she had warned him most earnestly about venturing upon the moor. No need to ask now who had broken open the cupboard and destroyed the evidence poor Jeremy had so painstakingly gathered. A slow, sullen anger was burning within Carter. He added another name to his list; that of the younger girl who waited on him at table.

The goat-priest had lifted a brass bowl covered with obscure symbols.

"Let the Bride of Satan be inducted formally!" he intoned.

The Tregorran woman came proudly in her nakedness to stand in front of the altar. A few paces behind her came the girl Pauline. Both were smiling and their eyes shone with some secret fulfilment.

"Is this your chosen neophyte?"

"It is, Master," the older woman said.

"Then prepare for your initiation."

The two women knelt submissively on the flagstones as the congregation gathered in a semi-circle, silent now. The goat-priest urinated quickly in the brass bowl. He held it out to the figure in the black and gold robe. Carter looked away. He knew what was coming though even Sennen's revelations had not prepared him for this.

There was a triumphant shout from the congregation which seemed to split the dark sky above Rats' Castle. When Carter looked again the girl Pauline had mounted the altar on all fours. Mrs. Tregorran quickly climbed on her back, turning over as the goat-priest rolled her gently, so that she was face upward, the girl's back acting as the altar surface.

The priests swiftly bound the women together with straps in two places, one at the breast, the other at the loins. There was a deep silence within the ruins. Both women's eyes were closed but the smiles remained on their faces.

The skull-priest was penetrating Pauline now, standing at the right-hand side of the altar, concentrating very deliberately on his task. Mrs. Tregorran arched her body, lifting her legs in the air. The goat-priest had taken his place in the ancient tableau in front of his colleague, straddling Pauline.

He in turn penetrated the dark-haired woman at the front, her legs resting on his shoulders. There was wild chanting from the congregation as the group on the altar redoubled their efforts. The men in the black cloaks and white masks replenished the braziers and stoked the flames higher.

"O, Bride of Satan, prepare for thy sacred task!" the goat-priest shrieked, redoubling his efforts.

"I am ready, O Master!" the dark-haired woman intoned. Spittle ran out at the corners of her mouth.

"O, Hand-Maiden of Satan, prepare for thy sacred task!" screamed the goat-priest.

"I am ready, O Master!" the girl Pauline groaned.

The third man in the ass mask had appeared at the back of the altar. The wooden donkey likeness also concealed his features from the congregation. He held a bowl of incense in benediction over the writhing group.

"What is the Law?" he shouted.

"Do as Thou Wilt Shall be the Whole of the Law!" the congregation shrieked as the group at the altar collapsed in a writhing heap.

Then the worshippers rushed in to kiss, to touch, and to fondle the four participants in the rites, before the goat-priest ordered them back so that the women's straps could be unbuckled.

He stood erect, his eyes glittering beneath the mask.

"The time of the Sacrifice is Come!" he screamed.

"Prepare!"

FORTY-NINE
Satan's Hounds

1

THE FAINT SQUEAKING noise which followed had furrows of fear creasing Carter's skin. He rolled over, his eyes fixed on the shadowy thing swaying above the flames of the braziers. He had forgotten it in his absorption in the scene before him. He then saw it was a large iron cage, such as those used for torture and imprisonment in the Middle Ages.

Nearer and nearer it came to the ground, and as it approached so did the sinister growling noise from the crowd become louder. Before Carter was really aware what was afoot, a naked, shivering wretch, bound hand and foot with leather straps and with chains about his wrists, had been dragged before the altar.

The goat-priest stood, tall and secure in his authority, his voice like brass above the babble of the congregation.

"Here stands the guilty one! How stands the penalty?"

"Death! Death is the penalty!" screamed the crowd, evidently in a long familiar ritual. Carter saw with sick horror that the wretched man's mouth was gagged with a linen band so that he could not cry out.

The sudden brutal demonstration of his friend Jeremy's own fate seemed to hold him in a paralysis or suspension of will. He felt sweat icy on his brow, and he trained his eyes and ears to note what happened next, while his hand crept toward the flare pistol in the satchel at his side.

One more shock was dealt him, before the raw terror of the moment robbed him of all volition for a brief space of time. Everyone within the shell of Rats' Castle had drawn close, in a tight circle round the doomed man, in a way Carter had noticed the healthy and the strong congregate about the dying victim of a traffic accident.

In that moment, when normal human intercourse was suspended and senses were relaxed and careless, the third figure at the altar surreptitiously drew aside his ass mask and mopped his overheated brow. Crater saw, with sick loathing, the fat and bloated features of the gross, bald-headed landlord of The Bassett Arms.

Then his eyes were again fixed on the unfortunate victim who was instantly secured within the iron cage by a dozen willing hands. Terrified, half insensible with fear, Carter saw the girl Pauline pour the pitch on to the naked flesh; the nude Tregorran woman, mistress of the vile ceremonies, kindle the logs beneath the victim's feet; and the torches thrust into the mass as the great cage was instantly hoisted into the air by means of the heavy iron chain.

Carter felt, rather than heard, the horrified moans of the dying man as the flames licked his feet. He writhed within the iron tomb his tormenters had made for him, and as the bandages actually burst from his lips with the heat of the fire, his scorched lungs gave vent to screams that seemed to echo to the far edge of the moor.

Half-crazed, unconscious of his actions, trying to blot out not only the screams but the mad, cruel jeering of the naked crowd, Carter moved his hand from the satchel to the pistol in his overcoat pocket. He was left with the memory of the Tregorran woman, still holding her torch beneath the cage-bars as the structure rose inexorably aloft; and the fantastic gyrations of the thing which blazed and burned alive within the ironwork.

He had the pistol up, the two cracks of the explosions cutting through the madness of the crowd, seeing with joy the jerking of the naked puppet as the bullets found him, the sudden slumping into the merciful oblivion of death. He was on his feet now, the satchel scooped up in his left hand, the pistol in his right as the crowd of worshippers broke up in screaming obscenity.

Then, his sanity restored, he heard with fear the baying of the dogs. The acolytes at the Temple edge had acted with alarming promptness. Lanterns lent their beams to the flames of the braziers; orders cracked in the wintry air; and the goat-priest at the altar and the man in black and gold cloak were adding their own instructions, steadying the maddened worshippers.

Carter slipped from the ridge of boulders in the confusion, conscious that he had no time to re-load. He was rolling desperately down the rough grass slope, the screams from Rats' Castle echoing in his ears.

He found brief refuge in the narrow tunnel between the rocks, the tongue of the hounds louder now. Desperately, he squeezed the trigger of the flare-pistol, aware that something was wrong.

The thing had misfired, either damp or defective; perhaps he had mis-read the instructions. With the vague feeling that the mist was encroaching and that might give him a fighting chance, Carter knew with numb despair that Sennen would not receive his alarm signal this night. He was on his own now.

He turned, his nerves aflame, firing the pistol point-blank at the slavering jaws as the first of the hunting dogs inserted its head into the narrow crack between the rocks.

2

Carter was running for his life. Behind he had left two dead hounds, wedged in the narrow place. That and that alone had saved his life. The bodies of the dogs had prevented the rest of the pack from getting at him. How Carter had squeezed through the narrow defile he did not know. Now, dazed, frightened half to death, muddy and with his knees and elbows skinned, he ran clear of the rocks, the breath rasping in his throat and the wide and clear sky above him.

Ahead, the merciful mist and the covering ground of the boulders; the darkness of the ravine; behind him, the raw insanity of the witch cult. Carter had dropped the satchel, its canvas literally torn from him by the nearest hound. No possible chance now of warning Sennen. He would scour the moor in vain with his telescope on the tower-top, while Carter was run to death by the Hounds of Hell on the fastnesses of the moor.

Despite his intense fear Carter had several factors in his favour. He had no time before to assess them but in the last few moments they had come filtering back into his brain much as ideas for escape seep into that of a condemned man. He had a few minutes' start only over his pursuers, but already a faint thread of hope ran through the darkness of his thoughts.

Firstly, there was the element of surprise. It would take a little while for his pursuers to dress and pursue him on foot, though they had had the swift response of loosing the hounds. The dogs were, in fact, the only thing he had to fear at the moment, and he might outwit them should the opportunity present itself.

Secondly, he was young and strong, sound and fit, and had a fairly clear idea what he intended to do. Thirdly, and most importantly, he was armed, and he knew how to use the pistol. He had a plentiful supply of ammunition, some 200 rounds in fact, and with those he could give a good account of himself, both against the hounds and against his human pursuers. He did not know if the latter were equipped to follow him on horseback across the moor. In any case this terrain was against them.

Lastly, and mercifully, he was absolutely unknown to the people gathered together at Rats' Castle. They had had no time to see him, as they were in the light and he was in comparative darkness. Further, it had taken only a split second to loose the two shots, and they were already absorbed by the spectacle of the dead man slumping in the cage before he had slithered off the saddle of rock and down to the clean freshness of the icy turf.

If he played all the cards still in his hand they would never know his identity; until, at least, they were in the dock at the Assizes with himself, Sennen and Magistrate Hemmings arraigned against them, but that was far off. His survival during the next hour was the all-important thing.

Carter conserved his strength. At the earliest opportunity, lost in a tangle of boulders, his ears attuned to the faint baying of the hounds, he re-loaded. He had only two shots left in the chamber, and it was essential to meet any new onslaught with a freshly-loaded weapon.

The stars were faint and far away now, and as Carter watched, faint wisps of vapour passed between him and the outer heavens. The mist was closing in; it had a two-fold effect. It would cloak him from his enemies; but it would also cut him off from all outside help. He must determine his ultimate destination within the next few minutes or be lost, for the hounds would be sure to find him, mist or no mist.

He did not know how big the pack was but he could not hope to fight them all off on the open ground, even with the pistol. He could remember still the glinting eyes and the red jaws of the first beast. He had fired point-blank into its muzzle but its place had been immediately taken by another. In the open they would tear him down or at least incapacitate him until the goat-priest and his followers came up.

Carter went on now, picking his way with care, anxiously listening for any sign that the pack was gaining. He could hear no sound of human pursuers but then he would not have expected to. They would hardly waste time in conversation with the pack in full tongue.

Carter briefly knew stark fear then; he realised fully the terror inspired among remote dwellers in lonely places on the moor, their reluctance to become involved, their hasty barring of cottage doors when the hounds gave tongue on the night wind. He marvelled again at the courage of Jeremy Hands, who had ventured out completely alone, without the reassuring presence of a Sennen or a Slade at his back.

Then, spurred on by strengthening in the sounds of the pack behind him, he conserved his energy. Slipping from boulder to boulder, going downhill now, his heavy overcoat plastered with mud, his left hand out to fend off obstructions in the darkness, his right holding the pistol ready.

His breath was sobbing in his throat when he again came out on open space, but he noted with satisfaction the thick, oily tendrils of mist which rose and cloaked the ground ahead of him. If he could evade the humans he might hold off the pack long enough with the pistol for help to arrive. But even as he formulated the possibility, he knew what he hoped for was unlikely. If he were to come out alive from the night's adventures, it would be through his own strength and wits and courage.

Despite the mist he knew where he was now; roughly retracing his steps of the earlier evening. With that came a fresh access of strength and cunning; the sort of native stealth that must have been given to man's early ancestors on ancient moors such as this, when they felt the hot breath of a hostile tribe on the back of their necks; with only their own resources and a stone club between them and oblivion.

With his heart thudding in his chest Carter's shaky nerves gave a jump as a dark shape slid toward him out of the whiteness; then he recognized the sharp outlines of one of the ancient Bronze Age dwellings that dotted the moor. Mere stone slabs now, tilted crazily on their sides, to give scant shelter from the weather.

At the same time he heard the sharp click of claws on the icy rocks behind him. Carter wormed aside quickly, making his way behind the stone hut, his eyes and nerves alert. For a second or two he saw nothing; then the wreathing mist parted and he saw the low, shaggy shape.

The big brute was running mute, its nose low to the ground as it followed the scent, the growling in its throat louder as the trail grew stronger. Carter had the creature's body in his sight now.

He squeezed the trigger carefully, aiming low. The explosion and the flash of the muzzle-flame was greeted with a mournful howl and the great hound somersaulted, its body arched against the background of mist, its jaws snapping ineffectually.

Almost before it was still Carter was up again and running for his life, his jumpy nerves reacting now. He shuddered as he ran, and his imagination played him tricks; first, he thought he heard the jeering shouts of his pursuers and then, more sinister, that faint clicking of claws as the more persistent trackers followed on.

He went downhill, winded, half-defeated, black fear in his heart. Three minutes later he hurled himself without hesitation into the white, brawling chaos of the stream.

FIFTY
Hunted

1

BREATHLESS, BATTERED, CARTER let the tumbling water take him down. He still held the pistol in his right hand, careless of the spray, but he kept tight hold, aware that it was his only means of survival. Icy cold invaded all his limbs and he instinctively closed his mouth against the freezing torrent.

He was drowning, dying, *in extremis*, but at least he was safe from the unholy crowd of unclean things at Rats' Castle. Then his head broke clear, he saw a faint glimpse of stars and sanity reasserted itself. His heavy overcoat was dragging him down and he thrashed ineffectually for a few moments before the current took him closer to the bank.

The stream, swollen by the winter rains, was running faster than a man could walk. If Carter could only survive the numbing cold he could use the swift spate in order to evade his pursuers and gain some sanctuary. The dogs could not follow, for they would lose the scent, but Carter knew that his implacable enemies would guess that he had gone downstream and pursue him with all the speed at their command.

It must be about one A.M. now, and if they discovered him before dawn and prevented him from going to ground they would be sure to kill him before Sennen or any other of his friends could reach him. All these thoughts passed through Carter's brain only too truly as the last moments of a drowning man, and then he had seized a tree-branch and dragged himself into the shallows.

He still held the pistol and it took only a few seconds to free it from water and to confirm it would fulfil its purpose should he need to fire it again. Too late, Carter regretted that he had abandoned the cognac flask in his headlong flight from the Castle. It would have come in extremely useful now.

A numbing cold still deeply penetrated his limbs, exacerbated by the chill breeze, which sent the folds of mist swaying in oily undulations. He was on the far bank of the stream and he kept on splashing through the shallows, careful not to venture on to dry land where his scent might once again be picked up by the dogs.

His overcoat was sodden and clinging about him but he kept it on, having read somewhere that the best way to pneumonia was to divest oneself of clothing under such circumstances. With the thin suit he was wearing beneath, the wind would soon penetrate his body. Carter longed for his watch now. Was it one A.M. or two A.M.? Somewhere he had lost all count of time.

It might be important to know, but he would no longer hear the church clock of Thornton Bassett down in the depths of this ravine and so far from the town. The only good thing was that he had the width of the stream between him and his pursuers. He would make better time by letting the rush of the torrent take him down; and he was making steadily to the west instead of the east.

Eastward was only the high moors, the thin thread of the road, and the vast open spaces where he would quickly be recaptured. Carter shuddered again, and not only from the cold this time.

He could imagine the fate that awaited him if he fell into the hands of the goat-priest and his followers. He wondered who the unfortunate wretch in the cage could have been. And why he had stood condemned to such a dreadful end. Perhaps because he had threatened to give away the secrets of the sect?

Carter did not know and he had no time to puzzle it out during his headlong flight. He only knew he must assure Sennen of his safety at the earliest possible opportunity and that Hemmings and the magistracy must set the wheels of justice in motion. He wondered where the dragoons had got to this evening.

Perhaps Sennen had seen signs of fire and a disturbance to the westward on the moor, as he had foretold. In that case the dragoons would be in that direction. But it also meant some of his enemies could lie to the westward too. Carter must make certain of friend or foe before he made his presence known.

Something else obscurely troubled him, amid his whirling thoughts. It came and went annoyingly in his feverish brain but try as he would, he could not arrest it long enough to fix it permanently in his consciousness. He paused again and he became aware that he must have made a grotesque sight if there had been anyone to see. A half-drowned, soaked, muddy figure; drawing each breath raucously and painfully, as it staggered ever onward through the freezing water, winding in and out of the boulders.

But the energy of youth and the fear of what lay behind kept him moving, and presently, despite the numbing coldness of his feet and legs, something of warmth and returning circulation came to cheer his upper limbs and body. The fog was thicker now and it lay in long swathes above the water so that he must be invisible to anyone behind him, even a dozen yards away. That was a comfort at any rate; but Carter was perturbed, at one of his halts, to find the tongues of the hounds disturbingly close behind him. It might have been a trick of the terrain, or perhaps of the mist, but he had supposed at least two miles lay between him and his pursuers.

2

He urged himself onward at a faster pace, conscious of the pain and tiredness in all his limbs. He had put the pistol back in his overcoat pocket for safe keeping but his hand remained upon the butt for if he dropped the weapon through carelessness in scrambling through the rock-strewn shallows, then everything might be lost.

Once or twice the vision of the girl's face came very close to him, and he stooped to embrace her; he knew then that delirium had begun to seize him. He fought against it, just as he fought against his tiredness, and his tendency to close his eyes, even as he ran; and he knew with dim despair that if he did not find refuge within the next hour or two he was a lost man.

He paused again beneath the shattered branches of a stunted tree which grew at the edge of the rushing stream; it was difficult to hear above the sound of the water but he remained there for five minutes. A dangerous time, but in that period he heard nothing; perhaps his pursuers had caught up with the hounds, realised his intentions and had put the dogs on leash?

Worse still, knowing the lie of the land, supposing they had withdrawn to the uplands of the moor, and in the comfort of horse-drawn conveyances had set out to cut him off farther down? That was a thought almost beyond contemplation, and Carter came close to terror again in his freezing and demoralised state.

But his keen commonsense reasserted itself. There was one thing he had forgotten. The ceremonies at Rats' Castle had necessarily called for elaborate preparations, as well as elaborate ritual. As he ran onward through the shallows Carter remembered in minute detail the cage, the heavy tackle needed to raise it, the altar, the robes, the canvas screens, and all the other paraphernalia of the obscene ceremonial rites he had witnessed.

They would need to be re-packed, stowed on to wagons or some other form of transport, and removed bodily from the Castle ruins well before daylight. It would take time too to douse the fires in the braziers and to remove the braziers themselves before the military or the police came upon this damning evidence.

In daylight they would have no opportunity of moving upon the moor without detection. Carter's conviction grew as he ran onward, the breath burning in his throat. So they would need perhaps half, perhaps more than that number of the congregation for the heavy work of loading and transporting.

Discounting the women present, who had made up at least half of the number, there could not be more than about ten or fifteen men following. Not forgetting the hounds, of course. Carter would never forget the hounds as long as he lived. Even so, fifteen men was a formidable body; but he felt slightly more peace of mind.

For there was something beyond this. The time it would take them to dress and arrange a search-party, to formulate plans at such short notice, and then to catch up with the hounds. Unless they had some system of signals, or of re-calling the brutes, they might not even know initially in which direction they had gone.

Carter stopped again, catching his breath in the rear of a boulder, his heart thudding in his chest. He had discounted the legend of Satan and His Hounds at any rate. No-one could have followed him on horseback tonight. And he was certain that no-one had tried. The story had obviously been set about to play upon the superstition of the moor-folk.

The architect stopped the tide of his racing thoughts once more. Already, he had stayed too long perhaps. He forced his weary, frozen limbs into action, being careful to keep to the shingled bottom of the stream where it shallowed, the water swirling round his ankles. He heard nothing of the hounds now; but they might be running mute again, and he had no wish to find one of the brutes' slavering jaws in his throat before he had time to fire the pistol.

It was extremely dark; the stars were blotted out in shimmering whiteness, and if Carter had not the stream to guide him he would have been hopelessly lost. As it was the chuckle and gush of the water, though it sometimes sounded like obscene laughter in his ears, at least kept him moving though sheer fear; and if it cloaked his enemies' movements at least it shielded his from them.

The mist was thick now, so thick in fact that it was useless to think of aiming his pistol, and Carter let it remain in his pocket. He jammed his handkerchief down on top of it to make sure it would remain there and splashed on through the shallows, his breath whistling through his nose; his labouring lungs sucking in the life-giving air.

His upper garments were dry again; amazingly, his body-heat had done this, together with the great athletic effort he was putting out. It reminded him of cross-country runs in winter in far-off schooldays, except that there were no cups or prizes at the end of this event; nothing but bloody death if he failed and a greater prize even than he knew if he succeeded.

He rested once more, only half-conscious of what he did. The roaring of the stream had become like a lullaby in his ears. A dangerous lullaby, because it spoke to him of nothing but rest and oblivious sleep. It was an insidious sound, and he fought against it, the icy water on his lower limbs helping to keep him awake. Once he stooped to splash the droplets upon his face and, galvanised as though with some burning fluid, ran on.

Presently, with a shock, he realised that the paleness of the mist was merging with the paleness of the sky. Dawn was at hand, and if he were discovered here all would be lost. Then he rounded a bend in the darkness of the gully, and the stream was running through gently swelling meadows. There was a low clump of trees, strange on that barren moor, and cattle grazing in fenced fields.

Carter knew where he was now and he ran onward quickly, conscious of the rising dawn, glancing fearfully behind him from time to time; but nothing moved in the milky opaqueness of the moor.

He skirted the trees, working his way around, the contours of the great house rising before him in the pearly light. Here was the terrace, the shrouded scaffolding, and the new walls of the galleries he was building at The Priory.

Only semi-conscious, a shambling, half-frozen scarecrow of a man, Carter staggered on across the frosty turf, looking for some place of refuge. There was no sign of life in the house, except for the pale glimmer of lamps in a room with oval windows at the far end of the great mass.

Carter made for it instinctively, keeping in the shadow so far as possible. It was Hemmings' study and he had grave news for the Magistrate. A French door leading on to the terrace opened before he got to it.

Someone in a plaid cloak stepped out at this extraordinary hour; someone who had been expecting him. Incredulously, Carter saw the tawny yellow hair of the girl shimmering in the strengthening light of dawn. She took in his condition, her eyes wide.

"John!"

He collapsed, conscious of strong young arms about him.

"I must see your uncle!"

The girl shook her head, her eyes clouded with anguish.

"He has gone to Plymouth for a magistrates' conference, John, and will be away for several days."

Carter's body sagged. Then he had turned around to strain his eyes across the milky vastness of the moor.

"Then for God's sake hide me, Fiona! Even if only for a few hours. No-one but you must know that I am here."

Fifty-One
Plans

1

"WILL YOU NOT tell me the truth, John?"

The girl's face was anxious as she sat at Carter's bedside, steam from the breakfast tray rising toward the ceiling. She leaned forward and put another spoonful of hot soup in the young man's mouth.

He lay in a remote, little-used room on the ground floor of The Priory. That much he had gathered from the girl when she had carefully unlocked the door. It was still only nine o'clock in the morning but despite the fact that he had only a short sleep he felt immensely rested.

"I will tell you all, just as soon as I am able. But what does this mean, Fiona? And why were you there?"

The girl frowned and ceased her ministrations with the spoon. Carter used the opportunity to sit up and took the bowl from her. His eye fell on the chair where his clothing, cleaned and pressed, lay ready for him.

"I might well ask you that, John. I had a message in strictest confidence, from Mr. Sennen, through Slade. I was to keep an early morning watch on the terrace in case I might help you and give you refuge. No-one else was to know."

"And no-one else does know?"

The girl shook her head, a faint hint of amusement behind her tense expression.

"No-one, John. I had already prepared this room. The divan needed only pillows and rugs, as you see. And the breakfast you are eating is my own. I told Mrs. Arkwright I would take it to my room."

She smiled openly then, the shadows of the night lifting from her face.

"She is more used to my unorthodox ways now, John. I hope I have done right."

"You have done splendidly, Fiona. I am immensely grateful."

He drew her to him, her cheek and hair against his own. Then, conscious of his nakedness beneath the plaid blanket he drew back. The girl's smile widened.

"Will you not tell me what this all means?"

"I cannot for the moment. Save that it is something terrible. And extremely important. Is there any further message from Mr. Sennen?"

"Only, if I did see you, I was to take you in the greatest secrecy and in a closed carriage, back to Thornton Bassett."

Carter gazed at the girl thoughtfully.

"Without anyone in this house knowing, of course?"

Fiona Hammond nodded.

"Which means I must stay here until after nightfall."

A little expression of irritation passed across the girl's face.

"If it is so much of an ordeal, John . . ."

The young architect shook his head, laying his hand on her arm.

"You would not say that if you knew what I know, Fiona. I can only say that this business is one of deadly seriousness. A matter of life and death. I would tell you more if I could. And I will tell you everything when I can. That is my solemn promise."

The girl's tense face relaxed then, and the pressure on her patient's hand grew.

"Eat the rest of your breakfast, John," she said gently. "You will not be disturbed here, and the outer shutters are closed. Sleep, and I will bring you lunch in due course."

She put a warm hand on his lips and pressed him back on the divan.

"No-one shall know you are here but me, John. I can assure you of that."

Carter thanked her again and already felt his senses leaving him as soon as he had finished his breakfast. He put the tray down on the table, conscious of the aches which now pervaded all his body. His flight through the fog had been a severe test of even his youth and strength. He knew no more until he was again conscious of the girl's blurred image above him.

"Is there any news?"

She nodded.

"Mr. Slade has been. I was able to convey to him, verbally and in confidence, the situation here. You cannot imagine the relief on his face!"

The girl smiled at the recollection and Carter thought he had never seen anything so beautiful.

"He has taken the message back to Mr. Sennen. I told him you would be at the Rectory after dark tonight. I hope I have done right."

Carter put his hand on to the back of her own, where it rested on the coverlet. Today she wore a green silk flowered dress and she looked cool and fresh and competent. The horrors of the night were lifting now. He raised the dish-cover, inhaling the fragrance of the lunch she had brought him.

"I hope you are not starving yourself to feed me?"

She shook her head, smiling again.

"I brought enough for both of us, if you do not mind sharing one knife and fork?"

"Not at all!"

Then, as the meal progressed, the pair became serious again.

"Slade is not coming back here for me?" Carter asked anxiously. "You will take me in?"

The girl assented.

"I thought it best. People might think it curious if Slade came to and fro continuously, especially when you are not supposed to be here."

Carter thought of something else then. He bit his lip in vexation.

"What about the office? I had quite forgotten. How am I to explain my absence from Pollard, Bassett today?"

Fiona Hammond shook her head.

"You are forgetting, John. Today is Saturday. The office is closed, is it not?"

The young man felt his memory was failing. He coloured for a moment.

"It is true, Fiona. It had escaped my mind. Though sometimes the partners put in an appearance on Saturday mornings to catch up on urgent work."

As the events of the past night flooded in again he thought once more of the ghastly ceremony and the living incineration of the wretched being in the iron cage; and all the blood drained from his face. The girl sat watching him sympathetically in the shadowed room, not knowing the reason.

"My landlady . . ." Carter began, to cover his embarrassment. "I have been away all night."

"Slade is calling there on his way back," the girl continued. "He has a story of a commission on the far side of the moor, of your missing the last train back to Princetown and of your staying at a small hotel. I am sure it will sound plausible enough by the time he has polished it."

Carter joined in the girl's smile

"I am sure," he agreed.

He felt he could not face the woman again; he would, in any case, abide by Sennen's sound advice this evening. He had the names and some of the faces. They were as far as ever from identifying the ring-leaders. Perhaps Sennen would have the answer. He would not worry now.

With the encouraging eye of his young nurse upon him Carter continued his lunch with the healthy appetite of returning strength.

2

"Mr. Carter, I cannot thank you enough for the information you have brought! And I can only apologise again for the appalling danger into which I led you!"

Carter shook his head.

"I went there with my eyes open, sir."

The two men sat in the shadowed comfort of the Rector's study, a crackling fire between them. It was ten at night and, true to her promise, Fiona Hammond had brought him to the side-gate of the Rectory not an hour since, when there would be few people about. She was, in any event, staying for one night with her friends at the far side of the town, and so had a perfect excuse for being there. Carter carried with him still the vivid image of her face at parting.

Sennen's expression had been grim as he listened to Carter's long recital, drumming impatiently with his thick fingers on the arm of his chair. Carter had interpreted the questions in his eyes correctly.

"We cannot move until we have the ring-leaders, sir?"

The Rector shook his head.

"But I still have one more card to play, Mr. Carter. If your nerve hold and you be willing."

"I am willing, Mr. Sennen," Carter said steadily.

Sennen nodded, again studying the list Carter had given him, and the torn-off sheets of sketches which the architect had thrust into his greatcoat pocket before he had taken to his heels.

"You took a great deal on trust last night, Mr. Carter. The time has come to be a little more frank with you. I did not count, of course, on the mist being so thick, or the factor of the flare-pistol malfunctioning."

His sorrowful eyes sought and held the other's own.

"You were not alone out there. Slade was stationed on the upper road, as a link. I also had a picked squad of police on the moor, at a pre-arranged spot on the tors, ready to move in at a moment's notice. Under the direction of our friend, Inspector Pepper of Plymouth Detective Force."

He smiled faintly at his companion's surprise.

"I have been in secret communication with Pepper for some time. He is an admirable man. I do not entirely trust our local officers. They have been remarkably ineffectual ever since these mysterious events began."

He put up his hand holding the stubby pipe before Carter could interrupt.

"My proceedings would have been these. At the sign of the flare I would have given a red signal with my hand-lantern to Slade, stationed with the trap on the shoulder of road above the town"

He shrugged.

"In the event, both the flare failed and the mist would have prevented me from seeing. I signalled Slade anyway. He could not see me on the tower because of the thickness of the fog. Normally, he would have himself given a red signal to the police on the tors and they would have taken action."

"Against a hundred men, sir?"

Carter could not keep the surprise out of his voice.

"Against a thousand men, sir!" said Sennen.

His eyes were hard and blazing now. Something of the fires which burned beneath his placid surface briefly flamed into the open.

"Remember, Mr. Carter, there were only some fifty men there, in a state of nudity. The police, small in number though they were—some ten in all—were hand-picked, determined and heavily armed. They would have been match enough for these creatures."

His eyes had already picked out Carter's next question from the architect's eyes.

"They have been staying at private houses in Princetown, so as not to arouse suspicion here. To the local people there they are prison officers under training and so have stirred no unusual interest."

"You think of everything, Mr. Sennen."

The cleric shook his head.

"Not entirely, Mr. Carter. You say Mr. Hemmings is from home?"

"Yes, sir. He has gone to Plymouth."

The Rector bit his lip.

"A pity," he said.

He became brisk again.

"However, we shall just have to proceed without him."

He got up and took a turn about the room; through a gap in the window curtains Carter could see fog thickly encroaching round the house. It was such a night as last night; he shuddered again as he thought of his headlong flight from death across the moor. He could not face such a situation again. The Rector caught his expression and was instantly at his side.

"Fear not, Mr. Carter. Tomorrow's expedition will take place in daylight and at minimum risk to yourself. I have given the problem some thought and I think I have the answer to some of the puzzles which confront us."

He poured Carter another cognac and went across to the small round table between them to replenish his own glass.

"Where is Miss Hammond spending the night? Back at The Priory, I suppose?"

Carter shook his head.

"She is staying with friends in Thornton Bassett and driving back tomorrow morning."

Sennen had relief on his face.

"That is good. I think it best that you make no attempt to see her for the moment. We will keep her informed."

Carter hesitated, disappointment flooding across him. He bit his lip.

"Just as you say, sir."

Sennen smiled wryly.

"There is good reason for what I say, Mr. Carter. It will emerge as things take shape. When Slade arrives we will go into conference. He is my link between myself and the police, as I have already noted."

He re-seated himself opposite the architect and looked at him sharply in the flickering firelight.

"You have been remarkably patient, Mr. Carter. Let us hope that this blackness will have been lifted for ever within the next day or two."

"Amen to that, sir," said Carter fervently.

"In the meantime you will be comfortable here," the Rector went on. "I will make up this leather divan near the fire, and you can pass the night well enough. I always keep my study locked so there is no fear of the housekeeper disturbing you. It means rising early in the morning, of course, but I take it you have no objection to that."

Carter shook his head.

"I am quite recovered, sir. I have been asleep most of the day."

The Rector gave him a strange, twisted smile.

"That is good. You see now my reasons for the pistol. You made good use of it, then."

Carter nodded.

"I accounted for at least three of those brutes, sir. Will not the police discover them on the moor?"

The hard look was back in Sennen's eyes.

"The police are keeping off the moor in daylight," he said. "It is essential these people know nothing of our activities. They must think they are dealing with one person only, as on previous occasions. They will have disposed of the dogs long ago."

He passed a heavy hand across his chin.

"My one fear is that last night may have frightened them off. If they go to ground now we are lost. We must just hope for the best."

Carter felt faint surprise.

"Why so, sir?"

The Rector gave him a wry smile.

"You have much to learn of the ways of the world, Mr. Carter. Because, my intrepid young friend, the goat-priest, as you insist on calling him, will not have overlooked one vital factor of last night's adventure."

"What might that be, sir?"

Sennen chuckled throatily.

"Simply your remarkable capacity for survival. If he has found your satchel he will know of the flare-pistol, the sandwiches, and the dark-lantern. That denotes careful preparation, does it not?"

Carter agreed.

"Then, people run down by the hounds in the past usually died, frightened and exhausted. If the hounds did not finish them, then The Black Death would. Either way these creatures incinerated their victims, alive or dead, not only to shroud their identities but to terrify people off the moor."

He spread his hands wide, his eyes twinkling, despite the horrifying subject of his discourse.

"You not only refused to die, you were fully armed and an accurate shot. You despatched several of their valuable hounds and then escaped into thin air."

He laid his finger alongside his nose.

"Or should I say thick air, in view of the fog. All those factors, Mr. Carter, make you unique."

His face was serious again now.

"There is something further. There cannot be many young, strong men on the moor who can outrun hounds, who are expert pistol shots, and who are purposeful enough to give the Hounds of Hell their quittance. The chief of these villains is unknown to us. But he is free to walk abroad, not only upon the moor, but in places like Thornton Bassett. It will not take him long to narrow the field. Fortunately it is a week-end, and I have services to prepare for tomorrow. We must keep you under cover as long as possible."

He leaned forward until his brilliant eyes were staring into the other's.

"We must make the most of our conference tonight and lay our new plans with care. I have ideas which may or may not invalidate the theories I have formed in my long years here. Where, for example, is all that material you saw in Rats' Castle last night? I may have the answer to that also."

Carter nodded. He saw where the other man's talk was tending.

"I have my own views on that, Rector."

He got up to stretch his legs, going over to the cleric.

"And what of that poor wretched creature I despatched in the cage? Have you given any thought to him?"

Sennen's haunted face clouded to an even darker hue.

"I have, Mr. Carter. There is a certain farmer upon the moor, who reported to the authorities some while back that his daughter was missing. I believe you were present at The Priory when the subject was under discussion."

"That is so, Mr. Sennen."

The Rector's lips were set in a thin, grim line.

"He was reported missing on Thursday, Mr. Carter. The last his employees heard of him was when he set off across the moor that night to search for his daughter."

Sennen went forward to knock out the dottle from his pipe at the metal fire surround. He straightened, his black hair a brindled mass in the firelight.

"I have no doubt his daughter is now a member of this unholy congregation," he said.

There came a sudden tap at the far window, facing the churchyard, which set Carter's nerves jumping. Sennen went to the door as the tower clock started tolling the hour of eleven.

"That will be Slade," he said. "Now we can formulate our plans."

Fifty-Two
The Stone is Lifted

1

IT WAS A piercingly cold, dark Sunday afternoon with even the birds falling silent, as Slade drove the closed carriage out of Thornton Bassett, through thin streams of people on their way to church. Out of sight upon the cushions at the rear lay Carter, his thoughts endlessly revolving. He could not see any flaw in Sennen's schemes, though they might go awry, as they had on Friday night. And if Sennen's suppositions, like Carter's, were untrue, then they were back at the beginning once again.

But he had the pistol and with Slade on guard and the police dispersed unobtrusively the plan might work. Crouched uncomfortably among coils of rope and cable, a light ladder, and other material which Slade had gathered from somewhere, Carter was uneasily aware of a vital blank in his memory.

It had something to do with the night on the moor; he had done his best to blot the horror from his brain. Perhaps he had succeeded too well for there was surely a central clue eluding him, which he struggled to unravel from the rest of his clouded impressions.

Slade sat forward, preserving absolute silence, his face sardonic and unreadable beneath the brim of his hard hat, and the air was so cold that Carter could see a faint rime gathering on his features as they clattered slowly uphill. Presently Slade got down, presumably to rest the pony, and Carter, still pressed to the floor of the carriage, heard him give a greeting to someone at the roadside.

Meticulous as ever, Slade was delivering several parcels today on his way to their destination, which gave him a perfectly valid reason for being abroad upon the moor at that time of a Sunday afternoon. Carter, fortified with a picnic lunch on the tower with the carrier, brought to them surreptitiously by the Rector, had also borrowed another cognac flask, as it was likely to be cold work up there today. Strange, Carter thought, that it would soon be Christmas, and the holly-decorated shops of Thornton Bassett made a garish façade for the horrors all about them.

They had spent the morning cautiously scanning the bleak slopes of the moor with the telescope, but had seen nothing out of the way; a scattering of sheep and ponies, a farmer in his trap. There was still some mist on the far hills and Rats' Castle had not been visible. Now, Carter longed only to get to work and to put Sennen's bold scheme into execution. He knew he could rely on him absolutely.

His one regret was not being able to get a message to Fiona. She had left the town before he and Slade had ascended to the tower-top, and he had had to be content with a brief glimpse of her through the telescope eyepiece as her vehicle ascended the far slope on its way back to Tor Bridge.

Carter had looked long and scrupulously in that direction and on the lonely, mist-enshrouded tors that the telescope traversed, but once again they held their ancient secrets.

Slade had stopped now at a lonely cottage and handed in another of his packages; whether they were Pollard's commissions or some errands of his own Carter did not know, and he would certainly not enquire. He knew better than to probe Slade's poker-faced exterior.

He thought again of the few brief months since he had come to Thornton Bassett and of the incredible and horrific happenings in which he had become inextricably involved. Thought too of the charred remains of his friend Jeremy lying shrouded in the secret vault of Sennen's Norman church. His eyes were hard and vengeful as he checked over the pistol and ammunition for the third time since leaving the town.

He was glad to relinquish such sombre flights as occupied his teeming mind when Slade abruptly stopped the trap in a wild and lonely countryside and told him it was safe to descend.

2

Carter got out, glad to stretch his legs. The place was a perfect one. They were in a sort of sunken side-lane that led off the high road across the moor. Carter had never been here before but Slade led him to the edge of the screening rocks.

Across the deep bowl before them, already lost in bluish haze despite the fact that it was only early afternoon, rose range after range of wild moorland, shading to the savage buttresses of the tors. The lowering sky pressed heavily on the hilltops and the bitter wind, with a hint of snow, blew mercilessly in their faces.

Carter had no time for the general view. His eyes followed the white scar of the road they had left, which curved round in vast ellipses until it eventually linked with the thoroughfare that led back to Tor Bridge. He remembered then that this network of roads was like a giant circle, running east-west, with Thornton Bassett at its base, like a pendant on a necklace.

Below, in the middle distance, and partly hidden by the jumbled rocks of the foreground, was Rats' Castle. Slade spat grimly, jamming his hat on to one side of his head.

"No chance of the pony and equipage being seen here, Mr. Carter," he said with satisfaction. "But I don't want to be caught on that open ground."

He grinned crookedly.

"I hope you're feeling in a strong mood, sir, because we must try and avoid two journeys."

The pair quickly returned to the carriage and unloaded all the material they needed. Slade produced a long rope and tied it to the pony's reins. He secured the other end round a protruding spur of rock, so that the animal could range widely to graze the rough turf, but could still not be seen from the road.

The carrier looked expertly across the moor, his keen eyes missing nothing.

"We could have done with the portable winch, Mr. Carter, but I told Mr. Sennen it would have been too heavy with just the two of us. We have to be practical, you see."

"Of course," said Carter, inwardly amused.

"But I think we can manage the slab between us, sir," Slade went on. "I've thought of a way."

He looked at Carter apologetically.

"Forgive me, sir. I was forgetting you were a full-blown architect and so on. You would know all about levers and fulcrum and stresses and that sort of thing."

"I think so," Carter smilingly agreed. "But on this occasion I am happy to leave the arrangements to you."

Slade gave him another tight grin in the depths of his beard.

"That's uncommonly civil of you, sir. If you'd take the baskets there, with the tools, the dark-lanterns, and the ropes, I'll manage the ladder and the chest."

Carter looked at him dubiously.

"Are you sure?"

"Trust me, sir."

Slade had already lifted the cumbersome objects with practised ease and was proceeding goat-footed over the broken ground, keeping a sharp eye across the moor. Carter followed more slowly, concentrating on retaining his footing amid the jumble of boulders.

Swiftly, they sank into the deep blue bowl of shadow and Carter felt more secure once the road had disappeared beneath the rim of encircling moorland. They were exposed up there and, as his companion had said, they did not want to be caught on the open ground.

Slade was already a long way ahead but he looked around encouragingly from time to time to supervise the architect's progress. Presently, Slade disappeared above as the ruins rose slowly toward the sky. Carter could not repress a shiver, but the presence of Slade and the revolver in his pocket soon restored his nerve.

Slade was back now, slithering recklessly down toward him.

"The coast is clear, sir. We won't be disturbed."

He took one of the cases from Carter and again disappeared from view. Three minutes later, blown and shivering, Carter arrived at the plateau on which the ruins stood and looked sombrely at the scene of the horrifying ritual. At first sight all appeared as it had on the afternoon he had explored the place with Fiona.

Here were the worn flagstones, the frowning walls, the dark shadows above. But there was a difference. There had been little rain in the interim and Carter could now see where heavy metal objects had been dragged across the slabs. Slade faced him, his right eye closed in a wink.

"You and Mr. Sennen were right, sir. The stuff must still be here."

He indicated blackened stonework far above.

"I smell burning, sir, even with the breeze."

Carter shuddered. He went over to look at the vast block set in the flags, the one with the heavy metal ring. When he came back Slade had already run out the ladder extension.

"Just hand me that rope-end, sir, if you please."

He took it from Carter and tied it round his waist. Then he placed the ladder in position and was already going up incredibly quickly while Carter held the bottom. His voice came down, sharp and excited.

"You were right, sir. This block is well greased and in regular use. Let out some slack!"

Carter fed him the rope and coil after coil disappeared above. Presently the end came down, and Carter secured it round his own waist. When Slade regained the ground his eyes were shining.

"We'll just rove this end round the ring, sir, and see how she goes."

When he had done this the two men took the rope and slowly exerted all their strength. The slab came up three or four inches and then fell back. The weight was enormous. Carter knew it would be so. He looked at the other in dismay. Slade's eyes were still bright.

"Just a moment, sir. No sense in killing ourselves."

He took the rope back to the edge of the ruins, flung it out one of the glassless casements, all the while his sharp eyes raking the far rim of the moor. Carter could see nothing at all but he knew Slade's eyes were even keener than his own. His companion had been well chosen by Sennen.

When he reached the tall man he had tied the loose end of the rope round an enormous granite boulder. He kicked it and it now hung halfway down the steep slope of the plateau on which Rats' Castle stood. Carter went quickly back, saw the rope taut and the slab raised by the ring some four or five inches. When he rejoined Slade the two men hauled on the rope, which quickly gave.

"That's it, Mr. Carter," Slade gasped. "Open sesame!"

Carter was inclined to take a more cautious view and he had the pistol out as they ran back within the ruins. As Slade had surmised the slab was turned to the sky, a black hole revealed. Quickly, Slade lit both of the dark-lanterns. He caught the ladder and lowered it into the darkness. He stopped Carter as he had his foot on the first rung. The floor was only about ten feet below, he could see now.

"You're certain you wouldn't rather me go, Mr. Carter? Surely you've done enough."

The architect shook his head.

"Mr. Sennen was most particular. You will be more useful here. And your quick wits will have some ready explanation if anyone chances along."

"More than that, sir!"

Slade slowly opened his large hand to expose the brown mahogany butt of a revolver.

"Perhaps you're right, Mr. Carter. But you might leave me the flask. It's likely to be colder up here than for you down there."

Smilingly, Carter handed it to him. He put his own pistol back in his overcoat pocket. Then he descended the wooden ladder slowly, taking his time and shining the full beam of the dark-lantern around. He soon saw he was in a large circular chamber made of closely wrought slabs; it was like a catacomb and of an ancient pattern.

He drew in his breath as the beam glanced across a jumble of tangled iron, braziers, curtaining, the wood altar, some trestles, rope and tackle, and, grimmest of all, the vast iron cage with its suspending chain. There was an arch ahead, and when Carter shone the lantern he saw a long passage leading off in a westward direction.

He came back to where Slade's head waited patiently in the grey square opening that framed the sky.

"Mr. Sennen was right!" he called up. "Everything is here; the braziers, the cage, all the infernal apparatus of that hellish ceremony."

There was excitement in Slade's voice.

"Then we are on the right track, sir. I will make my preparations now and let the others have a signal when it is dark enough. You will explore the tunnel for further evidence. Strange that Mr. Sennen knew all this! You'll be careful, sir?"

"You have no need to remind me," Carter replied, somewhat tremulously.

He tapped the pocket holding the pistol.

"They will not be expecting me. If I find an exit I will emerge there and rejoin you across country. If not I will come back the way I came."

Slade put his finger to the brim of his hat.

"Very well, sir. I will be here."

Carter left him then and went back across to the archway with a simulated confidence he was far from feeling. He eased down the narrow tunnel with his heart beating heavily in his throat. To his surprise the place was cool, with a faint breeze blowing from somewhere. He had expected the passage to be dank and airless.

He looked with professional interest at the beautifully bonded stonework. The passage was incredibly old yet it was in as good repair as the day it had been built.

The young man's heart grew sombre as he thought of the feet which must have advanced across the beaten earth floor so many times before him. Feet belonging to pagans of an ancient age and, more recently, those of evil persons whose perverted lusts had been responsible for the murder and cruel deeds in this remote corner of Dartmoor.

Carter had not gone more than twenty yards along the tunnel when there was a strange squeaking noise from the direction of the circular chamber he had just quitted. Then the slab fell back into position with a hollow thud that reverberated like the judgment of doom on the architect's heart.

FIFTY-THREE
The Tunnel

1

THE BEAM OF the lantern in Carter's hand trembled and then dipped suddenly toward the floor. Dismay, bewilderment and terror jumbled all together in his breast. Then he recovered himself. He knew that no accident could have lowered the slab, that if Slade had done so he had good reason.

If Slade had not, that was another matter. But a few seconds' more thought and commonsense had reasserted itself. Slade had had a clear view all round for miles across the moor. He was a man unlikely to be surprised by accident. So he had lowered the slab deliberately.

Perhaps he had noticed a vehicle or someone coming along the road. His best plan then would be to hide the ladder and other materials and conceal himself until the intruder had gone by. Yes, that must be it. There was no point in going back to the circular chamber for the slab was six inches thick and he could not make himself heard; neither would Slade shout down to him if the circumstances were as Carter feared.

He had to go on as arranged. If he were forced to return no doubt Slade would by then have again raised the slab, perhaps by increasing the number of boulders at the other end of the rope. It was the only sensible course.

Carter realised also that his colleague must have lifted out the ladder before dropping the stone; so the thing was not a sudden, perverse action but something premeditated. The supposed interruption of a stranger's appearance was the most likely cause.

He went on, his head bowed in thought, the lantern beam dancing before him, his heart steadying at last. The passage ran straight to the westward. Carter had a vague recollection of having passed a wooden door standing open, leading from the circular brick chamber beneath the slab, but there were no other obstructions.

At any other time his professional interests would have been absorbed by the wonderful construction of this ancient tunnel, but he hardly noticed the smoothness of the walls or the cunning jointure of the stonework. He guessed again that Sennen's antiquarian studies may have envisaged something of the sort.

What the tunnel's purpose was or where it led was more than his mind could compass. Now that Carter's eyes were accustomed to the gloom he adjusted the shutter of the lantern to lower the intensity of the light. The smooth walls stretched endlessly before him and now the passage was going steeply downward.

So far as he could judge it still led toward the west, and he realised also that the ancient builders had worked out the contours of the ground so accurately that they were following the exact curvature of the moorland, at least where it fell sharply into a valley.

Already he judged he had gone more than a quarter of a mile and still the tunnel bored inexorably on. There was no sign of life anywhere, either animal or insect, and the earthen floor, dry and hard, was as smooth as asphalt, beaten level by feet over hundreds of years.

The thing was an unexpected marvel to find in an area like Dartmoor but Carter had other problems to occupy his mind. If he were a long while underground would the air give out? There was certainly no sign of that for the moment. It was not exactly fresh, but there was a steady current, breathable and faintly earthy to the nostrils.

More important to the architect was the quantity of oil in his lamp. It was freshly filled; Sennen had seen to that; and the reservoir was a large one. It would last some hours but who knew how long he would be down here? Once left in the dark he could crawl about for days and end in gibbering madness.

He clenched his teeth in irritation. He put the lamp on the floor at his feet, removed the top and trimmed the wick before turning it down as far as it would go compatible with reasonable illumination. Then he opened up the dark section and went on again. That way the life of the lamp would perhaps be doubled and should see him through to the end of the tunnel.

It had turned in a gentle dog-leg now and was going down steeply again. But the same marvellous workmanship was involved and the same care evinced here as on the level sections. Many men must have toiled for many years to achieve this prodigality of mediæval engineering.

For it must date from mediæval times at least, Carter felt. He would ask Sennen when he next saw him; once exposed to public view these artefacts would be one of the wonders of the country. For the effort needed to produce such effects was colossal. As the tunnel progressed the rocks and boulders dislodged had been dressed and used for the construction itself.

That much was plain. Some of the dressing was moor stone, he knew; and that was found close to the surface. But much of it was igneous rock, which originated at considerable depths beneath the earth; the commonest in building use was granite, the hardest of the igneous rock formations. But it was also difficult to cut and would thus need not only sophisticated tools but an enormous labour force.

Such conditions did not exist in pre-history, Carter knew; so the tunnel must be mediæval in conception. Stressed as his mind was, he did not fail to note these points as he walked steadily downward, and it helped to keep his imaginings from darker things. He was surprised to find there were no facilities for lighting here, no ironwork for torches or candles, no brackets for lamps.

He glanced at his watch once and was astonished to see that more than an hour had gone by. He must have walked an enormous distance already. Presently he felt moisture underfoot and, shining the lamp, saw where seepage had occurred, the water glinting and glistening on small cracks in the stonework.

Carter realised with awe that he must be somewhere below the stream in which he had taken refuge in his headlong flight across the moor. It was inconceivable that he should not soon emerge at some point on high ground, secluded and secret enough so that the sect-members could assemble and make their way unseen to the venue of their rites. Or perhaps this was a secret route for their leaders. It was a possibility.

Again Carter remembered the oil painting in the hall of The Priory; the man being hunted by the hounds, and the figure of Satan on the hill-top. His instincts had not deserted him. Legend or not, Satan and His Hounds had a solid basis in historical fact. If he could discover the artist he might yet learn more of the tunnel's history.

Carter walked on for another hour. He had lost count of time and only realised its passage when the watch-dial informed him that it was early afternoon. He had given up all idea of returning to Rats' Castle now. As he must surely be at the end of the journey, it would be far easier to emerge at the entrance and make his way overland. That there would be an entrance was obvious; Carter refused to contemplate the awful possibility that it might be sealed by such a slab as they had found at the other end.

Presently, he had left the stream-bed far behind and after descending to what seemed like an immense depth, the tunnel was rising steadily again. Something that had been gnawing at Carter's mind for two days past was surfacing once more. He had tried to blot from his memory much of the awful events of the Friday but one factor obstinately remained, half-buried in his brain and struggling to free itself.

He was absorbed with this problem when he suddenly and without warning came to a broad, open space which was quite level. A faint breeze blew from somewhere. Ahead of him he saw that the passage divided. To the left was a gloomy flight of stone steps.

To the right was another short tunnel. Faintly, at the end of it he could see the lower rungs of a set of large wooden steps. Carter unhesitantly chose the right-hand passage.

2

He checked the revolver at the foot of the steps and replaced it in his overcoat pocket. His heart was beating unsteadily as he eased slowly up the wooden stair, tread by tread, to where a timber hatch came floating out of the darkness above his head.

Cautiously, scarcely daring to breathe, he pushed with his shoulders, holding the lantern to one side. Daylight flooded in; Carter saw a wooden floor littered with fragments of straw and other debris, leather straps and harness, a sword laid across the seat of a chair.

As he raised the hatch higher into the timbered room, whose light came from dusty windows high up, the fragment of his nightmare fused with reality. He stared without speaking at the unusual boots, which had a red thread running through their leather uppers, to match the piping of the military trousers above them.

Captain Michael Henderson sat at a rough trestle table, polishing the equipment before him, whistling noiselessly through his teeth.

His eyes narrowed with shock, and he stopped as Carter levered himself through the hatchway. The two men's eyes exchanged a wealth of accusation and denial in the few seconds before either spoke. With an immense effort of self-control Henderson forced a false smile to his lips.

"Well, well. Mr. Carter. That is the last direction I should have expected you to appear from."

"I can well imagine."

Carter was keeping his emotion well in check. He was up the stairway now and stepped out on to floor level, taking in the details of the tack-room. The Captain's hands lay quiet and still on the rough surface of the table. To his left lay the big service revolver he had been oiling and cleaning before he turned his attention to the brasswork of his cuirass.

His eyes flickered to the pistol and back to Carter. The young man kept his right hand deep in his overcoat pocket.

"Is that not somewhat menial work for a Captain of Dragoons?" Carter asked.

He was fully in control of himself now. A half-smile flowered at the corners of Henderson's lips.

"The troop has gone on leave, Mr. Carter. They left hours ago by the moor-road. I do this to amuse myself in an idle hour. Nothing more, nothing less."

He drew in his breath quickly, easing back in his rough wooden chair.

"Now that you are here, Mr. Carter, it will end the boredom."

"I can promise you that, Captain," said Carter crisply.

Henderson shifted his position very slowly in the chair. Carter noticed that he kept his eyes on the pistol.

"You have found your way from Rats' Castle, then?"

Carter gave him a tight smile.

"I should have thought that was fairly obvious."

The architect looked significantly at the Captain's boots.

"When taking part in unholy rites you should remember to change all your clothing. Your boots were too distinctive for me to overlook."

The Captain's firm mouth was trembling now beneath the thick black moustache and the face was sallow below the curling ringlets of hair which had once, so Carter thought, given him a Roman aspect.

The arrogance had drained out of his features, leaving them mean and haggard.

"So," he said in a very low voice. "So."

He nodded a few times as though inwardly convincing himself of something Carter could not read.

"It was a clever conceit," said Carter. "Leading your troop across the moor to hunt yourself! And the white horse you rode differentiated you from the black mounts of your dragoons. So that the moor-riders would not shoot the wrong man. I suppose your men are what they seem to be?"

Henderson shrugged, his expression blank.

"Even I cannot subvert the British Army,," he said. "I suppose it is no good appealing to your sense of self-interest?"

Carter smiled then.

"Self-interest lies in my continuing to ally myself with the forces of the law. You cannot escape in any event. The net is cast for all of you."

Henderson's ashen pallor deepened but his eyes continued to weigh the possibilities. Carter stood very still, watching the other's every move.

Henderson gave Carter a last, thin smile.

"As you say, Mr. Carter, I should remember to change my boots in the future. So it was you we were hunting across the moors! It could only have been someone of your energy and enterprise."

"You flatter me," Carter said.

The Captain had been holding his eyes with his own but the architect had kept his attention firmly on the dragoon officer's right hand.

As rapidly as he moved, Carter's reflexes were quicker still. Henderson stood, the pistol halfway to his shoulder when Carter shot him through his overcoat pocket. The muzzle-flash was so severe he felt it burn his outer thigh.

Henderson was slammed up against the opposite wall by the force of the heavy bullet. He looked at Carter incredulously, seemingly pinned against the woodwork by the bloody stain that was spreading on the breast of his uniform.

The barrel of his weapon was pointed at the floor as acrid smoke filled the room. Carter's teeth were chattering now and his legs had turned to water. Henderson slid to the floor and tumbled on to his face. It was the first time Carter had seen violent death at close quarters, and he had difficulty in breathing.

Then he forced himself toward the crumpled figure, felt for the pulse. The man was quite dead. Carter dragged himself to the door, looked through the dirty glass panel. For the first time he realised he was in the stable quarters at The Priory.

Now that he thought of it it could be the only logical destination for the passage, given the history of the two buildings. No-one seemed to have heard the shot. There was nobody in sight, though the distant clink of a hammer from the farrier's shop went on.

The smoke from his pistol had still not dispersed in the shadows of the ceiling before Carter made up his mind. He did his best to straighten the room, found a thick blanket and covered the body. Then he went to the tack-room door and turned the key from the inside, leaving it in the lock.

He surveyed the chamber from the doorway. The huddled figure in the blanket was hidden from sight by the bulk of the trestle table. It would be dusk soon anyway. Carter would leave it all to Pepper and the official police. He had other things to do.

It was the work of a moment only to regain the ladder and lower the trap-door. He carried the dark-lantern back in with him. His thigh was beginning to sting but he had no time for that now. He went down the ladder very slowly, like an old man, still sobbing for breath. He did not know that death under those circumstances would generate such emotion.

But no court of law would convict him. And Henderson had undoubtedly intended to kill him had he not acted first. He stood aimlessly at the bottom of the wooden staircase, collecting his wits. Then he noticed the bolt on the underside of the trap-door. He went back up and secured it. He did not want anyone behind him in these dark passages.

He remembered then Henderson's strange appearance in the hall of The Priory, on the night that Carter had surprised him there. Undoubtedly he had used a passage that gave secret access to the house. Carter must examine that panelling now.

Somehow, he found himself back in the wide concourse where the two tunnels joined. He looked at the stone staircase leading to the one he had not yet tried. He made up his mind. He lifted the lantern high and took the left-hand fork.

Fifty-Four
The Guardians

1

CARTER HAD RECOVERED himself before he gained the head of the steps. He felt energy and vitality flowing through his limbs again. He no longer thought about the situation, merely forced his body to obey the commands of his brain. He had arrived in a cold stone passage which branched away in a shallow curve before descending quite steeply.

The ancient brickwork was interrupted by evidence of newer work, of a more hurried and less craftsmanlike sort; the walls, in places, were shored by heavy beams of a modern pattern; and, here and there makeshift wooden stairs, roughly nailed and secured, led up and down.

Presently the dancing beam of his lantern was interrupted by a massive oaken door. Carter's spirits rose as he saw that it stood ajar. He pushed it cautiously, but the hinges revolved silently, well-greased and evidently in frequent use. Carter found himself in a winding passage of antique pattern, that was vaguely familiar. Lanterns stood on brackets and there were the indentations of many feet on the dusty stone floor.

He went on less cautiously now, revolving the beam of his lantern, the wick turned up to full intensity. If further doors were locked then he would either have to return all the way to Rats' Castle or to risk going back through the tack-room where the body of Henderson lay.

Carter's intuition told him that the end of his quest must lie here. He had first to reach the authorities before his new-formed theories and those of Sennen could be put to the test. His breathing was normal again and all his senses alert.

He went on down a straight and level corridor, the lantern brushing the shadows ahead of him, his footsteps making faint pattering echoes beneath the vaulted arch that soared above him. He had had enough of subterranean wanderings; Carter felt his experiences this afternoon would suffice for a lifetime.

The girl's image was in front of him, as ever, as he found the far door ajar, went on through; the golden light showing him yet another passage, bare and empty. There were wine-bins here, indicating that it connected with regions that were familiar to him. He went up a last flight of stone steps.

There was a scarlet curtain in front of him. Cautiously, very cautiously, Carter drew a segment of it back. Faintly, he could see cold light gleaming on parquet flooring; the long windows in here were covered with shutters outside the glass, through which the daylight leached meagrely.

The rest of the large apartment appeared to be empty and was in any event in deep shadow. He pulled back the curtain and went boldly through, his feet rousing slight clicking echoes from the parquet. Something flashed in the darkness and he half-stumbled, conscious that there was a sharp pain in his right calf. At the same instant panelling rumbled to behind him.

There was a curious whirring noise as though some gigantic bee were vibrating its wings in the dimness; Carter felt fear then, as his eyes adjusted to the light. A soulless metal face blinked into his own and a sabre glinted as the effigy lunged at him with murderous precision.

2

Carter moved frantically backward, conscious that he had animated another trip-wire. He understood many things as the life-size mechanical figure lumbered on, cannoning into another that was coming up at a tangent.

By the low illumination which penetrated the shutters he saw other slumbering forms, not yet animated, his senses unnerved and demoralized by the weird whirring sound of clockwork. He ran back quickly toward the panelling; it was firm and resisted his finger-tips.

Fortunately, the dark-lantern had dropped to the parquet just inside the curtain and was still alight. He set it upright on the floor and removed the shield. The flare revealed a scene of nightmare proportion that was to remain with him for the rest of his life.

He bit his lip at the sight of the immobile metal masks, having difficulty in remembering that they were inanimate, mechanical things that had no heart, no mercy, and certainly no possibility of appeal. The beam of the lantern stretched halfway across the room, dividing it equally in two.

The side nearest the windows, which admitted chinks of light, was necessarily brighter and it was here that Carter determined to make his stand. That it amounted to that was now clear to him. The mechanical men, dressed as soldiers, each bore a sabre or similar weapon; he could see by the light of the lantern that the swords were extremely sharp and that they had a fairly wide arc.

He guessed they would have lead counterweights in joints and elbows, and the thrusts and slashes could have lethal consequences if they connected in the right places. His only hope lay in quick movement and equally adroit thinking. He did not know how long the clockwork mechanisms ran, but it was obvious that his only hope lay in exhausting them before he himself became exhausted in turn.

He estimated there were at least a dozen of the dim figures ranged before him; a miniature army which barred him from the far end of the room, where he could see a door. There were two figures only coming slowly toward him at the moment, and he had already guessed that they were initially animated by his breaking or engaging fixed trip-wires.

Presumably, the other automata would be set into action if and when he tripped further wires; by the exercise of extreme care he might prevent this. Carter realised he had little but his wits to rely on, for it was useless to shoot at them unless he hit, by some lucky chance, upon the vital mechanism; and he had no weapon to hand to parry the sabre thrusts.

As he pondered, his back against the panelling, the nearest figure gave a tentative slash in the air with its sabre, as though it had by some devilish intent divined his thinking. Carter stepped back swiftly, colliding with the wall. He still kept the instinct of self-preservation and quickly slid the lantern toward the panel with his left heel, so that it would be unlikely to upset from the ponderous stalking of the mechanical figures.

For one wild moment he had the idea of setting fire to the room in order to attract the attention of someone in the house but swiftly abandoned the notion; apart from the fact that such an action might burn the mansion to the ground, it could also have the effect of overcoming himself, particularly if he could find no means of egress from the chamber.

That this was another supreme irony of The Black Death was not lost on him; he crouched, watching carefully the first of the two soldiers advancing toward his corner. He realised the machines could not think and that they were acting blindly in fixed arcs, animated purely by clockwork and ingenuity; but there was something terrifying and fatalistic about them that seemed to paralyse the will.

There was another loud clicking noise and the thing slashed downward with the sabre; Carter ducked to the floor and felt the razor-sharp blade strike the panelling above his head. It lodged there, the machine buzzing angrily as the legs beat a tattoo on the floor.

Impelled by desperation Carter seized the figure's wrist; it was inflexible. It had been his intention to wrest the sabre from its grip, but try as he would he could not find the secret of the catch which might disconnect it from the metal hand. It could be that it was screwed in; if so it would be an impossible task.

Instead, he drew back against the panelling and kicked at the thing's body; the sabre came free quickly and the automaton flew backward, colliding with the second. There was more angry whirring and the blades of the sabres flew alarmingly about.

Carter had a glimpse of pale grey glass eyes revolving menacingly in the metal sockets and then he had quit the corner. But he had forgotten his own cautionary measures. He felt the quick tug at his ankle again and realised he had touched another wire. Two more dark shadows were lumbering from their corners.

Blades described a criss-cross pattern in the semi-darkness, and Carter realised in a moment of dry-mouthed panic that he had left the lit half of the room to go into the darker, most dangerous part.

The floor trembled as the things came on. The four figures met almost in the centre and instead of becoming entangled as Carter had hoped, they merely bounced off each other.

The realistic clash the steel made and the sparks which flew made Carter even more aware that the figures were in deadly earnest. He had the pistol out now, steadying it on his left wrist. The explosion was so loud it seemed to fill the whole room.

The bullet smashed the head of the nearest figure, spinning it round and adding another vicious sound as it ricochetted about.

The second punched in the chest and there was a mad symphony of clockwork dissonance.

Watching the sabre blade carefully Carter ran in with the strength of desperation and toppled the figure. It spun the soldier next to it but did not send it to the floor. But the first crashed downward and Carter, perspiration running into his eyes, wedged the flailing sabre-hand into the corner of the panelling until the clockwork ran down.

He scrabbled away as the three other figures began circling about him, the steel points describing dazzling arcs in the lamplight. He decided he would not use the pistol again. It was too dangerous in the confined space and he might only wound himself.

He thought for one moment to run swiftly through the room, risking the trip-wires. But if he did that and found the far door locked, then the entire body of mechanical men would be on him. They could hack him to pieces in the enclosed space unless help from outside arrived.

Carter could not count on that. His shots had brought no-one and they had reverberated enormously. The whirring of clockwork went on as the impassive silver faces of the automata closed in, the sabres jerking and slashing spasmodically, the metal feet setting the floor trembling.

Dry-throated, terrified, crouched against the panelling, Carter prepared to fight for his life.

Fifty-Five
Silver Sabres

1

THE FALLEN FIGURE had stopped moving now. Carter got his fingers beneath the bodywork. He rolled it across the floor with all the strength at his command, as its three companions came on. There was a tremendous crash which set Carter's heart jumping and he watched the sword-points anxiously as the upright figures whirled.

The nearest was toppling too, caught behind the articulated knees by the carcass of the first. It fell backward, the eyes blinking at Carter in a horrifying parody of human reaction; Carter felt panic rising within him again. It was almost impossible not to feel that there were brains working behind these grotesque masks.

The second figure had momentarily sent the other to the far end of the room. Carter heard further wires give, saw yet more shapes stirring. He ran forward, dragged the carcass of the first soldier back, took it quickly to the well-lit half of the room.

He swallowed, watching the lumbering shapes that swam out of the darkness into the lamplight. The room resembled the interior of some gigantic clock-case. The noise of gears, of springs, of wires, of cogs and ratchets working in well-oiled unison made a mockery of his racing thoughts and his own brain calculating the risks he was facing.

The things were clumsy and slow, of course; but if he did not exercise all of his strength and energy he was sure to be cut to the ground eventually by sheer weight of numbers. The figures had some sort of guard round the bottom of their legs for they did not fall over the second soldier, which was still flailing away with its sabre in the centre of the room.

They merely glided off at another tangent; Carter remembered a conversation that seemed like years ago. Obviously the problems had been surmounted since then. He kept low, crouched behind the metal bodywork of the figure he had immobilised, anxiously watching the menacing blades. It was only too clear that this room was soundproofed in some fashion; else people would have rushed to his aid minutes ago.

Perhaps the walls were of the same ancient stone, feet thick, and the windows merely gave on to the terrace and the encroaching darkness of the winter afternoon. Carter moved convulsively as a blade chopped at him; he had been momentarily careless and he wriggled desperately aside, hearing the panelling splinter at his back.

There seemed no time-limit to the creatures' endurance. Carter had heard of massive springs which could animate large pieces of machinery for hours at a time, much as the smaller clock spring did for its own mechanism.

The automata were tireless, apparently impervious to his barehanded blows. His only chance was to topple them all, so giving himself time to search for a way out of this sealed room. But in the interim there was deadly danger in the sabres these terrifying toy soldiers were wielding.

Carter was in a corner, having dragged the metal carcass there to avoid the plunging death. He saw another sabre descend, a silvery blur in the lamplight; he did not move quickly enough, felt a pain in his shoulder; watched stupefied as the tip of the weapon sliced effortlessly through the thick material of his overcoat. Blood ran down his fingers.

He moved with the swift reaction of an automaton himself as a second blade slashed at his face, wielded gravely by another soldier whose emotionless features stared pitilessly into his own. He shouted then, kicking and punching, keeping low as he pushed the recumbent metal body before him into the milling mass of ponderously marching men.

2

Amid the clashing of sabres, the groan and grind of metal, the whirring of the mechanisms, and the heavy trembling of the floor, Carter fought desperately, hoping no chance blow would pierce his unprotected head and body. Then he was at the far side of the room, by the second door, watching the melee at the end he had just quitted.

He felt his shoulder, clenched his fingers; realised the wound he had sustained was probably a superficial one. He got his handkerchief, balled it in his palm to catch the thin trickle of blood.

Fortunately, it was his left arm and it would not interfere with his defensive tactics. Carter moved toward the door in the far corner, stopped as another clockwork man glided toward him.

Something had happened to the mechanism because the sabre was moving in a horizontal instead of a vertical arc. Carter braced himself against the wall and kicked its chest with all his strength. The thing, its eyes winking unnervingly, flew back across the parquet and there was another grinding cacophony of metal.

A sabre-point broke off somewhere and went whining into the far corner; a second face slid out into the lamp-light, staring into Carter's own. He was near desperation this time and slipped aside. This time the sabre-tip was immobile, ready to skewer him to the wall.

It jammed solid as the point ran upon the thick oak and the thing vibrated angrily, as though a human being were involved; black fear was at Carter's elbow now. He sent the metal carcass from him for the last time and rolled it into the wild tangle of clashing figures. Then his hand was on the knob of the far door.

There was an hysterical moment when he feared it was locked and then he had almost fallen into the quiet corridor beyond. He slammed the door behind him and the panel splintered as something heavy charged it. He turned the key and went on down the passage, his nerves in shreds, almost dropping with fatigue.

He was on familiar ground now, though he was not at first aware of it. He was halfway descending a particularly handsome staircase, before he recognized the opulent surroundings. There was the chandelier shimmering on the cut glass, on flowers and ornamental bowls, on oil-paintings in heavy gilded frames, and on the elegant tiling of the inner hall he had crossed so many times.

Carter looked at himself in an oval mirror which hung on the stair. He hardly recognised himself; dusty, dishevelled, his face distorted with fear, flecks of blood on his collar and clothing, his face pale, and his eyes strained. He breathed deeply like an animal and fought to get hold of his nerves before he went on.

He could hear the murmur of voices. He quickly descended the stair and concealed himself behind the curtains in the semi-gloom of the entrance hall. Carter watched the dark-haired woman cross the vast floor and disappear through the far door. In her civilised well-bred routine, she seemed like something from another world; a world which Carter had once inhabited but which he no longer recognised.

He waited until the door had closed behind her, listening for the echo of any further signs of life in the house; there were none. Then and only then did he quit his position behind the portieres and cross the hall, the butt of the pistol comforting beneath his fingers.

The door of the study was wide open, which was unusual in itself. For a moment, as he tiptoed closer, Carter could not see any sign of life in the gracious oval room with its flickering fire and ranks of books.

Then he heard furtive movement, and saw the files of documents; the mass of paper burning in the fireplace; the expensive leather travelling cases piled in the centre of the carpet.

He kept his hand in his coat pocket as he walked noiselessly across and surveyed the back of the elegant, grey-clad man who was feeding the fire with yet more sheafs of paper.

"I am sorry to interrupt you on the brink of a journey," Carter said.

Fifty-Six

The Goat-Priest Speaks

1

SIMON HEMMINGS' GOLD-RIMMED spectacles caught the light as he slowly turned to regard Carter. His manner was unchanged and he beamed amiably as though the architect were merely an unexpected guest.

"Well, Mr. Carter! This is quite a surprise."

"I thought you'd find it so," said Carter drily.

Hemmings' eyes changed as he regarded the other more closely.

"But you are hurt, Mr. Carter. What have you been up to? Not another accident, I hope?"

Carter shook his head grimly.

"Not this time, sir. The surprises have all been on my side, today. So you had not gone to Plymouth."

The Chief Magistrate chuckled, as though they were sharing some secret joke, his strong yellow teeth gleaming in his full-fleshed mouth.

"You have a remarkable sense of humour for such a young man."

He put his hand to the long hair tinged with grey, moving to pick up his cigar from the desk.

"I hope you have not damaged any of my mechanical toys, Mr. Carter."

Carter shifted over, catching a glimpse of himself in a mirror opposite. The glass echoed back his own face, distorted like that of a stranger.

Hemmings gave him a curious smile.

"What goes on in the mirror is far more important than what goes on in the room, Mr. Carter. Think about it."

Swift as a striking snake he had lifted the pistol from the desk, where it was concealed by a small bronze group, and levelled it coolly at Carter's chest. The shock was not entirely unexpected but Carter felt it just the same.

"I could not miss at this range, my bold young friend. Please remove that weapon from your pocket and drop it over here."

Carter hesitated. He saw the steel in the man's eyes and his finger tighten beneath the trigger guard. It was not worth losing his life at this late stage of the game. He did as the other suggested.

The Magistrate relaxed then, giving him another wintry smile.

"That is better, Mr. Carter. Now, kick it over."

He shrugged ironically.

"We are all voyaging on our separate ways to death, Mr. Carter."

He glanced from the pistol barrel to the architect.

"Except that some of us arrive there sooner than others."

Carter gave him a bitter smile.

"Why, sir, why? You—an upholder of the law . . . the goat-priest!"

Hemmings shook his head, the light glinting on his spectacles, the benevolent look back on his face again.

"You are very young, Mr. Carter. And we have so little time for explanations."

Carter glanced round the luxurious study in puzzlement.

"But you are rich . . . I do not understand why you grovel in the mire so."

Hemmings went over and closed the study door, turning the key in the lock.

"I can give you ten minutes, Mr. Carter. Then I shall require you. But perhaps I owe you something."

He shook his head regretfully, the pistol barrel aligned steadily on his companion.

"If only the young would learn to mind their own business."

He motioned with the pistol to indicate the study and, by implication, the house.

"I was rich, Mr. Carter. But I have a very extravagant mistress in London. She has run through most of my fortune. Please don't look so shocked. We are men of the world."

"I am not shocked," said Carter firmly. "Merely astonished. At both you and Henderson."

The Magistrate smiled.

"But then it is an astonishing world, is it not? Put briefly, I needed some distraction and also something which would produce money. A witch-cult seemed the answer. I have studied the subject extensively and I have a firm belief in the efficacy of the Black Arts. Human nature is a most amazing thing, Mr. Carter. I have seen much of it in my exalted position upon the bench. I used that knowledge and my office in the magistracy to ensure that the two strands of my private and public life never came into collision."

The eyes beamed with recollection behind the gold spectacles.

"Captain Henderson has been an invaluable aide. I knew him from a long time ago when we met in London gaming clubs. It was not very hard to recruit green young girls and bored older women for our rites. They were mainly sexual, as you have no doubt observed. Strict discipline was enforced. Rich men were recruited in London and introduced into the circle for large sums of money. Henderson organised the hounds to frighten off the locals and add to the aura of legend."

He waved the pistol with a smile.

"There you have the story in a nutshell."

"When the dupes were sufficiently compromised you blackmailed them!" said Carter suddenly.

"A nasty word, Mr. Carter."

"And when they could yield nothing further and threatened to expose the proceedings upon the moor they were disposed of."

"Through the effective example of The Black Death," said Hemmings. "We rarely had to discipline the local people. That way, we risked losing our most fervent disciples."

Carter again thought of the hopeless sobbing of an unknown woman in the night. He knew its cause now. Obviously a reluctant disciple.

Something else flickered into his mind.

"Your local agent was the landlord of The Bassett Arms."

Hemmings nodded.

"He knew everyone and everything that went on in the town. He has himself a criminal record. He confined his activities to London, but I got to know of his upsets through my duties on the bench. He was approached through Henderson. No-one knew my identity except that admirable officer."

Carter licked his lips.

"Why are you telling me all this, Mr. Hemmings?"

The Magistrate smiled a smile of bland benevolence.

"Because there is hardly any likelihood of you informing anyone else, Mr. Carter."

The pistol barrel steadied again as Carter sought for something to distract the Magistrate's attention.

"But surely, such money as you derived from your cult-victims could not keep this great house and estate going?"

Hemmings pouted his lips regretfully.

"Alas, no. It was a stopgap only. You are forgetting Miss Hammond. I have expectations there, you see."

Carter's eyes had grown hard.

"What expectations?" he said softly.

The older man shrugged.

"Miss Hammond is an immensely wealthy young lady. At the moment I have only the use of the interest on her fortune. She will be twenty-one in a few months' time when she comes into the entire estate."

Carter licked dry lips.

"I see."

The Magistrate sat down on the edge of his desk, his back to the fire.

"I had thought of introducing my ward to the ceremonies at Rats' Castle," he said very deliberately, "As a sort of vestal virgin. But I had no wish to share her. I might even marry her, Mr. Carter. I have not yet decided."

His voice cracked out in the silence of the study.

"Please do nothing foolish, sir. I should hate to shoot you here."

Carter came steadily toward him.

"I do not think you would shoot. It would only bring Mrs. Arkwright."

The Magistrate shook his head.

"The servants are on the other side of the house. I have told my housekeeper I am not to be disturbed for another hour. I could just as easily dispose of you in the chest in the corner there until such time as I found a more permanent method of interment."

Carter stood back. The Magistrate continued to stare at him with bland indifference.

"That is better, sir. And if anyone should hear the weapon go off?"

He waved his free hand in the air.

"I was cleaning the pistol and it discharged accidentally. There is always a way out. There is always a way . . ."

Carter's face was grim.

"You planned the fight with the dragoons, the gathering of the hounds from remote places for the nights when the rites took place; you wrote your own note warning yourself off the moor. I understand all that. But why risk killing me on your own terrace by ordering that stone dropped?'

Hemmings' face clouded.

"That was a piece of supreme stupidity, Mr. Carter. The foreman is a member of the sect, of course. Naturally, he did not know my true identity. Possibly some word of your snooping had got about the moor. He will be disciplined in due time, when I return from my honeymoon."

His fleshy tongue moved across his lips. He looked at Carter evenly.

"You are remarkably durable, sir. I had hoped that the mechanical toys would have relieved me of the necessity of disposing of you myself. As it is, your gallery rooms, completed by another hand, will remain your visible memorial."

"The situation is more difficult than you may think," Carter said.

"I cannot conceive of any loopholes, Mr. Carter. My ward and I have need of some sea air. We are leaving for a short voyage from Bristol the day after tomorrow. She lies in a deep sleep upstairs."

He raised the pistol barrel suddenly.

"Merely a mild drug, Mr. Carter. When she awakes she will be aboard, and it will be too late to do anything about the situation then."

He chuckled in the silence of the great room.

"I think I have covered everything. The Captain will be here soon with the carriage. And it will be quite simple to drop you off on the way."

Carter could not keep the triumph from his eyes.

"I think not, Mr. Hemmings. The Captain is dead."

There was a long silence. The Magistrate drew in his breath with a little implosive sound. Then he smiled again. Carter came close to admiring his self-control at that moment.

"I see. You took the right-hand passage first. A pity. I did not count on that. Of course, Mr. Carter, I guessed that it was you at the Castle the other night. And I wondered what you might get up to next. So I ordered the subterranean passage doors left open to lure you here, in case you discovered the secret of the stone slab. That mediæval tunnel has been of the greatest importance. I knew you would come alone."

"Even you could not think of everything," Carter said.

Hemmings nodded.

"A slight change of plans, that is all. And perhaps it is as well. The police may be looking for you for Henderson's murder."

He went over quickly and unlocked the door, throwing it back.

"In front of me, if you please, Mr. Carter. I shall need you to carry the young lady down to the carriage."

The two men were halfway across the silent hall when there came a sudden interruption.

2

The sharp clatter of footsteps from the stairhead broke the hush. Hemmings whirled, his pistol ready. Carter seized the opportunity. He went across the hall in a long dive, making for the shadow of the portieres. Hemmings' bullet chipped marble from a pillar before he was into the safety of darkness.

At the balustrade above he recognised the sardonic face of Slade beneath the hard hat and, next to him, the heavily moustached features of the Plymouth police officer, Inspector Pepper. His thoughts a boiling tumult, Carter had no idea how they had got there.

Sparks again flew from the marble as flame flickered from the Inspector's pistol but Hemmings had put himself into shelter beneath the stairwell. His own pistol made a grossly exaggerated echo in the vast space of the hall, and the officer sagged, scarlet splashes against his shirt front. Slade caught him as he fell, lowered him gently to the floor.

Hemmings faded from his consciousness as Carter ran toward the staircase, taking it two treads at a time. Slade met him, his face serious and concerned. The two pumped hands briefly before they turned to examine the wounded officer. Footsteps sounded then as Hemmings ran across the study floor; there was a brittle tinkle of shattering glass.

"Leave him!" said Carter. "He cannot get far."

He bent with Slade to examine Pepper. The officer, face white and strained, tried vainly to regain his feet.

"He will be all right," said Slade with relief. "The ball went through his shoulder."

"Look after him," said Carter. "I must find Miss Hammond."

He met Mrs. Arkwright halfway up the stairs, her face strained, her eyes wide.

"Take me to Miss Hammond's room! It is life or death!"

To her credit the housekeeper did not argue; he might have been asking merely for another pot of tea, so admirably had she been trained. She led him unquestioningly to a large chamber on the flight above.

Fiona lay, white-faced and insensible, fully clothed on the silk bedspread. She looked like some mediæval carving of a female saint, Carter thought. His heart turned cold and he felt for dark moments that he was too late.

Then she breathed shallowly and slightly changed her position, one small hand held close to her face. Carter's lips brushed her cheek; he felt moisture on his own.

"Take care of her," Carter said urgently. "She has been drugged. I will explain everything later."

He ran back down the corridor, gained the floor below. Slade had already transferred the wounded officer to a divan against the far wall, staunching the blood with a pocket handkerchief.

"How did you come here?" Carter asked.

Slade shook his head.

"I must ask your pardon, Mr. Carter. I had to drop the slab. The dragoons were riding along the top road and I did not know what they portended. I made all normal at the Castle ruins just in case. I waited until they had passed and then signalled the police, as arranged. It took time, of course. But we got the stone up and followed on."

He smiled grimly.

"You have made a mess of those mechanical men, sir. I'm afraid I had to break the door down."

"You have done well," Carter said. "You will find Captain Henderson lying dead in the stables. You had better send some officers there."

Slade nodded, his face incurious. He had remarkable self-control, Carter thought.

"The rest have gone to the right of the passage, if that leads to the stables," he said. "Do you wish me to come with you?"

Carter shook his head.

"I have my own personal score to settle."

He descended the staircase rapidly, his heart light. All that mattered was Fiona's safety, and that had been assured.

He found his pistol on the study floor, saw the shattered window where Hemmings had left the house. He went back into the hall.

"Where is Mr. Sennen?" he called.

Slade's hard hat appeared at the stairhead.

"With the main body, sir. They will be here directly."

Carter nodded.

"Tell him I have gone across the moor."

He ran out through the front door into the vast arcade which followed the façade of the house. For one who had been so long in darkness, he was astonished at the blackness of the winter afternoon.

He rounded the corner of the house, came out upon the terrace, looking wryly at the never-to-be-finished museum rooms where the workmen still toiled, oblivious of the drama which had been played out so close to them.

The black clouds pressed on the dim distances of Dartmoor with an almost palpable presence. Despite the bitter coldness of the air upon his cheeks, there was an underlying warmth as though a storm impended. To Carter's astonishment a distant crack of thunder sounded.

He gazed with incredulity across the rolling contours of the moorland, to the far distant tors wreathed in mist; conscious that behind him the workmen had paused upon their scaffolding, arrested in equal surprise.

The whole plan of the terrain was laid out before him, clear-etched as in a steel engraving. Carter felt he could almost see every blade of grass that shivered in the wind. He seized the butt of the pistol, noting the guilty figure of the distant Hemmings as he fled on foot from retribution.

Then he plunged from the terrace in swift pursuit.

3

Carter ran until the breath sobbed in his throat. Hemmings, despite his years, must have been incredibly fit. His stamina was remarkable, and he seemed to know every hollow, every swelling shoulder of hillside, and every granite boulder; using each to his advantage to hide his advance from Carter's menacing pistol.

A deep, dark anger burned within the architect now. He paused at the top of a crag, conscious of another clap of thunder, though the sky continued dark and cold. Behind him he could see the house and a thin skein of ant-like figures following on. That would be the police.

He wondered why the Magistrate had not made for the stables, where there would be quicker mode of transport. Then he realised that the geographical location of the house had made that impossible. The fleeing man would have had to come back up past the main entrance of the mansion; there was no other way. And that he dare not do.

Had he, in fact, some other bolthole on the moor which might give him shelter until nightfall, when he could make further arrangements to escape to Bristol and the open sea? Carter did not know. Only his burning anger and his own implacable will stood between the fleeing felon and the safety sought. That Carter was determined to deny him.

He noted carefully the last position in which he had seen Hemmings' figure and plunged headlong down the next slope, threading carefully between the boulders, holding the pistol in his overcoat pocket, the cardboard box of ammunition in his left, all tiredness forgotten now as he followed on, like the Hounds of Hell themselves.

There was a rich irony in the situation in which he pursued this terrible man across the barren landscape, and Carter savoured it with bitter relish.

He gained the next upward slope, noting the running figure on the opposite shoulder of hillside; there was a flame low among the dark rocks and something scratched a white scar on a boulder some fifteen feet to his left. Carter smiled thinly. His own pistol cracked, more for effect than anything else, and he relished the sight of the Magistrate staggering as his shot set the pebbles scattering at his feet.

Then Carter zig-zagged on the downward slope, again conscious of the bitter coldness of the air and the strangeness of a storm in such conditions. The heavy clouds were rolling across the moor, close to the tops of the rounded hills, and as they parted they brought with them a strange, bloody luminosity, as though an oven door had been opened.

The sky was alight with the fires of sunset as Carter ran down the steep, rocky path, the hurrying figure of Hemmings ever before him, scrambling from boulder to boulder, with incredible agility for a man of his age. Carter guessed that the galvanic energy of desperation was animating him, and it merely fed his inner satisfaction.

Many images whirled about him as he ran; the tranquillity of Thornton Bassett; the woman sobbing in the night; the hellish sect at Rats' Castle; Hands' solemn face in the midnight solitude of his room; Mrs. Tregorran's treacherous smile; the banked fires in the eyes of the girl Pauline; the oily hospitality of the fat landlord of The Bassett Arms; Sennen's tired, saint-like face in the lamplight; Henderson's incredulity as the bullet expunged the life from him; the pitiful, charred victims of The Black Death; the farmer writhing in the flames; the light glimmering on Hemmings' gold spectacles; the pitiless metal faces of the mechanical men; the granite block falling toward him; the strong humour of Slade's features under his hard hat; and, above all, Fiona's steadfast eyes beneath the tawny hair.

He stumbled then and almost fell. When he arose he missed the fleeting figure of the miscreant in front of him. He looked behind; far back, toiling across the moor came a long, thin line of figures; in their van a form he recognized. That of the Rector of Thornton Bassett, determined to be in at the kill.

Heartened, Carter conquered his aching limbs and plunged downward at a more reckless rate, conscious now of the furtive form flickering among the boulders of the far slope. His legs were lightened, his straining lungs eased, the weight of the pistol no longer important.

He had his pre-destined goal straight before him, and he fled toward it as an arrow flies to its target. Then he was on the upward slope again, the rolling slopes of the moor, barren and purple in the dusk, shining with an unearthly hue. The thunder crashed and rumbled again as he stood at the foot of a tumbled granite tor, whose jagged outlines were all cloudy with fire.

He turned to see a stupefying sight, his soul awed, conscious too of Rats' Castle, far to the eastward. Outlined against it was the onward-fleeing figure of the man he sought.

Epilogue
Pillars of Fire

CARTER RAN FORWARD, the fires of the sunset about him, staining the humpbacked hills of the rolling moors, staining the fleeing figure before him; even tinting purple the half-seen ruins of Rats' Castle which stood out on its upflung pattern of rock at the rim of the sky.

The crashing of great forces was reverberating and dinning in his ears, but whether it was of exterior source or within his head he now no longer knew or cared. His breath sobbing in his lungs, his heart thumping, the perspiration streaming down his face; he had little heed of where his footsteps were taking him, so long as they brought him within striking distance of Hemmings.

The pursuit seemed to take an interminable time; indeed, Carter had lost all sense of the passing minutes. He was only vaguely conscious now that behind him, strung out over miles of ground, were the friendly figures of Sennen and the police.

In front was nothing but the purple moor, the slowly growing image of the Castle ruins and, occasionally, the flickering shadow of the man he pursued. Once Carter paused to gain breath and was appalled to see the western sky behind him; a great livid glow of blood-red fire which might have portended the end of the world. From within it, white flame trembled and shivered and now and again came a crashing as though a mighty hammer beat upon an anvil.

It was obviously a rare winter electrical storm, but a storm of which Carter had never conceived the like; the whole inflamed mass of sky was so sombre, so alarming, and it cast such a reddened image across the moorland, that Carter was glad to turn his back upon it and resume the chase.

Hemmings had paused too. His own figure was bathed in the reddish tints of the sunset and he stared at Carter from the opposite crag for a brief moment. The young man could sense his malignancy even from that distance and he raised his pistol in a futile gesture before lowering it again.

The crashing reverberation was so great this time that it seemed to split his head. Even Rats' Castle was outlined in the whitish fire. Then Hemmings had plunged on toward it, and Carter needed all his strength to keep up.

Presently they had come to that wild and remote part of the moor where the great bowl, its ravines, full of purple shadows and the silver splash of the stream bisecting it, seemed to reflect the coming night. Mist was faintly rising, and the shadowy mass was almost solid in its appearance as it began to fill the adjacent hollows between the shoulders of hill.

Hemmings had again paused on the opposing slope. He was all stained with the fires of sunset and so close this time that Carter could see the scarlet shimmer reflect and burn on the gold rims of his spectacles.

Then came a greater crash of thunder from behind Carter, and the white fire in the heavens seemed to split them apart. Something descended from the darkness of the sky with an eye-searing incandescence that set Carter grovelling on his knees, shading his eyes.

When he raised them again it was to see the livid finger of vaporous brilliance pin-pointed on the figure of Hemmings on his craggy eminence. Something ran down it with great rapidity; red flame grew and then a whiteness that appeared to fill the whole universe.

A gigantic crackling, bluish flashes, and then pillars of fire before him. Hemmings was screaming, the centre of the pillar whose heart burnt white and blue before dying to purple flame. The searing, liquid mass was buckled and awry now, toppling like a spent candle, rolling down the opposite slope; save that he still writhed and screamed within the charred heart, Hemmings was a dead man.

Still on his knees Carter watched, stupefied. Something seemed to feed on the heat of the flame, and white lightning played about the clouded ashes. Presently it was over except that the intense glare continued to play on the hilltops and the great oven door of the sky in the west glowed red and menacing.

Carter got to his feet, went shakily down the slope, unable to believe what his eyes told him. He put the pistol away, his energy spent. He sank to his knees again, his incredulous gaze fixed upon the smoking atoms.

Above the charred fragments of bone and flesh, the shell of Rats' Castle stood golden in the sunset. Carter's eyes were raised and held by something beside it. He leaned forward and retched into the gorse.

It was there that Sennen found him some ten minutes later, shaken and blown with the long pursuit.

"My dear boy! God be praised that you are safe."

He gently raised the other, his face paling as he stared at the remains of Hemmings above.

"The Black Death!" he whispered. "The Black Death in reality!"

The two men were silent until Carter's shaking had subsided.

"The young lady? Miss Hammond?"

The Rector put his arm around the other's shoulder.

"She is well and recovering herself."

Sennen helped the architect back to the top of the slope from which they had just come, his remarks trying to lighten the other's mood.

"Promise me one thing when you are married," he said. "You and Miss Hammond, I mean."

Carter smiled weakly, his legs still buckling beneath him. He sat down on a boulder, waited for his strength to come back.

"And what might that be?"

"That you will get rid of that oil painting in the hall of The Priory."

The two men stared at each other in silence. Then the Rector started back. His eyes were lifted from the remains of the Magistrate, still smoking on the rocks above them, to the far vista of Rats' Castle and the mound some half mile from it, now all bright and fired with the scarlet glow in the sky.

Carter followed his glance; gasped and came to his feet. He did not know what Sennen saw. What he saw was the unmistakable silhouette of the Black Huntsman, as depicted in the painting, standing on the knoll, clear-etched in the livid light, leaning on a long staff as he gazed broodingly across the moor toward them.

Sennen's deep-set eyes were haunted and sombre as he stared back, his cheeks white. He shivered suddenly, again turning his glance to the charred remains of the Magistrate. Behind them came the faint rattle of stones as the body of police officers came up.

"Did you know about Hemmings?" Carter asked.

Sennen's voice was low and trembling.

"It had to be someone connected with the authorities. But I had never guessed . . ."

He slowly shook his head.

"Poetic justice," Sennen said.

Carter's eyes were still fixed across the moor, at the tremendous figure in the strange tricorn hat.

"No, sir," he disagreed. "The Devil came back for his own."

He remained staring as the silhouette of the Black Huntsman slowly faded into the mist; only the remains of Rats' Castle, red-tinged in the glare of the dying sun held in view, until the moor was again plunged into primeval darkness.

The Black Death
First Edition
1991

The Black Death by Basil Copper was published by Fedogan & Bremer, 700 Washington Avenue, S. E., Suite 50, Minneapolis, Minnesota 55414. Twenty-five hundred copies of the trade edition and one hundred copies of the limited edition were printed by Braun-Brumfield, Inc., Ann Arbor, Michigan from ITC New Baskerville.